THE
WALL
STREET
GANG

Ney Chasse les Marchands du Temple

Edward Sorel '70

Reproduced by permission of Edward Sorel. First published in *New York Magazine*.

Richard Ney

THE WALL STREET GANG

FOREWORD BY
SENATOR LEE METCALF

PRAEGER PUBLISHERS
New York • Washington

The following charts are reproduced by courtesy of Trendline, a division of Standard & Poor's Corporation, 345 Hudson Street, New York, New York 10014: 6–1 to 6–14, 7–1 to 7–6, 7–12 to 7–14, 9–1, 9–2, 9–4 to 9–8, 9–10 to 9–20, and 10–1 to 10–6. Some additions to these charts were made by Richard Ney.

The following charts were reproduced by courtesy of Securities Research Company, 208 Newbury Street, Boston, Massachusetts 02116: pages 128, 129, 130, 133, 141, 158, 169, 170, and in Chapter 10.

Published in the United States of America in 1974
by Praeger Publishers, Inc.
111 Fourth Avenue, New York, N.Y. 10003

Library of Congress Cataloging in Publication Data

Ney, Richard.
  The Wall Street gang.

  Includes bibliographical references.
  1. Speculation—United States. 2. Brokers—United States. 3. Stock-exchange—United States.
I. Title.
HG4910.N46   332.6′45′0973   73-13050
ISBN 0-275-33390-5

Printed in the United States of America

For Pauline

Contents

Foreword

by SENATOR LEE METCALF

I approach this commentary on Richard Ney's *The Wall Street Gang* with a mixture of pride and trepidation. I am proud that Mr. Ney has seen fit to single out in Chapter 2 an exposure of some of the activities of the Wall Streeters I have tried to bring to the attention of the American people; and I am concerned that perhaps I cannot do justice to a book that is more knowledgeable, more comprehensive, and more informative than anything I have achieved.

When Richard Ney published his earlier book *The Wall Street Jungle,* I read it with interest and amazement. In that book he enumerated some rules to guide investors through the jungle. Rule 12 therein was "Do not have your stock with your broker in street name. It is his power to vote this stock as the owner of record that gives the NYSE its power over the nation's political-industrial-military complex."

When I read that, just one of more than a score of admonitions to the investor, I recognized that my search for identification of the names on the nominee list and identification of the security holdings of the New York bank were significant not only in the utility field, in which I was concerned at the time, but in the entire area of business activity in America dominated by Wall Street and the financial institutions. Hence the inquiries started and the results described in Chapter 2 of *The Wall Street Gang*.

But that is just one chapter of a book that is devastating in its attack on the financial system in other areas.

For years we have suspected that the regulatory commissions have been the captives of the agencies that they purport to regulate. But not until we had the documentation of the failures of the Securities and Exchange Commission and the Interstate Commerce Commission in protecting investors was suspicion brought home to investors.

In his chapter on the SEC Mr. Ney demonstrates an understanding of the esoteric operations of the Stock exchange. Operations are controlled for the benefit of the insiders who have the special information and the clout to profit from all sorts of transactions, regardless of the actual value of the stock traded. The investor is left out or is an extraneous factor. The actual value of the listed stock is irrelevant. The name of the game is manipulation.

The SEC either is not interested in or cannot find out about these insider deals that are actually frauds upon the millions of small investors.

The failure of the regulatory commissions to regulate the insidious complicity between the government and the insiders on Wall Street to defraud investors is spelled out. (This includes the judiciary; although Mr. Ney does point toward a new and more favorable trend in recent decisions.) Case histories are given so that each investor can recognize the symptoms of a fraud if one is being practiced upon him. And Mr. Ney tells such an investor what to do about it.

The charts and the tables are informative and illuminating, as might be expected from a technician of the stature of Mr. Ney. But they are more than that, more than the similar charts that appear in the daily papers and the business periodicals because of the lucid explanations that accompany them.

The Wall Street Jungle was an impressive work. It recited the little known facts about the perils and obstacles of Wall Street. But *The Wall Street Gang* is even more impressive and informative. It is a guidebook and road map through and around the pitfalls in the Wall Street Jungle. It belongs in every investor's library; it should be required reading in every business school. Besides, it is a fascinating study that has all the suspense of a book of mystery stories. Mr. Ney has performed a great public service in using his analyst's skill, his knowledge, and his perception in a book that could save Americans millions of dollars.

Preface

Truth is not only stranger than fiction; it is a vital necessity. At a time when the vision of a better world seems to be growing dimmer, when the comfortable convictions about the relation of the few who rule to the many who are ruled have disappeared almost completely, the ability to distinguish between fact and fiction carries an exponential factor. The need for truth about the stock market, for real knowledge instead of pseudo-knowledge as the principal motivator of individual and collective action, becomes more urgent when it can be seen that the crisis now existing for investors is caused by the absence of truth.

Even the most generous appraisal of how the Stock Exchange extends its favors when it extends them, and for how much, cannot disregard the plain fact that the truths of the marketplace are reserved for the very rich and the complex of financial interests concerned with the maintenance of the *status quo*. The Exchange insider's ability to suppress the truth, however, is due less to his economic power than to his control over the nation's media and the machinery of information. Regrettably, those like myself, who know the truth and seek to share it are no match for those who know it and seek to suppress it. For this reason and because access to the media is limited, it can be much more difficult to tell the truth than to hide it. Though the lords of the press and the heads of the media clamor for the acquisition of positive knowledge and the play of ideas, if the ideas are unfamiliar to them or threaten the sanctified beliefs of the Stock Exchange, they will come down on these ideas like a carload of bricks—or else seek to silence them by ignoring them. No matter.

This state of affairs is not only fixed by custom and sanctioned by government but also proclaimed by an invisible system of myths and institutions that makes it next to impossible for the investor to do anything except indulge in self-deceiving rationalizations that have no lasting validity and propositions that cannot be verified in practice. Since cause is linked by an umbilical cord of piano wire to effect, the investor is inevitably ruined.

As both a market professional and an ordinary being who is deeply disturbed by the ill will and folly that seem to go hand in hand in the market, I am, perhaps, more surprised and distressed than I should be by the covert partnership between government and Wall Street that serves to keep the market's essential truths from investors. The only difference between the New York Stock Exchange and a dictatorship is that the dictator confiscates your money outright whereas the New York Stock Exchange merely says you've made a bad investment. This is a situation I find difficult to understand and impossible to accept.

As for the average investor, he is confused and apprehensive. Only a fool wouldn't be. He has discovered that, while he has been working longer hours for more money than ever before, he's being outrun by taxes, inflation, and the high cost of living. Whereas his parents were able to get along with less than half of what he earns, he isn't half as secure financially as they were. Indeed, because of the technical limitations imposed on him by his ignorance of the market and the losses he has sustained, he wonders if there are any solutions to his problems.

Wherever I go I am asked: "What shall I do with my money?" "What can I do to protect myself against inflation?" "Shall I take my losses in the market or hold on?" Implicit in these questions is the final question: Why in a country with the highest standard of living in the world should almost everyone who isn't a millionaire have suddenly come to the conclusion he is no longer competent to manage his own affairs?

These are questions I have been trying to answer for the layman long before he thought to ask them. As early as 1962, on radio and television and in my appearances before Congress, I pointed to the Stock Exchange as the source of the country's future financial problems. But it is one expression of the Exchange's power that education and improved methods of communication, instead of bringing investors closer to the truths of the stock market, have enabled the Exchange to so organize the community's myths that it is now able to totally dominate not only the private interests and potentialities of the investment community but the whole of society. Indeed, the most complex truth about the stock market is that the ceaseless motion and commotion imposed on investors and their centers of direction can be attributed to a directing dynamism imposed by traditional ways of thinking and reacting. The fostering of these traditions and myths explains the paradox of why a community of investors dedicated to information are constantly defeated by the information at their command. It is curious how the common sense of so many investors has ignored this fact and its corollary: The more the real order of things is revealed to the many, the less the order of things will be to those few who manipulate the market.

In the pages that follow, I will show investors how, by scrapping traditional approaches to the market and learning how to buy when Stock Exchange insiders buy, and to sell when they sell, the investor can beat them at their own game. Knowing full well that a taste for such things must be created, I will also seek to show that what the investor needs who has been defrauded, apart from convincing evidence of fraud, is a good attorney.

Finally, I would point out that, although it may be that many who have failed in the market have made hay of their failure by writing books to tell how they were "wiped out," be sure there is nothing of the sour grape in this volume. I have no regrets nor any fears as I lead my stable of clients into and out of the market. For the rest, since I am under no financial compulsion to change the system, I can only say I have written this book, which completes the set I intended to write on this subject, because I must. Someone long ago said, "So long as you believe in some truth you do not believe in yourself. You are a servant, a man of faith."

That, I suppose, describes my situation as well as any. The book is about a subject that is important to me. I can only treat it honestly. I naturally hope most people will agree with me and find in it the answers that bring them security and success in the market. I shall not be surprised or disappointed, however, if it offends those who, because of their desperate bias or their efforts to suppress the truth, are unconvinced. Their rejection is of no concern to me. Each of us according to his lights must choose whether he wishes truth or tranquility. We cannot have both.

Acknowledgments

Not the least of life's joys is to work with someone beautiful; it becomes something of a miracle when she also happens to be brilliant. For many reasons it is impossible to define or adequately describe the gratitude I feel toward my friend and associate, Mei-Lee. I cannot help but think that her total grasp of my methodology and her financial expertise gained its momentum more from the character of her culture and ancestry than from her earlier financial background as a stockbroker. Her imaginative authority over my writing and her sense of choice and value in the book's organization was paramount and unchallenged.

I have also acquired an altogether amiable set of obligations toward others. First there is Léon King of Praeger whose mind reached out to select my book and who then earnestly gathered in all the preparations and necessities needed for its publication. His long hours, enormous experience, and editorial help are deeply appreciated.

I would also like to express my gratitude toward Suzy Koniecy, another dear friend. Her discerning gifts as a photographer have a peculiar interest for anyone seeking hints and revelations of personal awareness. A talented visionary of the small fact, her photographs compel a maximum of meaning from a minimum of evidence.

Then there is Mei-Lee's husband Steve Fox of the Associated Press who read the manuscript and who knows so well how to impart a suggestion without stating it, but who approaches it again and again in such a way that you yourself come in contact with it. A former stockbroker, he, too, long ago began to question the assumptions of Wall Street.

I am grateful to the librarians at Beverly Hills, as also at UCLA, for their assistance; to Lucky Roberts, Joan Gluck Young, Mia Miyashiro, Teresa Calabrese, and Les Dornfeld.

Lastly there is my friend and agent, Scott Meredith, whose imaginative enterprise and professional ability to cope, assist, and guide have provided me with everything I could wish to have, and more.

In sum, I cannot help but reflect that, it is the presence of friends that measures a man's success.

THE
WALL
STREET
GANG

If you will be persuaded by me, pay little attention to Socrates, but much more to the truth, and if I appear to you to say anything true, assent to it, but if not, oppose me with all your might.

Socrates, in Plato, *Phaedo,* 360 B.C.

The truth has always been dangerous to the rule of the rogue, the exploiter, the robber. So the truth must be suppressed.

Eugene V. Debs

1. Confessions of a Croupier

In which it is shown that I could have learned the truth about Las Vegas East a lot sooner if only I hadn't allowed its pit bosses to help me.

The extent of our insights no more rests with us than the chance events that fate places in our path. This at any rate is the interpretation I put upon the evidence at my disposal to explain my entry into the securities business in 1961. As I look back to those earlier days, a sense of the inevitability of things seems to run through the course of my life. This, I believe, more than anything else, caused me to leap overnight from the optimism of the actor into the nihilism of the securities industry. I am not a creature of compulsion; the essential paradox of my life is that my present surefootedness springs from an extraordinary uncertainty of judgment. If I have gained some measure of control over my decisions it is because I am aware of the thinness of the ice I am skating on.

Aware of the moment's potentials for disaster, wherever possible I have tended to evade the necessity of exposing myself to risk until I have examined my materials to determine how well they can be expected to serve my purposes. I used to be critical of the time it took me to accomplish my tasks, until I realized that the world is in a state of collapse because most people are too willing to act on the basis of hastily improvised perceptions that leave them in the grip of delirium—a condition in which they must obey rather than command their society's secret processes. During the twenty-year period in which I was an actor, my reserve served as a handicap; in my present profession, this limitation has become a tangible asset.

Generally the momentum of one man's instincts is much the same as everyone else's, so I cannot help but wonder what causes me to evaluate things and people so differently from others. Why

3

is it, I ask myself, that I am lacking in the allegiance to tradition
that seems to strait-jacket my contemporaries? And why, almost
all my life, have my legitimate aspirations caused such an estrange-
ment from the leaders of society? My conspicuous alienation from
my contemporaries in the securities industry exists largely because
I cannot take seriously every idea of the businessman or politician
simply because everyone else does. Nor am I eager to choose
or judge until I have examined methods and purposes to see if
they form a logical chain. If all is as I think it should be, and as
I am told it is, I will be able to judge for myself whether their
methods are the best or the worst.

When I consider these things I can only conclude they are the
legacy that springs from the soil of my origins. My mother was
descended from Irish-English parents, my father from Alsatian
and Viennese. Thus I am the beneficiary of a mother's great sensi-
bility, and the analytic power of a father who separated ideas from
objects and emotions from labels.

My father's prudence, thrift, and simplicity asserted themselves
at an early age against his new-found traditions. He was without
ponderous academic pretensions or religious dogma, guided instead by solid instincts, experience, and common sense. Two
things he told me were typical of his skeptical philosophy. When
I was in my senior year at Columbia College, he admonished:
"God gave you talent, you must wait for luck to give you opportunity." Then, in late 1962, after he'd read one of my market
reports, he commented, "You seem so shocked at the behavior of
your friends on the Exchange. Yet it is only what men *won't* do
for money that should surprise you." He developed in me a keen
scent for the blindness of instinct, the habit of taking what most
men say and do with a grain of salt, and an understanding of why
they behave as they do without the wish to behave in the same
way.

My insights into people were, therefore, much more substantial
than my comprehension of the market when I entered the Bache
brokerage house in 1960. Although I had done some trading, I
was nonetheless ignorant in both my intuitions about the market
and in my facts. Only later did I come to learn that whatever spark
of intuition I might have had about the market was prejudiced
by my education in economics. Indeed, I attribute my early losses
in the market to my study of economics. I have no doubt that had
the subject appealed to me more than it did, I would long ago have
gone bankrupt. One thing, however, was not difficult to see: The
influence the hysteria in the Bache boardroom had over me and
the other traders was greater than the influence we had over our-

selves. Accordingly, I decided to take a leave of absence from active trading in the market the better to observe my fellow traders. I did this with the hope I could gain insight into our errors of judgment while I still had some money left to call my own.

An endless variety of market experts seemed to walk through that noisy, crowded room—chartists, fundamentalists, economists, and astrologers. The research on which they based their opinions on stocks made them biased and fiery. They would praise and denounce each other, pointing out how half the facts that proper understanding should have revealed had been overlooked. Costly errors of judgment were explored first from one quarter and then from another in order to show how wise they were and how stupid their fellows. If this taught me anything, it was that a few occasions of good luck could cause them to have more pride in their talents as market experts than their talents warranted. At first, however, I was naïve enough to take their self-inflating mannerisms and systems of analysis at face value. Then they would go off and demonstrate that they were, in fact, men after Humpty Dumpty's own heart. Worse still, no matter how wrong their views proved to be they seemed always unwilling to abandon the approach they had taken. They had gotten themselves into a rut, and almost without exception each of them proceeded to dig deeper into it until they buried themselves.

I was fortunate to have as a friend the then active manager of this branch of the brokerage firm. His mission, it seemed, was to keep some sort of order in the asylum under his charge. His name was Bill Blatner. It was he who, with his puckish sense of humor, ultimately persuaded me to become an investment adviser.

As he walked from his office between the rows of desks in front of the ticker tape, there seemed nothing particularly different in his appearance from that of anyone else. Yet his passage rarely went unnoticed. Invariably, someone would stop him, in most cases just to pass the time of day with someone whose presence made you aware he cared about you. Although he might offer a recommendation on stock if asked, which often proved disastrous, he never repeated the commonplaces of Wall Street propaganda. He installed a small desk for me in his office, from which I could view, in private and quiet, what I came to think of as "the arena," where traders behaved like mystics who thought they'd heard the voice of God.

Blatner introduced me to the Bache partners who visited Beverly Hills from time to time and who impressed me enormously with the impalpable aura of their power. I was equally impressed to watch how many martinis they could put away at luncheon without any visible change in the outer man. I wondered that they had always so little to say about the market and concluded that, unlike everyone else at Bache, being inwardly illuminated they found no need to parade their wisdom before others. Their conversation tended to be about unimportant matters, as though nothing else happened. As such, they were an incentive to the practice of silence which I thought warranted imitation as much as it did praise. (I was to learn later that they were fed up with talking about the market and had come to Beverly Hills to get away from it.)

At that time, I found no reason to impugn their motives or to challenge their authority. Consequently, their stature and encouragement (I was not beyond the reach of their encouragement) caused me to entertain a warm admiration for them and the legends that surrounded them as Wall Street financiers. While they were materialists to the core, I told myself that it was better to model a life on their goals than to identify my interests any longer with Stanislavsky's acting methods. The more I esteemed these men the more my interest in their way of life grew. How better, I asked myself, to bring to an end the unsatisfactory compromise between my contradictory and often incompatible tendencies? On the one hand, I had wanted to act and write plays but had done neither as well as I would have wished; on the other, I wanted to make good use of the energy with which I was endowed.

Also by that time I had returned to trading on a daily basis. I assumed, in my ignorance, that I knew as much as the next fellow and that my understanding of the market had freed me from the danger of running my head into a stone wall. The fact that I had begun to be quite successful I attributed to exceptional talent instead of good luck or the fact that it was early 1961 with the Dow Average in a strong uptrend.

I finally decided to take the material of existence that lay close at hand and, by abandoning acting, strike out into fresh territory. I made this decision in the course of filming a segment on the "Wagon Train" series. I was again playing an Englishman, this time being chased by Indians. Neurasthenic as much from lurching counter-clockwise in a stagecoach as from combat with Indians, I called Bill Blatner that night and asked him to lunch with me the following day.

After lunch Bill and I were walking back to his office at Bache. "I think I will take the examination," I told him, "and become a broker." He stopped and, in a very sincere tone, said, "You'll do no such thing." When I asked him why, he suggested that anyone who held my strong opinions would loathe the oppression practiced on stockbrokers by the Exchange. He had always managed to remain uncritical of other people, but now he was outspoken enough for me to assume that he had been concealing a highly independent and reflective nature. "Become an investment adviser," he told me. "It will take less time and cost only $25." He pointed out that my educational background and my experience as a trader qualified me. In due course I filed the papers, and in July, 1961, I received my registration from the SEC. As usual, however, Bill's forecast was too optimistic. My entry into the investment business cost $50, not $25.

With more enthusiasm than expertise, I proceeded to compose my first market report on the day I received my registration. Thinking I had more wisdom than I possessed, I sought to share with others the exact value I placed on things. Blatner saw to it a copy was placed on each broker's desk. No sooner was this done than the resident partner worked his way through the boardroom confiscating each and every copy. He'd located what he thought was a phallic reference to his boardroom, which, of course, hadn't occurred to me until he mentioned it. Once pointed out, the metaphor seemed so apt, I came to consider it deeply integrated with the ideals and norms of the business.

Though aware that I had not discovered any transcendent or absolute truths about the market, I did feel that the charting techniques I had begun to develop, with the help of one of Bache's most successful investors, enabled me to make my journey through the market with a Baedeker of sorts. I owe this man a great debt of gratitude, since without his initial help I doubt I would ever have been able to see an inch beyond my nose. His name is Al Pepper, and it says a great deal about his educated intuitions and imaginative charting techniques that he has continued to prosper.

I was struck by the fact that no one had yet gone so far as to predict a market crash. For as we moved into August, 1961, I could see that, although the public had begun to regard rising stock prices as a never ending source of manna from heaven, the revelations provided by my charting techniques indicated that this allegedly beneficent period of prosperity would soon come to an end.

Where arrogance so exceptional for one with my behavior patterns began, or in what heredity it was rooted, is hard to say, but I was now publishing my views on a weekly basis. Five hundred subscribers received it—free. Over Bill Blatner's protests that I was going out on a limb unnecessarily, I announced that the investor's pleasure with the continuing advance of stock prices had blinded him to the imminence of a forthcoming market decline. Most analysts are always optimistic about the market because to be otherwise is bad for business. Thus, when I made my forecast it was axiomatic that it would be questioned by the stockbrokers at Bache. I had anticipated this. Stockbrokers tend to be very critical of others, if for no other reason than that their customers are almost always very critical of them. On August 25, 1961, my forecast was headlined on the *Los Angeles Herald Examiner*'s financial page:

NEY PREDICTING D-J AVERAGE WILL HIT 750

The Dow Averages will continue their uptrend through mid-September, into the range of 750, before reacting into the mid-July trading range, Richard Ney, Beverly Hills investment counsellor, predicts. He holds to this view despite the auto strike threat sell-off of the past two days.

Ney has his own set of market indicators, and in both general market trend and in individual stock price ranges has scored a substantial record of accuracy.

He advises a strategy of switching to the "few situations that offer growth and security," maintaining a cash reserve for the attractive situations that will present themselves in the next two months and a mental attitude that is willing to accept the proposition current market action is typical of the last swings of a bull move.

Last July 31, after calling attention to the week's huge Dow gains as confirmation of his oft-repeated prediction from mid-June on, Ney urged purchase of Studebaker at 7¼. Those who took his advice were well rewarded. Last Friday morning he predicted this stock would go to near 13 and that a reaction would follow. The stock actually went to 12¼ before being hit by profit taking.

This reaction, Ney told us Thursday, is following the pattern the charts indicate for Studebaker.

Shortly thereafter *Time* magazine interviewed me concerning my views on the market, but the New York office decided I was "too pessimistic" and killed the story.

Having established myself as the fugleman of disaster and suffered the stigma of Bache's thirty-odd critics, when the market advanced to the 745 level in December and then began to retreat, its death rattle was like the sound of violins to my ears. Had my profane auguries failed to materialize, I doubt I would ever again have dared to voice the warnings the Stock Exchange is always so anxious to stifle.

I had entered the investment business prepared to be enthusiastic, but no sooner had I established my credentials and overcome my initial timidity than I began to recognize the reasons for the absence of security in the market and the hazards attached to any attempt to achieve the hoped for success that lies deep in the heart of all investors. Failure did not come, I realized, because of some inscrutable, ungovernable economic event but because of the peculiar requirements of human nature on the floor of the Exchange. There can seldom have been a more abrupt recognition of this than when, on a certain occasion, I happened to pick up and glance through the sheets published by the Francis Emory Fitch Company. Although I had been an adviser for almost a year, I had no knowledge of this publication or even of the existence of a service that provided investors with a daily rundown of all the transactions that occurred in each stock listed on the floor of the Exchange. Studying the transactions in each stock, I became immediately conscious that, on too many occasions to be a coincidence, a stock would advance from its morning low and then, often during the afternoon, would show an uptick of a half-point or more on a large block of anywhere from 1,500 to 5,000 or more shares. This transaction seemed to herald a transformation in what was taking place, for immediately thereafter the stock would begin to drop like Newton's apple. Before I could find out what caused this, another question presented itself: What caused the same thing to happen at the low point in that stock's decline? For it was also apparent that a block of stock of the same size often appeared on a downtick of a half-point or more, after which the stock quickly rallied. Together these two facts seemed to give a stock's pattern continuity.

At the end of several days of investigation, I discovered that these transactions at the top and bottom of a stock's price pattern were for the specialist's own account. The probability was, I learned, that at the top it was either a sale or a short sale for his trading account—or a combination of sale and short sale. At the bottom, it was a transaction in which the specialist covered his short position and went "long" before rallying his stock.

Clod that I was, I had at last recognized that, although the study of human nature may not be fashionable among economists, it is never out of season. Herein lay the answer to the riddle of the investor's putting two and two together and coming up with zero. It was almost too good to be true, but there before me was the evidence: The big block at the top and the big block at the bottom were appearing at the boundaries established by my charts. The Fitch sheets were pointing out something that should have been obvious to the careful tapewatcher.

This time a bombshell had been added to my general store of knowledge concerning the imperatives of market analysis. The information streaming from the tape enabled me to break through every obstacle and to see through every illusion. While I had, in a sense, become a spectator at Wall Street's version of "crime without punishment," I was also slowly learning how to play with loaded dice in a crooked gambling casino. Everything else was as fictitious, obscure, and irrational as human effort could make it.

Through the keyhole provided by the Fitch sheets, I began to explore the minute world of the Stock Exchange. Studying the placement of big blocks, I perceived that substance, sanity, and the wisdom of the world had no place in it. It existed according to its own pulse of time, its own laws, and its own standards of behavior. I found an invisible nightmare world that haunted the rise and fall of the American empire. Its organization, its scope, and its aims, like war itself, explained why technological and cultural achievement had failed to bring with it a higher standard of living for all Americans; why the tremendous differentiation in well-being still existed between social classes; why so much was expended on military power; and why this power was enlisted to serve the wide-ranging economic interests of this ever colonizing, power-grabbing community.

As an investment adviser I'd begun a trek through a jungle that, for all its padded luxury, had dumped human conscience as excess baggage. It was a safari conducted by the Stock Exchange specialist in which the concepts of the kill and the overkill meant the maximization of profits—with an indispensable minimum of conventional fair play thrown in for the sake of appearances. It was a battle in which the stockbroker served as an extension of the Exchange. He was its mercenary in the field and received special fees for special kills.

Until I became aware of these facts I had been like an amateur big game hunter out to make a "killing" in the market. Although I had become an investment adviser, I was still vulnerable to Wall Street's long-time professionals. These were the heads of specialist and brokerage firms whom I knew and trusted, the white hunters in their pin-stripe suits and starched collars. Out of the warp and woof of the specialists' practices they had woven the pattern of their lives, their leaky old yachts (sitting in the water next to their Greenwich estates), their drafty old Fifth Avenue townhouses, and their homes away from home in Florida, Palm Springs, and the south of France.

Lunching with me at "21" or sharing a drink on Christmas Eve, they were always quick to point out the "safe sanctuaries" for me and my clients; the new and exciting investments that made it all as simple as "shooting fish in a barrel." These were the owners of the hunting preserve. I felt I was in my element as I rubbed elbows with them. Almost too late I sniffed the truth—that I was the hunted, not the hunter. The minds of these men were the mind of the market. The more I began to distinguish between their optical illusions and their practical effects, the more the signs and seals of their integrity evaporated. Because politicians and the press glorified them with all the reverence men give to the dead, the nation's investors had become like 33 million Humpty Dumpties with no chance of a soft landing.

Then, quite unexpectedly, *Time* magazine commented on my work as an investment adviser in a June, 1962, cover story. It cited me as having pinpointed the timing of the market crash then under way. Shortly thereafter, Mr. Ira Haupt, the head of the firm of that name (and one of the most important specialists on the floor of the Exchange) retained me as investment consultant for his Beverly Hills brokerage office. Bill Blatner had left Bache to manage Haupt's new offices. My own office was above Bill's— it was through him that I had met Haupt. I was able to increase my clientele and extend my services. But the nature of my new retainer bound me in a manner of speaking to the Stock Exchange. I was vaguely frustrated by the relationship and couldn't help but wonder if the retainer was meant to color my unbiased view of the Stock Exchange's mad world. Certainly there was no better lever for social control. I was now part of the team and shared the same interests as the team. My fee was a tacit reminder that by accepting the Exchange's way of doing things I stood to make a handsomer profit than I'd ever imagined possible. On the basis of my recent successes, when I visited my home in New York I was invited to dinner by the heads of major brokerage firms and taken on extended tours of the Exchange, where I had occasion to meet with the team's managers, the specialists. I recall meeting the specialists in RCA and Telephone and thinking of them as the mechanics who kept the Exchange mechanism in working order. I questioned them about their methods—as guilelessly as possible—but they would tell me nothing. They alone knew how to operate their multibillion-dollar juggernaut, and, whatever slight ego satisfaction telling me how they made their fortunes might have given them, it wasn't worth it. Indeed, knowledge of their good fortune was more likely to please their enemies than their friends.

The momentum of my self-interest had place me, it seemed, on the winning side. It was all so easy. Mr. Haupt was a cheery, benevolent gentleman. It was impossible to associate him with anything that didn't further distinguish the grammar of charity.

He was gentle to talk to; he never insisted on forcing his notions of the market on anyone. As much, perhaps, as anyone I'd ever known, he evidenced a genuine concern for the needs and wishes of others. But a knowledge of how to make money in the market ran in, around, and underneath every word he uttered. And when he called from New York and told Bill Blatner or myself to buy, we bought; when he told us to disregard the news stories and sell, we sold. He was never wrong. He had the gift of total insight into all that was happening on the floor.

It was all *too* easy. I began to sense something sinister in myself —and pathetic. More to the point, I was blurring the truth out of my consciousness. Where formerly as an investment adviser I had revered the rule of right, and where public service had occupied as chief a place in my work as my own interests, now I had adopted a Calvinist attitude. That made it easier to say I was doing what I did because I had to. This was the rule of every self-seeking power maniac who had ever lived.

But if peaceful coexistence with the Exchange caused the fun to go out of my work for me, for the first time, my new role had begun to contribute a measure of joy to my wife, Pauline. In the past she'd comment, "You have no idea how difficult it makes it for me, Richard, when you say those things about Paul Zuckerman on the very day I'm having luncheon with Ruth."

"But I didn't say anything about Paul," I'd tell her. "I just wrote about the specialist in Chrysler."

With superb logic she'd then ask, "Well, what's the difference? Paul *is* the specialist in Chrysler!"

The rinsing of rhetoric that had taken place since my Haupt retainer and what it had occasioned made her feel as though she was no longer the other half of a wrecking crew when we went out to dinner or joined a group going to "the Dancers" at the St. Regis. Her interest in people, her quick-witted pleasure in the pleasure of others, her inexhaustible sense of what is chic and what isn't, the elegance and charm of gracious conversation, the thin mist of impalpable, impeccable femininity with which she covered the crazy quilt of life's realities—each of these and all of them together made me wish for the ability to attach as much importance as she to the refinements of civilization. But while I valued courtesy, I could not help bearing a grudge against myself when I realized what I was doing. My wife's natural desire not to antagonize our many acquaintances in the securities industry could only be bought at the sacrifice of truth—which was the arid and stereotyped payment made by almost everyone in the industry. With the certainty that I was pleasing others I was equally certain I was not pleasing myself. Nothing was as it ought to be, nor could it be, so long as I wasn't doing what I wanted. I returned to Beverly Hills and resumed my radio and television broadcasts on the market. I also tried to give a scrupulous account of it in my market reports. The work was its own justification. Without it I knew I would lack the strength to follow through in what I thought best.

After one of my television appearances, I had a telephone call from Mr. Haupt. He made it plain that he understood why I was making appearances on television and radio and why I was discussing the practices of specialists. He said he knew that, in my mind, I was doing my best to improve the securities industry. He also said he was not telling me I had to stop what I was doing. He asked me only to understand that, as an investment consultant in his employ, it was incumbent upon me to teach my aspirations to conform to being in his employ, but it didn't seem possible for me to do this. I agreed and resigned as his consultant.

In June, 1963, I flew to Washington to testify before the Senate's Banking and Currency Committee, a group of legislators who were by accident or design controlled by the Stock Exchange. I tried to point out to them that a choice had to be made between the collectivism of the Stock Exchange and the sober needs of government regulation. I learned that, next to an empty stomach, a man's worst enemy would seem to be his own government. On the following day the senators greeted members of the Stock Exchange and their lawyers as though they were the heroes of all their daydreams. Through mutuality of interests, the egos of Washington melted harmoniously into the egos of Wall Street. Alas, there was no room left for the egos of the public. Year after year, they promise to reform the Exchange, which they no doubt mean to do until they assess what the Exchange promises them if they don't.

When I finished my testimony Eileen Shanahan of the *New York Times,* along with the reporter from the *Wall Street Journal,* interviewed me. I thought that, even if the senators had only reluctantly listened to my testimony (most of them walked out on it), their allegiance to the Exchange would be somewhat diluted when the press accorded wide recognition to my views about the Exchange's specialist system. But the newspapers' critical pronouncements the following day made me wonder at the personal code of reporters who could so enthusiastically interview a subject and then willfully ignore his documented assertions because they might be offensive to Wall Street. Their comments completely ignored the centrality and range of the issues I'd raised. They turned a cold shoulder to my testimony and, as though I were the devil himself, booted me into the bottomless pit. The *Wall Street Journal* stated: "It's unlikely Richard Ney will ever affect the course of securities legislation."

When I returned to Los Angeles, I had a letter from G. Keith Funston, the president of the New York Stock Exchange, who had written to tell me that I was "biting the hand that feeds" me. But was the Exchange feeding me or anyone else? Was it not, rather, biting the hands its suppliants stretched out to it for help? Had Funston, I wondered, begun to deceive himself so that he might deceive others with impunity?

Since what men assumed to be true about the Stock Exchange establishment had great influence on what happened to them in the market, I decided to attack its fortress and open its doors so that they might examine it before they placed their trust in it. It was with this determination that I laid plans for the writing of *The Wall Street Jungle*.

Looking back on all these events from my present vantage point, I can only wonder that I ever entertained the notion that my indwelling conviction of wrong would carry me through the seven years it would take to complete the first of what I realized in the writing would probably be two volumes. Nor do I deceive myself that it could have been accomplished without guidance from others whose imaginative resources made it possible for me to express my experiences sincerely. Most notable among these was one whom I dared mention only as "Kip" in the first book's acknowledgments, lest its possible lack of success reflect unfavorably on him—Clifton Fadiman. Perhaps one day, in another volume, I will be able to describe the cumulative effect his long hours of editing had on my thinking and on my work.

Nor was I disheartened that it took so many years to prepare. Indeed, to have abandoned the effort for any reason would have seemed self-incriminating heresy. Seized as I am by the notion that all our efforts are grounded in eternal sources of cosmic experience, there wasn't a moment's doubt the task would be completed. I could think of nothing more rewarding to do than take up my slingshot, say goodby to my friends, and start up the hill to do battle.

2. Who Owns America?

In which it is shown that wealthy revolutionaries substitute stock proxies for gunpowder.

It is no accident that most investors lose money in the stock market. Their losses are an inevitable by-product of their ignorance of how little they know about the invisible world of the Stock Exchange. Like machines dominated by external influences, they are capable only of mechanical action.

Regrettably, the arrangements that exist to preserve the traditions and legalize the frauds of the securities industry are inseparable from the general organization of a society controlled by the financial establishment, a society whose laws and principal customs have been contrived to serve the special interests of the financial community. Thus, although the Stock Exchange's most profitable practices clearly compromise the freedoms granted others by the constitution, Exchange Insiders are granted immunity from the legal obligations and penalties that should be imposed on them.

We find ourselves in a situation where government not only has no intention of controlling the distinctive features of covert Stock Exchange power, but exists to enhance it by implementing its monopoly powers over the financial markets and the entire community of investors. The Exchange's monopoly could not have been achieved without assistance from the Federal Reserve System and the Eastern banking establishment. More important than anything else, however, has been the government's cooperation through the Securities and Exchange Commission. Strange as it may seem, great strides have been made in the growth of the Exchange's uncontrolled power since the passage of the Securities Exchange Act of 1934. By pretending to address itself to the investor's needs and appealing to his greed, the SEC has almost succeeded in masking the objectives of the Stock Exchange.

To compound the investor's problems, the information he draws from his newspaper's financial page affects him like chloroform one day and an irresistible aphrodisiac the next. The heads of the news media do not inform investors, largely because their collective morality is determined by stock prices and those who control them. As lords of the press, they are conditioned by their culture and by their position in the world of big business. The public's deferential attitude toward the Stock Exchange, therefore, is the product of an invisible and anonymous type of human engineering that shapes and dominates its imagination. Through proprietary ownership of the stock of publishing houses, newspapers, magazines, television networks, electronic means of information storage, and so forth, the Exchange is able to exert control over their policies and administrative procedures. The Exchange's achievement in this area provides a primer on the art of the coup d'état. What we're talking about is the greatest financial conspiracy in modern times.

As a people, we nourish a national faith in the ethical probity of our super-rich and respected fellow Americans. It is beyond our comprehension that Exchange insiders, bankers, and billionaires might underhandedly seek to gain control of the country's economic wealth and power. The traditional attitudes of most Americans embody a mawkish admiration for Wall Street. The public naïvely assumes that the possession of great wealth and position somehow makes it impossible for the American billionaire to run off the track in search of greater wealth and greater power.

Although most investors will believe that "Communist conspiracies are now increasingly in the ascendency"; the "Nazi conspiracy" was the most significant political experience of the late 1930's; and Greeks, Turks, Asians, and South Americans are even now conspiring against the middle-class traditions of their respective countries, it is considered paranoid to assume that such a thing could happen here. Certainly, American bankers would never think of themselves as "Communists," Fascists," or "Socialists." For that reason, it's a mistake to employ such labels. Even the Watergate conspiracy was not so much a conspiracy of Republican politicians as a covert plan of action by Wall Street investment bankers and lawyers (it should be pointed out that Maurice Stans is a stockbroker and John Mitchell a bond expert) to entrench themselves in power. These men are all high up in the pecking order of a financial establishment that believes in law and order only if it is *its* law and *its* order. Let a situation arise contrary to this establishment's wishes, and you find yourself faced

with revolutionaries as radical as any bomb-thrower who believes
"the end justifies the means."

The fact is, as an investor (or just as an ordinary citizen) you
need be far less frightened of the Communist specter than of
Washington's obedience to the sacred imperatives of Wall Street.
If you wonder for a moment how it exerts its invisible will over
the securities industry, you have only to read the New York Exchange's rules and regulations. The unswerving discipline, obedience, and loyalty it demands for its self-interest is more typical of
a totalitarian collective than a democratic institution.

One man who gave this conspiracy meticulous critical attention
and who claims to have been associated with its elite financial
group is Professor Carrol Quigley of the Foreign Service School
at Georgetown University. He says of this group or, as he calls it,
"network":

> I know of the operations of this network because I have studied it for
> twenty years and was permitted for two years in the early 1960's to
> examine its papers and its secret records. I have no aversion to it or to
> most of its aims and have for much of my life been close to it and
> to many of its instruments. I have objected, both in the past and
> recently, to a few of its policies . . . but in general my chief difference
> of opinion is that it wishes to remain unknown and I believe its role
> in history is significant enough to be known.

One of this network's "instruments" is the stock market, and I
doubt very much that the good professor understands anything
about the way it is being employed to achieve its end, which Professor Quigley states is "nothing less than to *create a world system
of financial control in private hands able to dominate the political
system of each country and the economy of the world as a whole.*"
(Emphasis added.)

Speaking before the Ecumenical Council, Father Pedro Arrupe,
head of the Jesuit Order of the Roman Catholic Church (which
is *the* order of scholars and educators), made essentially the same
charge about this small group of Wall Street conspirators. In a
story datelined October 27, 1965, the UPI quoted him:

> This . . . society operated in an extremely efficient manner at least
> in its higher levels of leadership. It makes use of every possible
> means at its disposal, be they scientific, social, or economic.
>
> It follows a perfectly mapped out strategy. It holds almost com-
> plete sway in international organizations, *in financial circles, in the
> field of mass communication, press, cinema, radio and television.*
> [Emphasis added.]

It is unfortunate that men like Professor Quigley and Father Arrupe are obliged to theorize from a position *outside* the financial establishment. The public is too easily persuaded to regard them as extremists and intellectual radicals.

Senator Lee Metcalf (D.-Montana), on the other hand, is a theorist in close touch with the realities of financial power. I had become accustomed to the typical responses of the Washington bureaucracy when, in 1971, I met Senator Metcalf. He was the *only* Senator who demonstrated an interest in assisting me in my investigations of the Exchange establishment and the institutional framework of which it is the guardian. It was Metcalf who intervened with Senator Gaylord Nelson (D.-Wisconsin) to have me speak as an invited witness in August, 1972, before the Senate monopoly subcommittee, and who introduced me at the hearings. And it was Senator Metcalf who revealed that the New York Stock Exchange, working hand in glove with major New York banks, has gained proprietary control of what appears to be almost every major corporation in this country.

On June 24, 1971, Senator Metcalf asked "Who Owns America?" and entered into the *Congressional Record* the "Secret Nominee List," which gives the corporate code names used by American companies to hide the identity of stockholders from the public. He began his remarks this way:

> Aftco, Byeco, Cadco, Bebco, Ertco, Fivco, Floco, Forco, Gepco, Ninco, Octco, Oneco, Quinco, Sevco, Sixco, Tenco, Treco, Twoco . . . may sound like a space age counting system. In reality, each is part of the corporate code. Each of these names is a nominee—a front name—used by the Prudential Insurance Co. of America to hide some of its interests.
>
> Use of nominees, also known in the securities trade as "street names" or "straws," to hide beneficial ownership of stock is a common corporate practice today. . . .
>
> How does one find out that Aftco is really Prudential, that Kane & Co. is really Chase Manhattan Bank, that Cede & Co., is the Stock Clearing Corp., which is a wholly owned subsidiary of the New York Stock Exchange?
>
> The answer is simple if you are a select insider. The answer is difficult or impossible to find out if you are an outsider, even a party to a case in which corporate ownership is an important issue.
>
> Many answers are found in the "Nominee List." It is published by the American Society of Corporate Secretaries, 9 Rockefeller Plaza, New York, N.Y. 10020. The executive director of the society is John S. Black, Jr.
>
> Last month the managing editor of a string of suburban news-

papers, W. J. Elvin III, of Globe Newspapers, Vienna, Va., asked the society for a copy of the "Nominee List." His request was denied. Mr. Elvin was told that distribution is limited to the membership.

Mr. Elvin then asked for a copy of the society's membership list. That request, too, was denied. Its distribution was also limited to the membership, he was told. . . .

At my request the American Society of Corporate Secretaries promptly furnished me a copy of its February, 1971, edition of the "Nominee List." . . . The information in this publication, nowhere else available to the best of my knowledge, belongs in the public domain. The press, counsel for the public and, indeed, Government regulators and administrators as well as the Congress and public generally need to know who owns America.

So, along with the code names for all the major Eastern banks, we learned that "Cede & Company" was the code name for the Stock Clearing Corporation of New York, the wholly owned subsidiary of the NYSE!

At a later date Senator Metcalf asked the Securities and Exchange Commission to identify the thirty top stockholders in each of the largest corporations in this country. The SEC responded that it did not have this information and suggested he make the inquiries himself. Senator Metcalf then sent his query to the top nine corporations.

The responses to his March 11 letter showed that Mobil, Chrysler, Ford, and General Electric supplied the requested information. Standard Oil of New Jersey, Texaco, General Motors, IBM, and ITT did not. On April 25, 1972, Senator Metcalf introduced into the Congressional Record the responses to his letter. In order to give the reader some understanding of the shares that are subject to control by the Stock Exchange, figures have been excerpted from the list of nominees presented by Senator Metcalf for General Electric and Mobil Oil.

TABLE 2–1

GENERAL ELECTRIC COMPANY

Number of shares at December 18, 1971

Tepe & Co.[1]	4,993,507
Kane & Co.	3,727,580
Cede & Co.[2]	2,822,602
Cudd & Co.	2,752,552
Atwell & Co.	2,309,912
Sigler & Co.	2,101,643
King & Co.	1,416,402
Barnett & Co.	1,321,360
Merrill Lynch	1,026,041

TABLE 2–2

MOBIL OIL CORPORATION

February 7, 1972

Registration:	Number of shares
Pitt & Co., Bankers Trust Co., New York, N. Y.	5,281,301
Kane & Co., Chase Manhattan Bank, N.A., New York, N.Y.	2,661,000
Cudd & Co., Chase Manhattan Bank, N.A., New York	2,607,491
Cede & Co., Stock Clearing Corp., New York, N.Y.	2,348,306

You will note that Merrill Lynch is listed as a large holder of General Electric stock. It is unusual for a brokerage firm to be named, since most brokerage firms' holdings are normally lumped with Cede & Company. The General Electric list gives us a good example, therefore, of the control that the country's larger brokerage firms are potentially capable of exerting.

Confronted with these facts, the New York Stock Exchange advised Senator Metcalf that its subsidiary, the Stock Clearing Corporation, acts only as a clearing agent and depository and has no power to vote the stock proxies it holds on behalf of its members and others; the proxies of all corporations whose stock is held by the Stock Clearing Corporation, it said, are voted by the beneficial owners of that stock. Yet the bylaws of the Stock Clearing Corporation of New York tell us:

ARTICLE IX. Corporate Instruments and Obligations

3194   Proxies

Sec. 4. The President, a Vice-President or the Treasurer may attend in person and act and *vote on behalf of the Corporation at any meeting of the Stockholders of any corporation in which the Corporation holds stock* or by his signature may appoint in the name and on behalf of the Corporation a proxy to attend and act and vote in respect of such stock at any such meeting. [Emphasis added.]

The immensity of the problems presented by the Stock Exchange's unprecedented control over the stocks held by its depository was revealed for the first time in January, 1974, when Senator Metcalf released the report he had prepared with Senator Muskie (D.-Maine), "Disclosure of Corporate Ownership." It documents the stock holdings of major banks of the Eastern financial establishment and other institutional investors. Senator Metcalf had written to the chief executive officers of 324 corporations requesting lists of the thirty top stockholders and the amount of common stock held by each. Only eighty-nine companies answered all the senator's requests for information. Others supplied partial answers to his questions or none at all. By this writing, the Central Certificate Service (the subsidiary of the Stock Clearing Corporation that actually holds the certificates) had been superseded by the Depository Trust Company. Cede & Company is now the nominee of that entity. Cede & Company was listed as the largest stockholder in 36 companies out of 132. (See Table 2–3.)

TABLE 2–3

THE LARGEST STOCKHOLDER OF 132 COMPANIES IN 1972 AS REPORTED BY RESPONDENTS TO SENATOR METCALF'S LETTER

I. HOLDERS WHICH ARE THE LARGEST STOCKHOLDER OF MORE THAN ONE COMPANY

Holder (Number of companies)	Percent of company's voting stock held by top stockholder
Cede & Co.[1] (36)	
Ashland Oil	7.0
Chrysler	12.1
Ling-Temco-Vought	39.0
Bethlehem Steel	7.2
Greyhound	8.1
United Brands	20.5
Raytheon	5.5
Trans World Airlines	10.6
Pan American Airways	15.0
Eastern Airlines	19.0
Braniff Airways	15.3
Continental Airlines	17.0
Pacific Southwest Airlines	21.3
North Central Airlines	10.6
Penn Central	18.9
Chicago, Milwaukee, St. Paul & Pacific	32.6
Kansas City Southern	13.9
Rio Grande Industries	7.7
Spector Industries	15.1
American Electric Power	5.5
General Telephone & Electric	3.8
Consolidated Edison	5.4
Philadelphia Electric	3.9
American Natural Gas	5.4
Niagara Mohawk Power	6.9
Northeast Utilities	3.0
Union Electric	5.3
Allegheny Power System	5.9
Baltimore Gas & Electric	4.2
Pennsylvania Power & Light	3.8
Potomac Electric Power	6.1
Western Union	6.9
Cleveland Electric Illuminating	3.3
Grand Union	13.6
Interstate Stores	18.7
Charter N.Y. Bank	4.1

Be assured that, when these facts are brought to public attention, the Stock Exchange will cry out "this is inadmissible evidence!" As for the financial press, it will proceed to ignore the central issues relating to the Exchange's nominee, Cede & Company. Yet here Senator Metcalf has revealed Wall Street's phantom parasites in the act of gaining title to the nation's corporate empire. The process for doing so shows all the arcane involutions and muscle of the twentieth century's master financial strategists as they fix a bone-crushing grip on the heavyweights of the industrial complex.

Here the problem is nothing so simple as a corporate takeover, nor anything so obvious as a Greek, German, Italian, or Chilean type of power grab. The harsh facts reveal a tough invisible web being spun across the length and breadth of a nation's business enterprise.

For its part the Exchange, when confronted and asked to justify its practices, instead of tanks and footsoldiers, sends in a platoon of lawyers. With murderous logic and legal rationalizations that border on burlesque, their lawyers direct the charge "irresponsible" at anyone who takes exception to the Exchange's monopolist compulsions. When the Civil Aeronautics Board director of enforcement writes suggesting that the extent of Cede's control is a source of incomprehensible wonder to him, the Exchange's lawyers, with consummate awareness of what they are about, depict what is actually a financial effort of a well-nigh revolutionary nature as an instance of dazzling public service and efficiency. In this case the Exchange is responding to a complaint that its elegantly forged proxy mechanism has effected a sharp break with the once dominant but ever diminishing American ethic of competitive enterprise. The complaint was filed by the Aviation Consumer Action Project, which alleged that: "Cede & Co. . . appears to be an instrument created by certain major stockholders of the airline respondents for the purposes of concealing the identity of such stockholders." In view of the amounts of airline stock held by Cede & Company the complainants further alleged "control by Cede over various air carriers."

In reply, the Exchange lawyers insisted that Cede cannot vote proxies of the stock it holds except on instructions, and that its brokers can take instructions only from their customers. These are the traditional arguments employed by the Exchange. Yet, New York Stock Exchange Rule 451.20 bears the heading "When Brokers May Vote on All Proposals Without Instructions." Upon reading this we discover that, through the use of proxies, control *can* be achieved—with all the finesse of a highly skilled pick-pocket. According to Rule 451.20, all the broker need do is send the following form letter with the proxy material to the beneficial owner of stock:

> To our Clients:
>
> We have been requested to forward to you the enclosed proxy material relative to shares carried by us in your account but not registered in your name. Such shares can be voted only by the holder of record.
>
> We shall be pleased to vote your shares in accordance with your wishes, if you will execute the enclosed proxy form and return it to us promptly in the self-addressed, stamped envelope, also enclosed. It is understood that, if you sign without otherwise marking the form, the shares will be voted as recommended by the management on all matters to be considered at the meeting.
>
> Should you wish to have a proxy covering your shares issued to yourself or others, we shall be pleased to issue the same.
>
> The rules of the New York Stock Exchange provide that if instructions are not received by the tenth day before the meeting, the proxy may be given at discretion by the holder of record of the shares.

Rule 452 states:

> If such instructions are not received by the *tenth* day before the meeting *the proxy may be given at discretion by the owner of record* when the proxy soliciting material is transmitted to the beneficial owner of the stock at least *fifteen* days before the meeting.

If the letter is metered by the broker one day and sent the next, or if the mails delay delivery, can it be received by the investor, examined, and returned in five days? The letter is a hollow gesture, form without content, a superb instance of deception.

The CAB enforcement director wisely felt that the issue of Cede & Company control over certain airline companies was not fully clarified by the generalizations contained in the first letter from the Exchange's lawyer. He therefore sent the lawyer a second letter, which read in part:

> Under Section 408(f) of the Federal Aviation Act of 1958 [49 USC 1378(f)], any person that holds 10% or more of the voting stock of an air carrier shall be presumed to be in control of such air carrier, unless the Board finds otherwise.
>
> In light of such a presumption and the law from cases such as *McClain, et al.* v. *Lanova Corp., et al.*, 39 A. 2d 209, we ask Cede to

fully explain its position that it has no control over any air carrier. The *McClain* case cited Delaware corporation law, to the effect that mere record holders of corporate stock could vote such stock without the directions of real owners, even where record owners were New York brokerage partnerships having no beneficial interest in the stock and notwithstanding any rules of the New York Stock Exchange to the contrary.

With a tone of intense legal scruple, a reply was forthwith addressed to the director of CAB enforcement in which it was grudgingly acknowledged that:

> Cede & Co., as recorder holder, of securities of New York issuers, is entitled to vote such securities (New York Business Corporation Law 612). A similar rule applies with respect to securities of Delaware issuers (General Corporation Law of the State of Delaware 219 [c]) and we assume, with respect to securities of issuers of most, if not all other states.

After admitting still another legal loophole through which Cede can vote proxies, the lawyer brilliantly attempted to cloud the issue by maintaining:

> The theoretical possibility that Cede & Co. *might* vote securities of which it is record holder without direction from a Depository Trust member is illusory. For Cede & Co. so to act would be a complete breach of the agreements under which it operates. It would also be a complete breach of Depository Trust's and Cede & Co.'s consistent and long standing practice and understanding with Depository Trust members. Any such action by Depository Trust and Cede & Co., would result in a complete lack of faith in Depository Trust and Cede & Co. on the part of Depository Trust members and would, of course, place such members in a completely untenable position with respect to those of their customers for whom they hold securities in Depository Trust and upon whose direction Cede & Co. is required to vote such securities. Depository Trust members would in such event probably have no alternative but to withdraw such securities from Depository Trust . . . they might even feel compelled to terminate their Depository Trust membership.

As we've learned, Cede obtains its instructions from the Depository Trust Company, which in turn receives its instructions from its brokers. Considering the influence it is able to exercise over its brokerage fiefdom and the community of interests shared by all these brokers, the thesis is casually passed over that the brokers would be only too happy to surrender these rights to the Exchange.

Aware of the power inherent in these rights, and unwilling to divest himself of their ultimate potential for control, Thomas P. Phelan, president of the Pacific Coast Stock Exchange, provides us with an insight into the attitude of the Depository Trust toward its members. On January 21, 1974, the *Wall Street Journal,* reporting that merger talks between the New York and the Pacific stock exchanges had collapsed once they got into discussions concerning the consolidation of their stock depositories, stated: "The Pacific president said the Big Board's plan as advanced, by its Depository's Trust Company subsidiary was, an attempt at a complete takeover; they didn't want any of our people. They would've come out here and opened up, and we would've closed down.' "

Worthy of observation is the Metcalf study's finding that "institutions as a group have a record of voting involvement that displays relatively little opposition to management." In this connection, it is important to point out that management finds it in its own best interests to do what its investment bankers recommend, since management is fully aware of the power exerted over their stock's price by this fraternity. If there is any doubt of this, one need only consider the records of the ITT hearings, as they show the total control exerted over ITT's decision-making processes by Felix Rohatyn of Lazard Frères. (I once spoke with the top official of a major corporation listed on the NYSE. When he complained to me about the performance of the specialist, I suggested he make his feelings known to the SEC. His reply was, "God help me if I did. If our multiple ever dropped, I'd be out on my ear.")

The CAB director of enforcement, however, was pointing to the control exercised over air carriers through the use of proxies by Cede & Company. In a final attempt to dismiss this idea, the lawyer evaded the issue by pointing to further differences between beneficial owners and holders of record. Curiously, the point he then raised concerning control required that he cite the *Boston and Maine* case:

> The decisions of the courts support the view that "control" as used in Section 408 does not necessarily depend upon the ownership of any specific minimum percentage of stock or other ownership rights, but rather depends, in the light of all the facts and circumstances in a particular case, upon whether there exists as a matter of fact a power to *dominate* or an actual domination of one legal personality by another.

One begins to wonder if he is arguing for or against control by Cede. In light of the several studies on the strategies of control included in Senator Metcalf's report, we must assume from the lawyer's statement that no matter what percentage Cede holds, it can exercise control if it can be shown to have the "power to dominate." Consider then the statement from the U. S. Securities and Exchange Commission Institutional Investor Study Report:

> To the extent that an institution holds a large percentage of a company's outstanding shares, it may be able more readily to mobilize the additional shares needed to approve or disapprove a corporate proposal. These institutions as a group appear to have substantial power which might be exercised through voting.

Then there is the House Banking Committee's conclusion:

> It is important to note that while an individual who holds a few or even a few hundred shares of stock in a corporation having several thousands or millions of shares outstanding does not regard his voting right as significant, a corporate trustee who can combine the voting rights of hundreds or thousands of such small holdings into significant voting power regards the voting right as a very valuable asset.
>
> This concentrated voting power can obviously be used for many purposes, among them the control of boards of directors and officers, as well as influencing the policies of the corporation in which the stock is held.

Finally, if anything further were needed, we have Senator Metcalf's conclusion:

> At this stage, then, it seems fair to conclude that the stocks held in nominee accounts of banks' trust departments and in other institutions do in fact put these institutions in a position where they can exert significant influence, through voting and otherwise, on corporate decisions and policies.

One need not stretch one's imagination very far to recognize who owns America when we add the last piece to the pattern provided by the CAB. Things begin to assume the design of a carefully contrived mosaic. The bulldog tenacity of the director of enforcement of the CAB compels him to write to the attorneys of Chase Manhattan Bank, who, as is fitting under the circumstances, also turn out to be the Exchange's legal counsel. Their response confirms his suspicions concerning the actual consequences of access to proxies:

MILBANK, TWEED, HADLEY & McCLOY,
New York, N.Y., May 17, 1973.

Mr. RICHARD J. O'MELIA,
Director, Bureau of Enforcement,
Civil Aeronautics Board,
Washington, D.C.

DEAR MR. O'MELIA: On behalf of The Chase Manhattan Bank (N.A.) and Kane & Co. we are glad to cooperate in furnishing the further information requested in your letter dated March 28, 1973. We regret that it has taken time to assemble the information.

1. *Voting of Proxies*

The number of shares as to which Chase, as trustee or agent, was authorized by the beneficial owners to vote proxies, in either sole or shared discretion, on June 14, 1972 was as follows:

Airline	Number of shares as to which Chase had sole voting discretion	Number of shares as to which voting discretion was shared with cotrustee or customer
American Airlines, Inc.	2,004,441	28,413
National Airlines, Inc.	611,644	5,700
Eastern Airlines, Inc.	1,338,067	3,878
Trans World Airlines, Inc.	460,275	3,329

Thus we see that, although it was hotly denied at the time by the Eastern banking establishment, it would appear that the Senator from Montana was on target when he added the following bit of memorabilia in the *Congressional Record* of April 25, 1972: "According to studies by the House Banking and Currency Committee, most of the stock held by banks is voted by the banks."

Under the myths and pressures of orthodoxy, tradition, and custom we can see the processes of bloodless revolution fully launched and under way. The conditions of the takeover may be different, but the objectives are the same. In the nature of things, the big businessman's principal weapon is now the proxy. Heretofore, the coup d'état was accomplished through military intervention—the junta declared martial law. So obsolete and dangerous an approach to power belongs to the militarist, not the investment banker. How much easier to do it with proxies and then secretly finance your puppet into the White House.

The control by Cede & Company and other members of the Exchange establishment over publishing and broadcasting com-

panies is also revealed in Senator Metcalf's report. The consequences are obvious: History is written not to inform the public
about Metcalf's revelations but to serve the establishment. In the
Wall Street Journal's comments on his subcommittee report,
buried on page 8, no mention was made of Cede & Company.
There was only the bankers' summary dismissal of the document.
Not for a moment did the *Journal* report Metcalf's opinions,
much less comment on the inconsistencies of the bankers' indignation in the light of the report's simple statements of fact. That's
the way things are nowadays.

If the individual hopes to survive financially in this society,
he must learn to take care of himself. To do that he must learn
to exploit the profit potentials and privileges extended to the
financial community by government. In my opinion, this is the
only way the individual can survive in what I believe has become
a total distortion of the whole concept of free enterprise. Also,
properly understood, the stock market provides the best way to
benefit from the existence of laws that sanction minimum taxes on
profits made gambling in the market while hard-earned wages
are taxed to the limit. If not dumfounding, it will be at least dis-
quieting to investors to learn that, because of the control the
Exchange maintains over the market, the market's daily fluctuations are not an amalgam of unanticipated and ever changing
events but are linked to each other so logically that they show a
perfect blueprint of past, present, and future market action. Hap-
pily, a close acquaintance with the complexities of the stock market shows us that, in fact, *investing in the market can be extremely
profitable once the merchandising strategies of Stock Exchange
specialists are explained*—and only if they are explained by someone willing to tell the whole truth about them.

Coming to the end of this first chapter, I sought to paraphrase
the meaning to Americans of this interlocking financial conspiracy. Like the revelation provided by lightning on a dark
night, I realized that many years ago my telephone had provided
the answer. I had discovered that if, instead of using numbers, a
resident of Los Angeles took one of Henry Miller's favorite words,
added "i-n-g" and then dialed F-U-C-K-I-N-G, he got Merrill
Lynch![1]

---

[1] After several years of publicity, Merrill Lynch decided to change the number in
May, 1973.

3. Stop the Press, I Want to Get Off

In which it is shown that, if in spite of your financial pages' hard sell you can keep your head while all those around you are losing theirs, then you are able to distinguish between what you want and what the Stock Exchange wants you to want.

Shortly after the publication of *The Wall Street Jungle* in 1970, it occurred to me that the organization of public opinion by the media is the secret of the Stock Exchange's power. Two factors supported this proposition: (1) The climate of opinion created by the financial press disposed investors to accept highly unprofitable theoretical constructions with no basis in fact to explain the market's fluctuations. (2) I had supplied financial editors and writers with the materials that had proved their predictive value and which should have enabled them to give investors a clearer structural approach to the market.

I had shown that the system created for investors was unwieldly and almost inevitably ruinous; that it enabled the Exchange establishment to compete with the public by employing deception and an array of secret practices. Yet almost every important financial newspaper appeared determined to see existing theory preserved and kept separate from the facts.

If what I had to say was in error or inadequate, why I wondered didn't the financial media deal with it in order to dispose of it? I could only conclude the media had taken their lead from the Exchange.

As for the Exchange, Christopher Elias, in his book *"Fleecing the Lambs,"* wrote:

> Richard Ney's well documented *Wall Street Jungle* roundly criticized practices among specialists and others on the floor of the American and New York Exchanges. This thoroughly enraged J.

29

William O'Reilly, vice president of the floor department, who for weeks after the book's appearance inveighed against Ney to all who would listen, especially during lunch in the senior staff dining room.

But long before Elias placed these facts before the public in his book, the Exchange's expressions of extreme hostility to my work had been commented on by members of the media not linked to the financial page. Joe Egelhof of the *Chicago Tribune* pointedly asked the Exchange to respond to the issues I had raised. But when the only comment he received was "no comment," he asked how the Exchange could remain silent in view of the specifics of my indictment. He was told, "There have been other authors like Ney and other books like *The Wall Street Jungle.* They have all disappeared and we are still here."

In the same spirit, the *New York Times* refused to review the book despite the fact it was on its best-seller lists for more than eleven months; in response to an advertisement submitted by Pickwick Bookshops, the *Wall Street Journal* stated: "We will not take an ad for *that* book." On June 22, 1970, the *Journal* published a review of the book that totally ignoring the book's principal arguments devoted itself to an attack on the design of the dust jacket and the typeface selected by the publishers. Because of the dilemma raised by what I considered to be the media's total compromise of their critical vision, I began an investigation of financial writing, the essential habits of financial writers, the uses of financial propaganda, and its crucial impact on the investor's behavior pattern. At first I found it difficult to reconcile the motivations of financial writers with their professed function. I had assumed that they were dedicated to a rational and truthful unfolding of financial events. Then I came upon the opinions of other journalists. The book *Reporting the News,* by Nieman Fellow journalists, quotes the Hutchins Commission report on "Freedom of the Press" as noting that the press "is acting increasingly like big business and increasingly in alliance with the interests of other big businesses." The report then concluded that

> *the American people do not realize what has happened to them.* They are not aware that a communications revolution has taken place. They do not appreciate the tremendous power which the new instruments and new organization of the press place in the hands of a few men. *They have not yet understood how far the performance of the press falls short of the requirements of a free society.* [Emphasis added.]

In *Blueprint for a Better Press,* another book of articles by Nieman Fellow Journalists, Leon Svirsky, the book's editor, had this to say: "The fetish of objectivity does not trouble most financial editors. Outright propaganda makes up the bulk of their business news."

In March, 1963, at hearings before the Antitrust Subcommittee of the Judiciary Committee of the House of Representatives to determine the effects of a continuing decline in newspaper competition, the publishers of the New York *Herald-Tribune* were asked, "What sense of social responsibility should the press have?" The *Tribune* answered, "The American newspaper has always been a newspaper affected with the public interest." The *Wall Street Journal* dissented, however, with the following comment:

> A newspaper is a private enterprise, *owing nothing whatever to the public* . . . it is emphatically the property of its owner who is selling a manufactured product at his own risk. Editors, except where they own their own newspapers, take their policy from their employers —but for ridiculously obvious reasons there are many newspaper owners willing enough to encourage the public in the delusion that it is the editor of a newspaper who dictates the selection of news and the expression of public opinion. He only does so, subject to correction and suggestion of the proprietor of the paper, who, most probably, considers his newspaper a plain business proposition. It is just that, no more, and certainly no less. [Emphasis added.]

Because of the Exchange's ability to dominate the financial page, it has proved almost impossible to expose the deceptions inherent in its practices. It has therefore erected a fact-proof screen between itself and the investor. For this reason, the existence of the Exchange specialist's practices have remained a greater mystery to investors than the composition of the atom. Hence investors are only "seekers;" they rarely become "finders."

The task of preventing disclosure has fallen largely to the Stock Exchange News Bureau. For practical purposes, it is the Exchange establishment's ministry of propaganda.

Housed on the fourteenth floor of the Stock Exchange, the News Bureau is the largest single unit in the Exchange's Department of Public Information and Press Relations. The men the Exchange has gathered together to service this propaganda machine include the most brilliant journalists, news analysts, and PR men in the business. Many of them are highly imaginative writers. They interpret the Exchange's personal prejudices and myths as critical market data.

The staff members work with reporters and others doing feature articles for newspapers and magazines; they prepare live broadcasts concerning stocks, the Stock Exchange, and the economy;

and they act as liaison with radio and television stations on business news presentations and as consultants to a number of listed companies preparing documentary films on the Exchange or on the corporations listed with it. Their department has also established very close links with the total spectrum of the news media.

The most obvious thing about this financial propaganda is the way it employs the comments of economists, businessmen, and government officials to precipitate buying or selling by the public or to alibi a fluctuation in the market. When the signal was given in April, 1971, that the Dow average was about to follow the rest of the market down, we find that, totally oblivious to the nightmare the investor was about to experience, the media were encouraging him to enter the market.

The ideological struggle between Exchange insiders and the public was further compounded when President Nixon during the 1970 decline in the market placed the interests of the Stock Exchange before the common man by allowing himself to be quoted to the effect that if he had any money at that time he would buy stock. On April 17, 1971, as the Dow began its dive, the President appeared for press photographs with friends from the Stock Exchange. Handed a stuffed leather bull by Bernie Lasker, a specialist on the floor of the Exchange, he affirmed that, because "next year is going to be a very good year" and because the stock market is the measure of all good things, the public should invest in the market. In all this there is not one phrase of useful information provided investors, merely the spectacle of a President using his office on behalf of the Exchange to influence the investor thinking.

On April 28, 1971, instead of protesting against deception and the substantial realities of a declining market, President Nixon circulated to 1,300 editors, editorial writers, broadcast news directors, and Washington bureau chiefs a list of the stocks of ten corporations that had advanced during the past year. The *Washington Post* of April 29, 1971, reported:

> Herbert G. Klein, Director of Communications, sent out the list as evidence of the stock market's confirmation of the President's "advice" that "it would be a good time to invest in the stock market."

In the course of every decline the propaganda machine is cranked up to provide investors with the assurance that, if they are losing money in the market, specialists and other Stock Exchange insiders are also having a tough time. For example, the market decline of 1969–70 brought us the following report by Philip Greer in the May 4, 1970, *Washington Post,* telling of another visit to Washington by President Nixon's good friend Bernie Lasker, then chairman of the NYSE:

> Wall Street made a pilgrimage to Washington . . . trying to find somebody, anybody in the White House to listen to the tale of woe. . . .
> For emphasis they only had to show off the battle scars in their checkbooks.

In its issue of August 10, 1970, *Time* magazine began an article with these words: "This year's slump has hit nobody more than the men who make the market on the Stock Exchange floors—the specialists." So the media exhibit a steadfast unwillingness to admit that specialists make as much money (from their short-selling) in a declining market as they do in an advancing market.

Financial columnists are too willing to take their lead from their Wall Street sources. On May 9, 1971, one month after the Stock Exchange had launched the market into a major downtrend, the *Los Angeles Times,* instead of providing information that might persuade investors to sell, ran the following propaganda-loaded headline in its Sunday editions: "EXPERTS TIP ON WHEN TO SELL: DON'T." Feigned stupidity is a commonplace of deception.

If any thesis rings hollow it is that network television is interested in factual reporting about the Stock Exchange. In July, 1970, a month after the publication of the *Jungle,* Bill Stout taped a twenty-minute interview that was to be aired on three successive CBS early morning network news hours. At the end of the interview, Stout commented, "It's good. I hope they use this one." The camera crew asked how to obtain copies of the book. A week later Stout told me that CBS had killed the interview with the explanation, "It is over the public's head." A few years earlier CBS cancelled another interview with Stout for the Walter Cronkite "Evening News" with the explanation, "He doesn't know what he's talking about." Subsequent to a taped interview on the Merv Griffin program in late 1971, CBS censored all references to the New York Stock Exchange and Merrill Lynch. I wrote Frank Stanton, the head of CBS, pointing out that my statements were fully documented. An exchange of letters ensued until it became apparent CBS was unwilling to allow me to make any comments about the Stock Exchange. CBS's censorship signified a distinct recognition of the importance of the censored material.

David Susskind assured me after lunch at a New York restaurant: "You've *got* to be on my program. I'll get my broker who is the specialist in Fanny May to go on with you." He spotted Ed

McMahon, called him over, introduced us, and repeated some of my comments to him. McMahon asked me to wait at the restaurant. He said he was going directly to NBC and would have someone there call me to arrange for an immediate interview for the Carson program. The call came, and I visited the Carson offices. After an interview I was told, "We can't have Nader on. I'll see if we can have you." Three days later I was told they couldn't.

When Freddie de Cordova took over as producer of the Carson program, I explained what had happened and asked him why the program wouldn't have Nader or myself on. He assured me that as soon as the show came to California he would like to have me on to discuss the market. But few men are aware of tomorrow's fears. A year later he commented, "The show is only geared to entertainment." As for Susskind, when we met again he told me his broker wouldn't go on with me and he couldn't get anyone else. "Naturally I couldn't have you on alone."

The television networks' news services have had a profound influence on the thinking of Americans about the stock market. All who can become big advertisers are presumed to possess supreme virtues, and the network news programs now list stock-brokerage firms, mutual funds, and financial tip sheets among their sponsors. Unlike those who were finally allowed to deliver anti-cigarette commercials, investor advocates are not granted air time to point out that beneath the superb façade of the sacred brahmins of the financial world life is arid, dark, and malign. Nor can other forms of information in this vein be provided investors, lest it offend important new advertisers.

The Metcalf and Muskie report mentioned earlier also included a Congressional Research Service analysis of ownership of broadcast companies and networks in 1972. It shows that Stock Exchange establishment banks like Chase Manhattan, Bankers Trust, and Bank of New York together had voting rights to almost one-fourth of the stock in both the Columbia Broadcasting System and American Broadcasting Company. The major New York banks also had significant voting rights in Metromedia, Pacific and Southern Broadcasting, Capital Cities Broadcasting, and fourteen other broadcasting groups. Senators Metcalf and Muskie commented, "Possibly, were he still with us, Ed Murrow would say: 'This is the news.'" The senators said Eastern establishment banks had violated FCC rules regarding concentration of ownership of broadcast companies:

> The FCC did not know that the banks were in gross violation of
> regulations until the banks told the Commission about it. It took

three years to get [the bankers'] material to and considered by the Commission, which then gave the banks three more years to get in compliance with the more lenient rules, which may be relaxed further.

On July 7, 1970, I left for Washington, D.C., to speak before Representative John Moss's (D.-California) Commerce and Finance Subcommittee. With the nation's press lined up behind the Investor Protection Bill, it looked very much as though the American taxpayer was going to have his other cheek bashed in—again.

Like all politicians who deal with securities matters, those on Chairman Moss's subcommittee are dedicated to leaving the cookie jar open for the Stock Exchange. They show indignation at such things as higher commission rates, but under pressure from the Stock Exchange, they capitulate. Senator Harrison Williams (D.-Connecticut), Chairman of the Securities Subcommittee, is a case in point. Seemingly, he had fought for the investor on two fronts: against the SEC by insisting it conduct open hearings between itself and its stockbroker-oriented advisory committees and against Chairman Needham of the NYSE when he sought to eliminate the third market. For reasons best known to the Senator, in March 1974, he joined forces with the Exchange by introducing an amendment to eliminate the third market. The Exchange has lobbied for years in order to achieve this total monopoly. Here we have the curious spectacle of an elected representative of the people eliminating a market in which investors can trade at commission rates 50% less than those on the Exchange. It is ever thus. Between Washington and Main Street there is a wide and impassable gulf.

My testimony before the subcommittee took more than an hour. By the time I'd finished it was obvious I wasn't going to turn Stock Exchange lobbyists into Nader's Raiders. I assumed the *New York Times* would at least point out that in my testimony I had concluded that the bill was a scheme in which the American taxpayer would be asked to pay for the losses sustained by investors when their brokerage firm failed. But, pretending to offer more to investors than it wished to deliver, the press was silent.

I asked Robert Metz, a *Times* financial columnist, why my arguments against the bill hadn't been mentioned in his paper. He advised me that "perhaps the reporter who covered the hearings for the *Times* didn't agree with what you had to say."

James Reston of the *New York Times* states in his book, *Artillery of the Press* (p. 94):

We need to question not only our old definitions of news and our allocation of space and time but also many other popular assumptions that have been accepted uncritically for much too long. . . .

The press has one extremely important job to do. We must try to keep the issues for decision clearly before the people, a task which is not really being done in the present jumble of the average American newspaper or news program.

Nor, indeed, is it being done by the *New York Times.* Long after the bill had been passed, however, *Barron's* had something to say about my opposition to it. Like the *Wall Street Journal, Barron's* is controlled by the Dow Jones Corporation. In the issue of November 23, 1970, *Barron's* editor launched a front-page attack on my testimony. I had testified that the bill ignored the fact that self-regulation by the Stock Exchange had led to the excesses that caused the bankruptcies of member firms. I had stated that the bill "stands to save the Exchange billions of dollars that they would otherwise be on the hook for." *Barron's* commented, "Mr. Ney may be an expert on some things and he's entitled to his opinion on others. With respect to the measure in question, however, he doesn't know what he's talking about. For the money will not come from the U.S. Treasury."

A rebuttal was provided by William McChesney Martin, a director of the Dow Jones Corporation—the publisher of *Barron's.* The *Washington Post* of November 24, 1971, quoted Mr. Martin as follows:

The Securities Investor Protection Act passed by Congress last year was "an unfortunate act" because it did nothing to upgrade the quality of the industry, William McChesney Martin, Jr., said today.

Martin, former Chairman of the Federal Reserve Board who last summer offered a report on restructuring the New York Stock Exchange, said the act, which created the Securities Investors Protection Corp., only accomplished half the necessary job. "You are not chartering brokers the way you are banks and *you're going to bail out the industry with a call on the federal treasury,"* Martin told a meeting of the New York Financial Writers Association. [Emphasis added.]

Unfortunately, truth can't be told on the installment plan. Martin's perceptive and thorough denunciation of the bill's limitations came too late to be of any use. With the help of the Securities Investor Protection Corporation, the Stock Exchange had perfected a new technique for spitting on the American taxpayer without having to open its mouth.

Now I was about to approach the problems presented by militantly biased media from another angle. I was also to learn that while force of habit causes us to make mistakes about people, friendships cause the most unexpected. The typical financial editor had thus far shown himself incapable of objectivity. I was expecting compensation for this unfortunate cultural condition from my friends on *Time* magazine. Few people had a closer acquaintance with the subject matter of my book than members of *Time*'s editorial staff.

I met Marshall Berges, the head of *Time*'s Los Angeles Bureau, through Charles Champlin, who was responsible for the June, 1962, *Time* piece on my work. Then, through Berges, I met the magazine's managing editor, soon to become vice-president, Otto Fuerbringer. Both Berges and Fuerbringer encouraged me in my writing.

They opened the doors—one might almost say the windows—of the magazine to me, and it was a strange but always interesting world I entered. Berges would meet with me regularly for luncheon. I found his insights into the American political scene charged with color, perception, and humor.

In December, 1967, because of a chance remark made to Fuerbringer that I would be in New York at Christmas time, he arranged a dinner party at his home in Greenwich, Connecticut. It was an altogether interesting evening. Otto introduced me to the heads of some of the country's most important corporations and to his magazine's editors. I felt I was making friendships that were both professional and personal. He also introduced me to G. Keith Funston, the president of the New York Stock Exchange. Funston remarked on our earlier correspondence and gave me to understand that his interest in specialists and such matters evaporated the moment he left Wall Street. Hence our conversation diminished into an amiable discussion of the weather.

I also made the acquaintance of Marshall Loeb, the magazine's business editor, and Henry Grunwald, who would soon take over as managing editor when Otto became vice-president.

Then, on August 10, 1970, in its always interesting style, *Time* magazine presented me with the melancholy spectacle of another publication asserting its solidarity with the Stock Exchange by attacking my book. The disappointment I felt at that moment is difficult to describe. The article was not only *not* a candid evaluation of my work, but in its consuming ambition to appease Stock Exchange specialists, *Time* surpassed even the *Wall Street Journal* in its failure to present its readers with the issues I had raised. It carried the headline "Rising Attack on Stock Exchange Insiders."

It described, with more imagination than insight, the enormous losses suffered by specialists during the 1970 slump in the market. It then stated, "Now insult has been added to financial injury: the specialists are under widespread attack." To wit:

> Richard Ney, a onetime movie actor turned investment adviser, has condemned the specialists in his sensationalist bestseller, *The Wall Street Jungle*. He charges that the specialists manipulate the market and more than make up their short-term losses by turning enormous profits when prices rise, as they eventually do. Most Wall Streeters find Ney's indictment grossly overstated.

The thinking in the piece was so totally out of step with the ideas I'd heard expressed in conversations with *Time*'s editors that I felt certain a meeting with Marshall Loeb would bring forth a follow-up article. I called him and arranged for an immediate appointment.

When I entered his office I noticed among the several books on his desk a copy of the *Jungle*. We talked about the book and the issues it raised. He asked an associate to join us and had me repeat my comments about the errors I'd found in the *Time* piece. When I finished, he said, "Very well, Richard, what do you want me to do?" I told him. He then put me in touch with John Tompkins, the correspondent who had written the article. I asked him how he knew that specialists had taken losses in the market. He got this information, he told me, from his Wall Street sources. I asked him where he got the rest of his material for the article. From his Wall Street sources, he said. I told him to imagine asking Dutch Schultz his opinion of Al Capone. Could he expect any answer other than that "the indictment against Al is grossly exaggerated"? I told Tompkins I wasn't interested in Wall Street's views and asked him, "What is *your* opinion of the book's argument?"

"I haven't had time to read your book," he said. "By the time I get home at night I only have time to work on my own."

The next morning I called Henry Grunwald, now *Time*'s managing editor. It was a Friday, and I knew he would be busy with editors and writers. I asked if I could see him "for three minutes." "Come right over, Richard" he said, "It's Friday, I'm under the gun, but if you don't mind waiting a few minutes I'd love to see you."

When we met, I told Grunwald I felt justified in stating that Tompkins's comments were a virtuoso composite of secondhand ideas. I gave him to understand that his financial propaganda would be swallowed by investors at great cost. I talked as fast as I could in order to crowd as many ideas as possible into three minutes. When my time was up, I thanked him and started out. He stopped me and said he would like to discuss the matter further. He added that he had wanted to do a piece on the book. I was delighted. Marshall Loeb joined us. When he learned of Tompkins's comments, he insisted that Tompkins and I meet again. I was grateful to Grunwald and Loeb for their vigorous expression of intentions to set things straight for once and all. In another hour's conversation with Tompkins, I described the massiveness of the deceptions confronting investors. When we parted Tompkins assured me he would prepare another piece.

As the weeks passed and the promised article failed to appear, my confusion over the magazine's seemingly conflicting tendencies increased. I wondered how Fuerbringer had reacted to the article.

On many occasions in the past we had discussed the book. After a small dinner I gave for him and his wife, Winona, we returned to my office. He said he would like to see my manuscript. He laughed at my opening statement: "There is more sheer larceny per square foot on the floor of the New York Stock Exchange than any place else in the world." We then discussed the book.

I was sure Fuerbringer would not echo the refrain taken by Tompkins. When he was managing editor, he had carried a lantern as well as cracked a whip. Would he now concede the faults, as Loeb himself had admitted and Grunwald had noted? I called him, and we arranged to have dinner. On that and two similar occasions I sensed an unwillingness on his part to discuss the book or the article. Except for the self-conscious give and take of dinner conversation, he said nothing. I had the curious feeling that there was something he didn't wish to discuss. This feeling was further compounded by Marshall Berges's (now assistant to the publisher) total unavailability for any further meetings once the book was published.

More than a year later, on October 12, 1971, Senator Metcalf introduced into the *Congressional Record* his findings from leafing through a copy of *Time* magazine.

WILL "TIME" TELL?

Mr. METCALF. Mr. President, last week, while paging through my copy of Time, I noticed some familiar names in an odd place. The name was the "nominees," "street names," or "straws" used to hide the identity of various financial interests. I found these street names in Time's ownership statement, which appears on page 92 of the magazine of October 11.

Periodical ownership statements are supposed to be published at least once a year. . . .

According to the weekly news magazine, it is owned by Time, Inc., of which 10 stockholders each own or hold 1 percent or more of the total amount of stock. . . .

First on the list is Carson & Co. Its address is box 491, Church Street Station, N.Y. 10018. . . . Carson & Co. really means Morgan Guaranty Trust.

Further down in Time's report on its principal stockholders appears the name Powers & Co. It has a different post office box at the Church Street Station—Box 1479 . . . you can see by the Nominee List that it is—also—Morgan Guaranty Trust.

Powers & Co. shares box 1479 with another of Time's stockholders —Tegge & Co. . . . Tegge & Co. shows up in this year's edition of the nominee list, as yet another pseudonym used by Morgan Guaranty Trust.

Time includes among its reported stockholders Chetco, at 35 Congress Street, Boston, and Ferro & Co., at the same address. Both, according to the Nominee List, are really the National Shawmut Bank of Boston.

Time likewise lists without further identification Pace & Co., Box 926, Pittsburgh. And who is Pace? It is really Mellon Bank & Trust, according to the Nominee List.

Another of Time's stockholders is reported as Cede & Co., Box 20, Bowling Green Station, N.Y. Persons who follow regulatory matters will recall that Cede & Co. shows up repeatedly on ownership reports of power companies, airlines, and railroads, and that not long ago the Interstate Commerce Commission expressed mild interest in finding out who controlled all those Cede & Co. shares. . . . The Nominee List shows that Cede & Co. is the Stock Clearing Corp., at 44 Broad Street. I would add that the Stock Clearing Corp. is a wholly owned subsidiary of the New York Stock Exchange. . . . I leave it to the would-be Lieblings to ferret out press ownership and its implications.

Perhaps university students and faculty will want to develop the larger issue of identifying the persons or groups who vote the proxies that corporations send, I suppose, to those post office box headquarters of phantom companies.

And perhaps the Vice President, or appropriate congressional committees, will want to pursue this issue. Could it be that Carson, Powers, Tegge, Chetco, Ferro, Cede and Companies have surreptitiously acquired more control of the country than either the radiclibs or the Mafia?

Will Time tell?

In June, 1972, Senator Metcalf delivered further testimony about *Time*'s links with the Eastern financial establishment before Senator Gaylord Nelson's Monopoly Subcommittee. It elicited a

reply from Andrew Heiskell, the chairman of *Time*'s board, who
included the following comment in his letter to Senator Metcalf:

> Now that the question has been raised, we propose to write to each
> shareholder of record who, on August 28, 1972, owns more than one
> per cent of the stock of the company and request that each inform
> us if he acts as trustee or in any other fiduciary relation and if so,
> the names and addresses of the persons or corporations for whom he
> is so acting. . . . We shall then include in our report for 1972 what-
> ever information we obtain in this manner.

This diffident defense carries a strong odor of presumption that
Senator Metcalf is unaware of the distinction between "beneficial"
and "proprietary" owners of stock. Information, however, is the
open sesame to consciousness. Metcalf is aware that invisible control hides under the alias of the proprietary owner. On August 9,
1972, he replied to Mr. Heiskell's letter:

August 9, 1972

Mr. Andrew Heiskell,
Chairman of the Board, Time, Inc.
Rockefeller Center, New York, N.Y.

Dear Mr. Heiskell: I appreciate your 3 August letter regarding my
Senate reference to principal stockholders of Time, Inc., and other
corporations.

I am sending two enclosures which may be helpful to you.

The first is my Senate speech of 28 June. I call your particular
attention to this paragraph:

"Let me emphasize that I do not propose identification of the
beneficial owners of the stock the people or institutions who receive
the dividends, even though their investments are sizable. What the
public, the stockholders, the regulators need to know is the identity
of the proprietary owners—the voters—of significant amounts of
stock."

You state that you proposed to write each shareholder of record
who holds more than one percent of the stock of the company, and
ask them to identify the persons or corporations for whom they act
as a trustee or in any other fiduciary capacity, and that you shall
include this information in your report required under the Postal
Reorganization Act.

That is of course your prerogative. It will, however, in my opinion,
lead to unnecessary paperwork and expense without providing the
identity of the proprietary owners who vote the principal blocks of
stock.

My second enclosure elaborates on that point. It is that portion
of a report by the American Bankers Association, furnished me by
Chairman Burch of the Federal Communications Commission, which

deals with voting strength in Time, Inc. by nineteen banks. You will see that one bank has sole voting rights to 360,167 shares of stock, and joint voting rights to 16,795 shares, comprising in total 5.2 percent of the shares voted. But these concentrated voting rights are divided among an estimated 256 accounts.

In another situation, as you can see, a bank has sole voting rights to 271,352 shares and joint voting rights to 37,257 shares. Together this amounts to 4.3 percent of the stock voted. But the voting rights of this bank are divided among 128 accounts.

If you wish to obtain and publish the names and addresses of the hundreds of beneficial owners of stock in your company, that is of course your privilege. If you choose to obtain and disclose voluntarily the names of those few institutions and individuals which have voting control of the principal blocks of stock, Time, Inc. will have made an important breakthrough in the establishment of the people's right to know.

Very truly yours,
Lee Metcalf

That was the end of the correspondence. How can you argue with a man who uses logic as though it were a hammer?

On September 22, 1973, I sent certified letters to Walter Cronkite, John Chancellor, and Howard K. Smith, advising them that a major manipulation was under way to raise stock prices in order to distribute stock; that the public should be rescued from the propaganda aimed at fostering a belief that a bull market was under way; and that the sharp advance in the market would be immediately followed by a major decline in stock prices. But, because the networks are controlled by the stockbrokers and investment bankers on their boards, they begin with a bias toward the Exchange and seek only to systematize the evidence to conform to the bias. Thus, nothing was said on the air, and hundreds of thousands of investors were caught in another bear trap prepared for them by the Exchange.

As has been suggested, television serves no purpose or function as a source of information for investors. Instead, it propagates Exchange handouts.

Many cities have stock market stations. An investigation of the comments of the brokers, investment advisers and others who use television in order to disseminate their views about the market reveals that, for practical purposes, they know no more than their viewers about the movement of stock prices.

Nor are the syndicated television shows on the market any better. "Wall Street Week," one of the most highly esteemed and successful of these programs, is, in my opinion, quite possibly the most dangerous. Its panel of experts are symptoms of a process in which, like bad bridge players, they can be counted on to play the wrong card instinctively. Not only have their bullish forecasts over the past few years proven uniformly wrong, but these forecasts are presented in the most attractive of possible settings by the most personable individuals. The persuasiveness of the format cannot, therefore, be overestimated.

To further compound the investor's desperately complex situation the hosts of these programs become recognized by the media as market experts. On Sunday, December 16, 1973, the *Los Angeles Times* ran an article called "Smart Money and Other Stock Market Myths," by the host and star of "Wall Street Week." Ignoring his own show's critical defects he pointed to institutional traders and told us that they

> . . . have vacillated recently between headlong selling, which caused the market to emulate a Polaris submarine on red alert, and unrestrained buying, which in turn caused the market to take off like the comet Kohoutek.

The interesting thing about the article was not his failure to grasp the manner in which the law of supply and demand actually works in the market, but that in a little box under his article there was the announcement that Doubleday & Co. was about to publish a book he has written, "How to Make Money on Wall Street."

The Exchange depends upon the tacit approval of the media, but beyond that it always harbors the expectation that the media will sanction its practices. On those rare occasions when a journalist appears who does not show proper team spirit, he is placed on its enemies list and watched carefully.

Writing in the *Washington Post* of July 1, 1970, Nicholas von Hoffman provided his readers with a remarkably candid two-page commentary on what he called "Wall Street's Bingo Game." The following is an excerpt from that column:

> The inside story does get out. A Joe Valachi talks. A Trappist monk sends a message out in the form of a book. A Ku Klux Klan member sells his version of the murder to a magazine for $25,000. A retired confidence man reminisces on a TV talk show. . . . Dead men's diaries are discovered and published. Old letters are found . . . the most recent inside story to surface is called "The Wall Street Jungle" . . . good material on the market is rare. Most of what we get is simple minded propaganda put out by the brokers and obscurantist propaganda put out by the Securities and Exchange Commission in the form of reports. Both have the same aim, which is to assure us that they're running an honest game up there in New York and if we play it we'll win. Ney, who describes himself as a "croupier in search of a legitimate profession" says otherwise.

Because of this article, the Exchange tried to get von Hoffman fired. Instead, Mrs. Graham, the publisher, offered Haack, then the president of the New York Stock Exchange, space in which to rebut the column. Haack declined the offer.

Richard Buffum, as it turned out, was less fortunate. Writing in the *Los Angeles Times* of June 2, 1970, he ended a column with the following statement:

> I hasten to lay to rest any notion you may have that Ney's sweeping generalizations remain undocumented. With a surgeon's precision, he carves a full-scale indictment of the ethics, the methods of those who direct American money. Having read his book during the stock market's recent dramatic fluctuations, I have come to believe that a whole series of reforms he recommends should receive the careful attention of Congress. It seems clear to me that a lot of arbitrary manipulation has been going on in the market that is unrelated to the law of supply and demand. It appears that Ney's reforms, if adopted, could reach a long way toward creating a safe and sane auction market for every investor, and not merely the exclusive, private club for privileged insiders which he describes.

From this column more than a million readers who had not read the book and would never read it gained some insight into the abuses of the existing Stock Exchange system. None of this was lost on the Stock Exchange. James F. Hill, the head of its propaganda wing, sent a letter with an article about me to Buffum. The Exchange had begun writing to columnists whose work was causing their readers to put their savings into the bank instead of the stock market. Buffum sent me the Exchange's letter with the comment, "I can only wonder why they sent me the article. It reads more like a puff piece."

NEW YORK STOCK EXCHANGE

DEPARTMENT OF PUBLIC INFORMATION PRESS RELATIONS

ELEVEN WALL STREET

NEW YORK, N.Y. 10005

JAMES F. HILL
  MANAGER, NEWS BUREAU

November 3, 1970

Dear Mr. Buffum:

   We noticed your review of Mr. Richard Ney's book, "The Wall Street Jungle," and thought you might like to see the enclosed story on Mr. Ney by Chris Welles.

It appeared in the November 2 issue of New York magazine.

Sincerely,

James F. Hill

Mr. Richard Buffum
Los Angeles Times
Times Mirror Square
Los Angeles, Calif. 90053

Mr. Hill neglected to mention that Armand Erpf, one of the founders of the magazine, was an investment banker, and that another owner, John Loeb, is the senior partner in the Loeb, Rhoades brokerage firm, or that the article was a covert attack on me by the Stock Exchange.

In September, 1970, I held a press conference in New York to introduce a proposal for a new Stock Exchange. My plan would employ computers instead of specialists to maintain an orderly market and provide safeguards that protected investors from manipulation by Exchange insiders. With the aid of two computer scientists from Rand Corporation I had developed the plan to enable the public to invest its savings on the basis of earnings and dividends. (The names of these scientists are Joseph L. Midler and Dr. Lawrence J. Watters. On a Sunday afternoon in 1971 they took me to Rand and gave me a demonstration of the computer in operation.) The plan would eliminate the ability of Stock Exchange members to trade for themselves along with the concept of the specialist system, hence it was not too favorably received by the financial community or, indeed, by the financial press. The story was not carried by any New York newspaper. Nor did the *Los Angeles Times* make any mention of it.

When I returned to Los Angeles I called Richard Buffum and gave him the material containing my concept for the new Exchange. On October 15, 1970, his column appeared in the *Los Angeles Times:*

> Richard Ney's book, "The Wall Street Jungle,"—astonishingly holding a modest position for several months on the best seller lists against powerful competition from books about sex—is more than an adroit polemic against unethical conduct in the securities industry.
>
> It is a literary extension of the character of the author, a reflection of his moral outrage over Wall Street's pious manipulations in the "great bingo game" which he claims is isolating more and more the stock market from the real business of real businessmen.

Dedicated reformers normally can be found rummaging about behind scenes trying to create a reality consistent with their convictions, and Ney is no exception. He has plenty of strong notions about how to reform Wall Street. Chief among them is to do something drastic about the specialists.

Specialists are a privileged group of brokers' brokers, 470 of them, who make the markets on the stock exchange floors. Specialists are supposed to buy when most investors are selling, and sell when most are buying. Theoretically, their purpose is to stabilize the market.

Tremendous Temptation

Specialists play a dual role, though. As a broker for other brokers, he also is a dealer for his own account. He stands to profit from his inside knowledge of the fluctuating demands for stock and from his commission on trades. A conflict of interest exists that would tempt a saint.

Business Week magazine commented that the temptations of specialists "are built in by a system that gives freedom to run a stock up and down, often with large gaps, and to trade near the end of those runs—'against the market,' to be sure—for their personal benefit and not always for the market's equilibrium."

Ney, a trim, ebullient 53, took time out from his vigorous book promotion schedule, to confess to me the other day about his behind-the-book activities. He said he is working at trying to establish "a fair and orderly market, with price spreads determined by computers."

Moreover, he plans to found a new kind of stock exchange in competition with existing ones.

Favors Computers

Ney's exchange would eliminate the human element in matching buy and sell orders by handing the entire process over to computers. The specialists would be eliminated.

Currently gathering financial and necessary congressional support for his preliminary 29-point plan, Ney described it as a nonprofit organization regulated as a public utility. All transactions would be a matter of public record. To avoid conflict of interest, brokers would not be allowed to trade for themselves or as principals.

As Business Week's William G. Shepherd Jr., remarked prophetically last July: "It may only be a matter of time before the market is regulated as a public utility and computers replace specialists." What he failed to mention was that Richard Ney, former movie actor turned investment counselor in Bel-Air, may very well be the father.

I suspect that a partial explanation why Ney's book is doing well against competition from "The Sensuous Woman" is that all that is not erotica is not dull when a behavioral revolution is waxing—even on starchy old Wall Street.

Some time later, Buffum visited my office. I used the opportunity to take him to my charting room. I showed him the Grumman charts (see Chapter 10) and explained my techniques and their implications. Like everyone else to whom I'd shown the charts, he was stunned. They confirmed for him what I had said in *The Wall Street Jungle.* "I want to do another column on these charts," he said.

Shortly afterward, I mentioned on television Buffum's reaction to the charts and commented that he intended to do another column on them. That was a mistake. Less than three weeks later Buffum called me to say he had been told his column would now only appear in the Orange County edition of the *Los Angeles Times.* His regular space would be taken over by Art Seidenbaum. Buffum had cared about my battle with the Exchange, and I couldn't help but feel he was a casualty of that battle. The Exchange had been unable to get to Nicholas von Hoffman's job, but apparently they had a better in with Otis Chandler, the publisher of the *Los Angeles Times,* than they had with Kathyrin Graham, publisher of the *Washington Post.*

As for Seidenbaum, who took over Buffum's space, he subsequently advised another columnist who wanted to do a story about the *Jungle,* "Stay away from Ney. He'll get you in trouble."

To understand Otis Chandler it helps to read what Upton Sinclair had to say about his grandfather, Harry Chandler, in *The Jungle.* His attitudes toward his paper's financial page are better understood when one learns that owners of his newspaper include mutual funds, financial foundations, and disciples of Wall Street. It is also interesting that Keith Funston sits as a director on the board of Chandler's publishing syndicate.

On May 18, 1973, a story broke that was covered in greater detail in the *New York Times* than it was in the *Los Angeles Times:*

> The Securities and Exchange Commission has accused 12 persons, including Otis Chandler, publisher of the Los Angeles Times, of involvement in a fraudulent investment scheme into which more than 2,000 persons poured about $30-million over eight years.

Chandler was accused of making false and misleading statements about these investments and failing to disclose he was being paid finder's fees, which, it was alleged, totaled $109,000. The fees were for getting people to invest in the fund. He was also charged with failing to disclose he owned 10 per cent of the stock of one of the companies involved in the scheme. It was further alleged that a clause in Chandler's contract agreed to indemnify him against any possible losses—from lawsuits or otherwise—arising out of his involvement with the plan.

It would be remiss not to point out that, while the principles of blind chaos and self-interest are the theme of most financial editors and commentators, there are talented exceptions who are pugnaciously intent on serving the traditions of public service. One of these is Carl Ritter, financial editor of the *San Diego Union-Tribune*. He has none of the servility of the ordinary editor who provides his readers only with stockbrokers' opinions. Then there are Patrick Owens of *Newsday*, Chuck Stone of the Philadelphia *Daily News*, and Joe Egelhof of the Chicago *Tribune*. Among television and radio commentators, there are people like Stuart Schulberg, producer of the "Today Show," John Bartholomew Tucker of New York, Lou Gordon in Detroit, Grady Randolph in Atlanta, Bob Morlan of Radio News West in Los Angeles, Jerry Williams, in Boston, and Ken Hackelman in Houston.

Most television network news commentators, and journalists, however, have no immediate experience of the stock market or the Stock Exchange. The raw material of their daily experience, with its attendant images, abstractions, and generalizations, is therefore incapable of providing perceptive propositions about the market. An understanding of the market involves an understanding of propositions that cannot be acquired, even by the most intelligent men, through interviews or luncheon conversations. An understanding of the market comes only by keeping a skeptical attitude toward its traditional dogma. This allows the commentator to develop concepts that have assignable meanings and can be operationally verified in the market, the way the propositions of pseudo-knowledge cannot be. Without this degree of understanding, it is impossible for a commentator to realize that the issues raised each day about politics and politicians are the consequences of a cause-and-effect relationship with origins in the multibillion-dollar activities of the Stock Exchange. Regrettably, the networks' men accept the gentle consolations of pseudo-knowledge rather than real knowledge. The image they have of the market, based as it is on pseudo-knowledge, makes them unwilling to face the dark possibility that they have been exposed to a truth that, because of their responsibilities to investigative journalism, they are obligated to examine.

The fact remains, so long as investors are persuaded to accept the teachings, preachings, and shamming rationalizations of the wire services, the master hypnotists of the financial page, and radio and television newscasts, the devouring genius of the Stock Exchange will continue to swallow them.

Investors must learn to recognize the mountebanks who drape themselves in sacerdotal robes in order to exploit stumbling mankind's ignorance. They must exercise their powers of judgment and make use of the knowledge that publishers like Dow Jones and Otis Chandler, the *New York Times,* and the heads of the major television networks have the strongest links to the financial establishment. There's a very good reason why *Time* magazine, in its August 16, 1971, issue, just as President Nixon delivered his new economic policy announcement, should complain that consumers "are increasing their savings at a spectacular annual rate of $64 billion. If they could be *tempted* to part with some of that cash . . . the stock market could soar." And then it added, "Administration spokesmen insist that the U.S. is poised to enter one of history's most prosperous and productive periods." The last thing needed is *Time*'s request for a "revival of consumer confidence." What we need is a revival of consumer prudence, thrift, and investor skepticism—particularly toward the Exchange's propaganda agencies.

In *Time* magazine, May 8, 1950, Arthur Hays Sulzberger, then publisher of the *New York Times,* commenting on "impartial news reporting," stated, "We tell the public which way the cat is jumping. The public will take care of the cat." Yet each and every edition of his newspaper is given to an uncritical admiration of the biggest tom of them all—the Wall Street Fat Cat.

4. Can the SEC Speak for Investors? Can Cannibals Speak for Those Who Make Them Fat?

In which it is shown that, although it's Nixon who refuses to accept anything except the worst regulators, it's Peter Flanigan who provides them.

The forces ranged against investors are essentially a historical process that began with Roosevelt's appointment of Joseph Kennedy in 1934 as the Securities and Exchange Commission's first chairman.

The size of the atrocity represented by Kennedy's appointment can be best appreciated if one visualizes an eleventh-hour pitch by Wall Street to Roosevelt to place its man at the head of the SEC. Four months before the appointment Ferdinand Pecora had uncovered the fact that Kennedy's stock manipulations had stomped more investors than an Irish bull at a St. Patrick's Day rally. Pecora singled out the Libby Owens Ford Glass swindle as a classic instance of Kennedy expertise. This manipulation was inspired by Kennedy and Elisha Walker, a Kuhn Loeb partner. The simple genius underlying the operation went a long way toward creating the boom of 1933. After Kennedy and company closed in for the kill the boom collapsed. Judged on its legal merits, this achievement should have sent Kennedy to Sing Sing instead of the SEC. Unfortunately, Roosevelt chose to ignore the distinguishing features of Kennedy's career along with the fact that Pecora's findings about these pooling operations were chiefly responsible for the Stock Exchange Control Bill. What gave the Kennedy appointment its special interest was that it established the precedent that was to govern all future appointments to the SEC.

The theory of an independent regulatory agency capable of disinterested judgment succumbs to a policy of self-interest. Lacking the concentration of will needed to be fiercely partisan to the needs of investors, regulatory policy became totally irrelevant to those needs. Appointment to the Commission automatically became a pushbutton to material success. The form of regulation was there, not the substance. Thus, despite the Securities Act, the Stock Exchange establishment was able to revert to what, for all practical purposes, was the earlier pattern of unregulated behavior. Unable to dominate and control stock prices by applying methods that are appropriate to an auction market, the Stock Exchange establishment mastered the market by employing unknown punitive processes and myths that excite passions but obscure insight— all with the approval of the Securities and Exchange Commission.

That is why, in a culture employing highly advanced machine technology, the specialist system must employ the old-fashioned, primitive manual method of an earlier era. In modern times, computer analysts have discovered ways to detect fraudulent programming methods. Again with the consent of the SEC, no insights are provided investors into the running of the system as a whole, into its complexities; nor is information provided investors that might enable them to compete successfully against the specialist system.

The possibility of reforming or regulating the Stock Exchange and the specialist system become ineffective when, despite the thundering commands of Congress, the enforcement of regulation is left to the initiative of lawyers and businessmen to detect and prosecute violations. For the most part, such regulators are all too easily made to see that their future incomes and status are totally dependent on their willingness to "carry the ball" in order to serve the objectives of the Exchange establishment.

Thus it is that, surrendering wholly to instinct with very little tutoring, new appointees to the Commission get the hang of things very quickly. In due course, the regulatory principle becomes the most powerful of all weapons for overriding rather than enforcing the law.

The Securities Acts of 1933 and 1934 were supposedly legal mainstays for the protection of investors. By the time the industry got finished working them over, the acts were a snarl of loopholes. Accordingly, investors celebrated the elimination of old abuses while continuing to be ruined by them.

Despite the critical intelligence of the dedicated career men and women who staff the Commission in Washington and those who work on the investor's behalf in its regional offices, no statement about the Stock Exchange by an SEC commissioner not made under sodium pentothal can be accepted as accurate.

In July, 1972, James Needham resigned his job as a $38,000-a-year SEC commissioner to accept a five-year contract at $200,000 a year (plus expenses) as the New York Stock Exchange's new board chairman. Appointed to the SEC by President Nixon on July 10, 1969, he took exactly three years to demonstrate that there is no real difference between serving the securities industry in Washington and serving it on Wall Street except the pay is better on Wall Street.

When Needham was appointed, Chairman Casey of the SEC, who in the ordinary course of events should have been rewarded with this plum, said he believed Mr. Needham would prove "a splendid leader of the broadened governing structure of the New York Stock Exchange."[1]

What "broadened" meant in this instance was that the Exchange had been forced by public pressure to place members of the public on its board of governors. These, presumably, would have a benign influence on the decision-making powers of the other half of the board, composed of stockbrokers. But only by the wildest stretch of the imagination could the tycoons selected by the Exchange be said to have anything in common with the public. The public members included luminaries like Donald Cook, a former chairman of the SEC and now president and chief executive officer of American Electric Power; James Roche, director of General Motors; and Robert Sarnoff, chairman of the board and chief executive officer of RCA. Then there was the executive vice president of American Telephone and Telegraph, the chairman of J. C. Penney, and the chairman of Owens Illinois. And, of course, now working on behalf of his stockbroker interests, was Ralph Saul, formerly a director of the SEC, former president of the American Stock Exchange, and now chairman of First Boston Corporation, one of the country's most important brokerage firms. Don Regan was also there, representing Merrill Lynch.

As a former commissioner who had "consistently asked industry leaders the toughest questions,"[2] Needham now revealed in a rather uninhibited way a sudden ability to deal with objects and ideas totally alien to regulators. As chairman of the Exchange,

1 *Wall Street Journal,* July 14, 1972.
2 *Ibid.*

one of his principal concerns is the cost of running this establishment.

In May, to get a 15 per cent raise in commission rates, he had argued to the SEC, "most small investors don't pay much attention to commissions." Investors soon made it plain that most of them *do* care. Informed about Needham's attempt for a rate increase, one investor commented: "Coming from a former SEC Commissioner, it's enough to blow the lid off your jar!"

Needham went back to the drawing board. After a long session with his board of governors he devised a new plan:

NEEDHAM SAYS PHONE COSTS JUSTIFY EXCHANGE RATE RISE

The NYSE, with former SEC Commissioner James Needham running interference as NYSE chairman, has asked for a 15 per cent rate increase on stock orders involving $5,000 to $300,000 by value and 10 per cent on orders between $100 and $5,000. The NYSE justification for the hike's inflation is the higher costs of doing business, such as telephone rates.

The SEC wondered aloud if such a proposal for raising commission rates might not be received with prejudice by the small investor.

Commissioner John Evans said the NYSE data might be an index but not a useful measure of what is really happening in the industry. . . .

Mr. Needham stepped in to say that although "the line of questioning is valid . . . I think we're going to be frustrated in reaching a conclusion with the speed which I hoped we could.

"I'm concerned we'll get bogged down," he said midway through the second day of hearings.

"I think we could get bogged down thoroughly. We'll become so lost we'll lose sight of what we're here for."[3]

Needham's comments provoked a round of applause. Indeed, the hearing had provided myriad opportunities for boffs. The only misgiving in the minds of SEC personnel seemed to be whether investors might conclude that the SEC commissioners were medically certifiable if they granted a further increase in commission rates on the basis of Needham's proposal.

Whereas the lesson of Commissioner Needham is that the exit from the SEC is the door to the NYSE, Ralph Saul's case suggests

[3] *New York Law Journal,* July 18, 1973.

that Commission officials differ only in the date of their arrival on Wall Street. Having joined the SEC as a $19,000-a-year analyst, Ralph soon displayed the one asset that ensured advancment: He was a diplomat. One by one, he mollified irate investors who questioned the manner in which they'd been wiped out. He became the SEC's totem of appeasement. When a market crisis or an investor problem of major proportions came up, the first thing the chairman would say was "give it to Ralph. Let him handle it."

On November 22, 1963, the day President Kennedy was assassinated, specialists used the alibi provided by tragedy to clean out their books down to wholesale price levels. After they had accumulated large inventories of stock, they closed shop for the day and walked off the floor. This prevented public buy orders from being executed at the day's lows. The specialist in Telephone, for example, dropped his stock on November 22 from $138 to $130. He opened it on the 25th at $140! Sacrificing accuracy for expediency, he admitted to making $25,000 for his trading account. Ralph Saul saw to it that his omnibus and investment accounts were left shrouded in mystery.

Such occasions were alienating millions of investors. Congress decided to investigate specialists' transactions on November 22 and November 26. In a context of political crisis, it directed the chairman of the Commission to review and report his findings concerning specialists' transactions and to assess whether they had performed honorably. Turning to his secretary, the chairman handed her the order from Congress and said, "Let Ralph handle it."

Ralph knew that the information needed by the public to comment on his analysis of the specialists' transactions was unavailable. Both he and the Exchange knew that had he wanted to make headlines, all he had to do was denounce specialists—especially the specialist in Telephone. That would have allowed investors to launch ten thousand lawsuits, and he would have been hailed as Robin Hood.

As events turned out, he submitted a report that praised the performance of specialists. The Stock Exchange labeled his report as "tough, but even-handed." The Commission and Congress said nothing, and the public was appeased. Soon thereafter, Ralph was given the chance to serve investors as president of the American Stock Exchange, proving that, if a simple man's words are worth a small fortune, it may well be his silence is worth much more.

With the appointment of Hamer Budge as SEC chairman on February 22, 1969, the Commission's prestige declined sharply. When Senator Proxmire (D.-Wisconsin) decided to investigate the chairman's frequent trips to Minneapolis, it was discovered that Budge went there to confer with the officials of Investor's Diversified Services, a mutual fund complex. Proxmire had wondered why the Chairman didn't order the fund's officials to visit him since an investigation into their questionable activities was even then under way at the SEC.

Learning why, Senator Proxmire then announced he had slated hearings for "conflict of interest charges against Hamer Budge," citing reports that Budge was "negotiating for a job with the nation's largest mutual fund complex. . . . Proxmire told the Senate that Budge's subsequent statement that he declined an offer to become president of IDS fails to deny reports that he is still negotiating with the firm."[4]

Then it was learned that Senator Harrison Williams (D.-New Jersey) of the Senate Securities Subcommittee intended to conduct an open hearing on Hamer's job negotiations. According to Richard Halloran of the *Washington Post:*

> ". . . The SEC currently is considering matters pertaining to mutual funds, negotiated commission rates, access to the New York Stock Exchange by financial institutions and public ownership of broker-dealers who are exchange members," Williams said.
>
> "All of these matters directly affect the fund which offered Chairman Budge the job," he said. "Absolute impartiality is required and the public must be assured that this will be the case. . . ."
>
> Williams said the criminal code prohibits officers of independent agencies from negotiating for employment with firms that have current transactions with those agencies without written permission of the President.[5]

Budge decided to "tough it out." With that in mind, he appeared briefly at the beginning of the hearing shortly afterward and asked to be excused. "The appearance for me," he said, "is a traumatic experience." He pointed out that Nixon had been a director of four of IDS's mutual funds from late 1964 until May, 1968, and that Ralph Saul had also served as a director.

During the rest of that year Hamer proved to be an embarrassment to his odd-ball friends on the Commission and a joy to his enemies—among whom he now numbered his onetime friend Nathan Voloshen, the lobbyist and apologist for Parvin Dohrmann. As the *Los Angeles Times* of December 18, 1969, reported:

> A federal grand jury, under Robert Morgenthau's direction, is also looking into the activities of Nathan P. Voloshen, the New York

4 *Washington Post,* July 31, 1969.
5 *Ibid.*

businessman who is a close friend of House Speaker John W. Mc-
Cormack (D-Mass.). It is known that Hamer H. Budge, the Republican chairman of the Securities and Exchange Commission, may be
called to testify. No wrongdoing is alleged but investigators are
anxious to learn more details of Budge's private meeting with the
Parvin Dohrmann Co. of Los Angeles and how it was arranged by
Voloshen through McCormack's office.

As it turned out, Voloshen had persuaded Hamer to lift the first
suspension of trading on Parvin Dohrmann. But Budge's intervention was discovered and headlined in the newspapers "PAR-
VIN CASE AND THE SEC." Possibly, in the hope that no one
would suspect he had ulterior motives in lifting the suspension the
first time, Hamer suspended the stock a second time, causing some
difficulties for stockholders—and Voloshen.

Hamer left the SEC in December, 1970. The *Wall Street Journal* carried three lines announcing his departure, but neglected
to mention that while in Minneapolis, with a thoroughgoing
attention to detail, he had contrived a scheme to maximize profits
for the Exchange and IDS that would qualify him for the top spot
at IDS. What he'd done was to virtually eliminate the payment of
commissions by IDS and its mutual funds. The scheme was to go
into effect on April 5, 1971, four months after Hamer had de-
parted Washington. He had introduced a rule that required commissions on big-block transactions in excess of $300,000 to be
negotiated. This was an achievement for Hamer. Whereas in the
past big block transactions required the payment of both a large
commission *and* a special fee, after April 5, 1971, IDS and other
funds and institutional investors would be able to move into and
out of the market paying just the fee and nothing or almost
nothing in commissions. Hamer had demonstrated he knew how
to maximize the cash value of an SEC chairman's job.

In addition to enabling mutual funds to increase their moves
into and out of the market, Hamer's rule ensured that many funds
would now wait until April 5 to initiate their selling, which in
turn meant that prices of Dow and other highly active stocks
would be maintained at their highs in order not to discourage
selling. As it turned out, April 5 provided the signal for the funds
to initiate major big block selling. For that reason, the Dow Jones
average was not allowed to decline until the second week in April,
1971. During this period, the commissions saved by IDS more than
paid for Hamer's salary up to his date of retirement, and his pension after that.

On May 19, 1971, in an attempt to interest *Fortune* magazine in
this matter, I commented on Hamer's accomplishments for IDS
to Carol Loomis, an editor of *Fortune*. She replied: "I am in favor

of big block discounts. My husband is a stockbroker." I assumed she meant her husband was higher up in the business who profited from the increase in big block fees.

The Exchange sought to compensate brokers for the loss of commissions from mutual funds by having the SEC increase commission rates for the small investor.

Hamer had introduced a surcharge on commission rates as early as April, 1970. Brokers got this raise in commission rates because, to quote Don Regan, "the evidence that help was needed by brokerage houses was everywhere." Concerning the increase in commissions via the surcharge, Regan adds: "The increase was subject to easy change or elimination, so that the SEC could not be pilloried for favoring the industry *excessively;* and the stipulation of a 50% maximum increase stood as evidence of the SEC's interest in the individual investor."[6] The following year the surcharge was dropped and the Exchange increased commission rates.

On September 24, 1973, I wrote to Chairman Garrett of the SEC:

RICHARD NEY & ASSOCIATES
INCORPORATED
INVESTMENT COUNSELLORS
BOX H
BEVERLY HILLS, CALIFORNIA 90213

September 24, 1973

Chairman Ray Garrett, Jr.
Securities and Exchange Commission
500 North Capitol
Washington, D. C. 21001

Dear Chairman Garrett:

A comprehensive response to the NYSE's request for higher commission rates should address itself *not* to the fact that the public is now out of the market but to the fact that the public almost totally committed itself to the market from October 1970 through January 1973. In other words, the public is already locked into the market in terms of its available cash reserves.

What is certain is the Exchange wants it both ways. It wants to eat its cake and have it too. To mix metaphors, it has swallowed the goose that lays the golden egg and it expects the Commission to supply more eggs. Accordingly, while other businesses are allowed to go into bankruptcy because of non-competitive methodologies, the Exchange is further subsidized with increases in commission rates and gimmicks

[6] Donald T. Regan, *A View from the Street* (New York: W. W. Norton, 1972), p. 120.

like the Investor Protection Corp., which, thus far have served only to
further compound the investor's problems.

Commission income—along with other income—for brokerage house
executives during the 1970-Jan 1973 period defies comparison with
most other businesses. The organic, self-informing nature of this income should make it apparent to the Commission that the Exchange
should not be allowed to successfully plead hardship during a period
of inevitable slack as prices move to lower levels preparatory to another bull raid on the market by insiders.*

The letter went unanswered.

In his crusading, uncompromising one-man (and wife) weekly
magazine, I. F. Stone had on numerous occasions cracked down on
regulators who had submitted to improper influence from those
they are supposed to regulate. When President Nixon designated
William Casey to take Hamer Budge's place on the Commission,
Stone reacted with characteristic candor in his March 22, 1971,
issue:

PICKING A MASTER OF ADVERTISING FAKERY AS CHAIRMAN OF THE SEC

The SEC was set up to protect investors from false claims. William
J. Casey, Nixon's choice for SEC chairman, has been his No. 1 agent
in fake advertising. In 1969 Casey turned up as head of a "grass
roots" organization claiming that 84% of the American people
favored an ABM. The "grass roots" turned out to be Room 495 in
the White House annex. A few months later he was appointed adviser to the Arms Control and Disarmament Agency. In October of
that year full page ads called for "silent Americans" to speak up
for Nixon's Vietnam policy. The chairman again was Casey. On
November 17 there was a full page ad in the New York Times,
"Hold Your Ears Hanoi: Here Comes America's Silent Majority."
There was Casey's name again along with other such silent Americans as Clare Booth Luce and Leo Cherne. Such fakery, if used to
sell stock, would violate the Securities Act. Casey has already been
in trouble under the Securities Act. Casey settled one investor suit
against himself out of court (along with a plagiarism case) and is
defendant in another. But his odoriferous appointment will probably be confirmed.

The dance of ironies is again apparent. Casey's appointment was
worth a full-column spread on most financial pages. The president of the American Stock Exchange was delighted. So were

---

* As of December, 1973, the round trip commission costs to an investor for 100
shares of a $10 stock are 5% of the sales price; for a $50 stock it is 3%.

members of the New York Stock Exchange. A short while later another barrage from the Stock Exchange News Bureau told us that Casey was being "tough." The president of the Amex found that Casey had taken the "years and years of problems" that had built up and "set them in order." A senate staff man was more outspoken: "Casey isn't interested in saving money for investors but for brokers."[7] Whereas in the past the SEC and the NYSE conducted informal get-togethers in which, over canapés and martinis, future administrative procedures, policy changes, relaxed compliance schedules, and security industry problems were discussed behind closed doors, Casey would formalize these secret meetings through the use of the euphemism called an "advisory committee." In other words, he would see to it that Wall Street's phantom parasites would now be able to walk straight through the front door of the Commission and upstairs to the Chairman's office.

Casey resigned from the Commission in 1973 to become Assistant Secretary of State. At this writing he has been named to head the Export-Import Bank. Having served the securities industry well, he is now on his way up. His place on the Commission was taken by G. Bradford Cook, who at the end of two and one-half months found himself in serious trouble because of his efforts on behalf of President Nixon's re-election. The consequences were published in the *Washington Post* of May 17, 1973: "SEC CHAIRMAN QUITS IN WAKE OF VESCO INDICTMENT: Cook Cites 'A Web of Factors.' " If Cook suffered from an attack of double vision, it was because a federal grand jury in New York had opened a can of worms, and the press had dropped on them like falcons.

It was alleged that, having been the plaything of financial charlatans, Cook had succumbed to the clandestine methods of Nixon's chief fund-raiser and friend, stockbroker Maurice Stans. In a frenzy of misdirected loyalty he had deleted from an SEC suit mention of $200,000 in cash passed along by Mr. Vesco as a secret campaign contribution to Nixon. The grand jury had alleged that this gift was part of a conspiracy among Mr. Vesco, Stans, and others "to influence, obstruct, and impede" the SEC proceedings against Mr. Vesco.

According to the grand jury indictment, while the SEC staff was investigating Vesco's financial dealings, Cook involved himself with stockbroker Stans in ways the staff knew nothing about. In the course of interviews Cook let it be known he had gone

[7] *Wall Street Journal,* June 4, 1972.

"goose-hunting" with Stans and that Stans had persuaded him to delete "specific references to Vesco's $200,000 gift. He also confided to Stans that he yearned to be Chairman of the SEC, and Stans said he would 'pass the word along to Nixon.' What some newspapermen wondered was whether 'the word' had a price tag."[8]

"This is all we need," one SEC official was quoted as saying in the same article. Another commissioner, Hugh Owens, who took over as acting head on Cook's departure, said, "Morale is a little bit low around here." (Soon thereafter he left to take over as president of the Investors Protection Corp, where morale is equally low.)

Cook said he felt as though he had become involved in "a web of factors." He was merely another in a long line of Nixon appointees who had been handed a passport to a nervous breakdown. As it turned out, recent testimony (March, 1974) in the trial of Maurice Stans and former Attorney General John Mitchell who were indicted for obstructing justice in the Vesco case revealed that Cook's predecessor had also been involved. At Mitchell's request, Casey had met with Mr. Vesco's emissaries on several occasions to try to iron out the financier's problems with the SEC. As for Cook, like so many other Nixon puppets, he was allowed "to twist slowly, slowly in the wind." As Stanislaws Lec said, it is "easy to hang puppets. The strings are already there."

The rhetoric of the Commission's newest chairman, Ray Garrett, Jr., suggests that he may have begun to entangle himself in his own "web of factors." A *New York Times* headline of November 13, 1973, proclaimed, "GARRETT PROPOSES ANTITRUST LENIENCY FOR WALL STREET FIRMS." In December, 1973, Garrett attacked mutual funds but saw fit to single out the Merrill Lynch fund. He cited it for its splendid performance, neglecting to mention it had just been formed in October and that while the firm's stockbrokers were committing their customers to the market on the advice of Merrill Lynch research information, the fund itself was still largely in cash.* On December 4 Garrett spoke before the Securities Industry Association. Traveling to Boca Raton, Florida, for the occasion he had this to say (in part):

". . . because of the central role played by the securities industry in our economy your problems, collectively, if not individually, are problems for our economy, and therefore, for our society and our political system."

[8] Philip Greer, *Washington Post,* May 21, 1973.
* The Lionel D. Edie Capital Fund, Inc.

I couldn't have said it better. But the ideas going on in Garrett's head pointed in a different direction. He is a spokesman for the Street: "Those in the securities industry are entitled to bemoan the fact that almost all of them have had a rotten year financially." But, as I had pointed out to him in my letter of September 24, they had had a beautiful year in '72, and before that in '71, and before that in 1970. They have one, in fact, whenever they can suck the public into the market to buy their shares. Then specialists "bemoan the fact" there's no one left to buy as the market drops, when in fact they are pulling prices down to wholesale price levels in order to reaccumulate shares. As SEC chairman, Garrett should have been thankful these chuckleheads had a "rotten year" in '73 as the market dropped. If they'd had a better year it would have meant that even more investors were being ruined than those the Street had gunned down from 1969 to 1973. In the final analysis, men like Garrett raise this problem: How can we hope to tell the face of the enemy from an SEC official when they are interchangeable?

Wall Street always places its hatchetmen next to the President. Peter Flanigan is the present incumbent. He decides who will be appointed or has the final say on all federal regulatory appointees. In the whole of the Commission's history, no group of regulators have more mercilessly sacrificed the interests of investors.

It was Flanigan who, with Felix Rohatyn of Lazard Frères, determined that the Justice Department would drop its antitrust suit against ITT. Such generosity is characteristic of Flanigan. He can be counted on to advance the Administration's "hands off Wall Street" policy, on behalf of not only the Stock Exchange but any company associated in any way with Wall Street—particularly when any of these companies runs afoul of the SEC or any other regulatory agency. As in the case of ITT, the good things in life go to those who can pay for them. According to the *Washington Post* editorial of November 17, 1973, "Mr. Nixon's money men did not have to make any specific threats. Their very touch felt like a strongarm to nervous executives. This kind of process has a simple name: extortion." ITT offered $400,000.

Flanigan's functions had been kept rather well hidden until the ITT affair reared up and it was discovered he was the mastermind behind the whole thing, that even Mitchell at the Justice Department took orders from him. Soon after the ITT affair stories began surfacing in the press describing the manner in which copper magnates sought his intervention when it became apparent that the Environmental Protection Agency was obliging them to shape up or ship out. Flanigan intervened on their behalf, and they kicked in to the Nixon kitty.

Ralph Nader, Senator Eagleton (D.-Missouri), and Jack Anderson all refer to Flanigan as "Mr. Fixit" and are quick to note how busy he is solving the problems of corporations listed with the Stock Exchange. He was the man who should have been called to testify before the Senate hearings on the ITT scandal. But no more than Flanigan did the senators conducting the hearings want to call him for fear it might focus on Wall Street's investment bankers, particularly those at Lazard Frères who masterminded ITT's affairs. Parenthetically, it should be pointed out that, during the period Senator Kennedy (D.-Massachusetts) was conducting these hearings, he called Casey in June, 1972, to ask him not to mention the name of Felix Rohatyn's boss, André Meyer, the head of Lazard Frères. He explained to Casey that Meyer was a trustee of the Kennedy family foundation, that "he was a man of high reputation and had been very helpful to the Kennedy family." Casey testified that the SEC had no intention of mentioning Meyer personally but that Kennedy was apparently concerned "that the firm name would be named and perhaps besmirch his reputation." This was made public on June 25, 1973. In my weekly radio broadcast out of Washington, D.C. on March 24, 1972, I stated:

Most of Senator Kennedy's, Senator Tunney's and Senator Eastland's financial support comes from the stockbroker establishment. Hence, in the hearings now under way these Senators have discussed everything except the influence on the Justice Department of the stockbrokers closely involved with ITT. Thus, the really important facts behind Jack Anderson's revelations concerning the decision-making power of these stockbrokers have not been brought out at these hearings. Nor have they by the news media since the media are also controlled by the Stock Exchange or those with close links to the Stock Exchange. For example, besides Felix Rohatyn of Lazard Frères, Donald Petrie, another partner of Lazard Frères, is a director of RCA and—get this—also serves as chairman of the executive committee of ITT. It should not be surprising, therefore, that NBC news commentators state: "Thus far, Jack Anderson has been unable to show any link between the ITT contribution of $400,000 to the Republican convention and the dropping of the ITT antitrust suit." *How* can an NBC newsman be expected to say anything else when one of his bosses is an ITT chairman and another boss, Sarnoff, the chairman of RCA, is married to a member of the Kuhn-Loeb family—nor should we forget that A. E. Friedman is a Sarnoff in-law, a general partner of Kuhn Loeb, and is a director of ITT. A somewhat similar problem exists over at CBS. As for the *New York Times* stories that sneer at Jack Anderson, but praise Felix Rohatyn and Harold Geneen, let me point out that another ITT director is E. R. Black who is also a director of the New York Times.

Where Wall Street is concerned there is always a pigswill rush-hour atmosphere in almost every government office.

Flanigan is a wealthy man as a result of his stockbroker activities with Dillon, Read. Although he has somehow managed to keep from being mentioned in the Watergate shenanigans, since his arrival in Washington he has been involved in almost every controversy surrounding big money and the Nixon Administration. In 1970 he used his influence to get a Treasury Department waiver permitting an oil tanker to engage in coastal shipping. This increased the ship's value by more than $5 million. The tanker, it turned out, had been owned by him and the partners of Dillon, Read.*

He saw to the cancelation of a government task force's recommendation eliminating the quotas on oil imports. He did this for the investment banking industry's friends in the oil industry who would have lost billions of dollars. What he has cost the American consumer can't begin to be comprehended.

On May 24, 1972, Senator Metcalf introduced into the Congressional Record an article by *Washington Star* columnist Stephen Aug in which Mr. Aug discusses the practices of regulatory agency chairmen in sending reports to Flanigan. The following excerpt from Aug's column is of interest:

> *Flanigan said his own contacts with other regulatory agency officials include extensive discussions with William J. Casey, chairman of the SEC.* Initially, the discussions deal with legislation involving the Treasury Department that set up the Securities Investor Protection Corp., which indemnifies customers of bankrupt brokerage houses. Flanigan, whose background is largely that of Wall Street investment houses, currently discusses with Casey "the legislation that continues to be put forward" as well as major operational problems of the securities industry. [Emphasis added.]

The major cause of investor unhappiness used to be money and sex. Since the only thing investors talk about any more is how much money they've lost in the market, it can be said that Flanigan has helped eliminate half the investor's problems.

---

* *Newsweek,* March 20, 1972.

5. Is the SEC Relevant?

In which it is shown that the predicament of power is that, while it may be necessary to enforce virtue, no one who has it need ever complain of a want of opportunity to associate it with vice.

More than half the investor's avoidable suffering springs from the manner in which the SEC has seen fit to accommodate the wishes of the Stock Exchange. It's generally agreed that this is because of the intimacy that has grown up between the NYSE and the SEC. Washington and Wall Street seldom doing anything together except at the expense of a third party—the investor.

A key to an understanding of the manner in which the SEC's tactics serve the desires, tastes, and interests of the Stock Exchange rather than investors is revealed in a letter sent January 10, 1974, to SEC chairman Ray Garrett, Jr., by New York Attorney General Louis J. Lefkowitz. In his letter, Mr. Lefkowitz stated:

> I would like to bring to your attention my disappointment with the Commission's failure to act on my recommendations to the SEC based upon investigations by my office. . . . Three years ago, I recommended a new approach to the regulation of new issues. . . . Many securities firms have continually over-extended themselves in this area to the eventual downfall of both the firms and their investors.
>
> Federal regulation in this field has permitted the surging of a hot new issue market wherein questionable securities are sold at quickly inflated prices. . . . Another area of great importance involves the stability and trustworthiness of stock brokerage firms. I recommended several years ago a full accounting to broker-customers, including the regular issuance of profit-and-loss statements by all firms belonging to national exchanges. . . . This was done by allowing each brokerage firm to determine whether or not it was to continue the system of "surprise audits," a policy which both my office and the Congressional Committee found objectionable.

In the confidential report made available to your agency on institutional activity involving the stock of Levitz Furniture Corporation, several key recommendations were made to help curb perfidious activities by large and small mutual funds engaging in transactions with the investing public. Although an SEC investigator spent an entire week reviewing our internal files in detail many months ago, to date my office has not noted any action by the Commission in this field based on many of such recommendations.

The indispensable habits of mind that are peculiar to a Lefkowitz are regrettably not often found among government officials. The reasons for this are obvious. Once investment bankers discover they are not to be allowed to do whatever is most immediately profitable, they lay plans for the dismissal of the regulator.

Indeed, there has been, to my knowledge, only one occasion in which people who held the balance of power within the Commission indicated they were willing to engage in a brawl with the Stock Exchange. That was for a brief period during the Truman Administration, and the issue was a proposal to limit the number of floor traders allowed to indulge in investor throat-slitting.

Floor trading was instituted long before an improvement in the Exchange's secret practices introduced the specialist system. An SEC study group in 1962 attacked the practice and recommended action, but a timid chairman ignored the recommendation. Ganson Purcell, who had been the chairman in 1945, however, was aware that on more than one occasion floor traders' relative immunity from any sort of regulation had more than once caused a total breakdown of stock prices on the floor of the Exchange (for some reason no one ever observes that it is the manipulated bull raid by insiders, which, then, makes a decline in stock prices possible). Purcell commented particularly on the impact of floor traders on short-selling and price manipulation. His 1945 report was based largely on studies conducted by the Commission in 1944. The most important section, relating to floor trading (see Special Study Report, Part II, pp. 229–32), stated:

Floor traders "beyond a doubt" enjoy "formidable" trading advantages over the general public.

Floor trading cannot fail to divert and distract brokers from their duties to the public. Nor does the floor trader help in the filling of public orders. By and large, floor traders compete with the public in their buying and selling. When public demand exceeds public supply at a given price, the floor trader is likely to step in to increase the disequilibrium; he is more likely to augment the demand

and compete with the public for the available supply than to do the opposite.

Floor trading engenders excessive trading and excessive fluctuations in price. The floor trader typically "trades with the trend." If there are times when he tends to re-establish equilibrium in prices, such trading is very likely the aftermath of a course of action which threw prices off balance in the first instance. Cases other than these may sometimes exist when floor trading acts as a stabilizing influence but, if so, the voluminous data which we have accumulated shows that they are certainly not common, let alone typical.

In answer to the Commission's findings, the Exchange proposed a new set of rules that purported to restrict the floor traders' activities. The Commission found them loaded with loopholes and issued the following release:

> For all practical purposes [this method] is already in effect and has been for many years. For a long time, the exchanges have had adequate power under existing rules to restrain undesirable floor trading. . . . But a review of the exchanges' enforcement of these rules over the past 10 years demonstrates that neither these nor any similar rules administered by the exchanges serve to restrain floor trading in the slightest measurable degree.

The Commission also cited the Exchange's earlier failures to restrict floor-trader short-selling:

> The Commission's one effort in this direction—the short-selling rule—has met with limited success at best, insofar as floor traders are concerned, for it has not adequately prevented heavy short-selling from this source at critical junctures in the market.

Heretofore the SEC majority (with Robert Healy and Pecora dissenting) had demonstrated a willingness to sanction the habits and attitudes of floor traders. All that had changed. The SEC report now recommended that floor trading be prohibited and with it the competitive on-floor cost advantages and other privileges enjoyed by members. The Exchange was dumfounded. The following release was issued:

> It is our conclusion that, if floor trading is to be judged solely on the basis of the manner in which it has affected liquidity, continuity, and orderliness in trading, then the record justifies a continuation of this practice. . . .
> A certain proportion of the traders' activities, as discussed above, tends to be directly nonstabilizing and therefore presumably initiates or accentuates price trends; the indirect effect on price stability of a large number of their transactions has yet to be satisfactorily

measured, and, in certain specific instances presented in the Trading and Exchange Division's report of January 15, 1945, some of the effects of floor trader activity do not appear to have been in the public interest. It would therefore seem that every effort should be made to explore the possibilities of modifying floor trading practices as they now exist to the end that specific deleterious effects may be eliminated and, on an overall basis, the net favorable influence of floor trading may represent a larger proportion of all floor trading than currently seems to be the case.

The Exchange's proposal reveals the absence of any attempt to effect anything except the usual delaying action. Meanwhile, Stock Exchange members devised another set of rules and forwarded them to the Commission, along with a letter to the SEC chairman suggesting that these new rules covered the questions raised by the Commission:

> The Exchange will observe closely, as we feel sure the Securities and Exchange Commission will, the operation of the new rules to the end that their usefulness and effectiveness may be determined on the basis of a fair trial. A period of 6 months should be sufficient for such a test; I earnestly request on behalf of the New York Stock Exchange that, meanwhile, the Commission withhold action with respect to the proposals which its Trading and Exchange Division has made on the subject of floor trading.

Chairman Ganson Purcell rejected the Exchange's request. The Exchange repeated it on August 2, 1945. However, on August 8 the Commission voted to abolish floor trading. Unwilling to accept the Commission's edict, the Exchange sent a deputation of its most important members to appeal to Truman. They advised the President that any interference with existing Stock Exchange practices could have severe repercussions on the bull market then under way.

The fiction employed by Wall Streeters that any interference with its practices or any information that might be embarrassing to the Exchange will cause a severe drop in stock prices is always used to prevent action that needs to be taken. It was also used as an argument for dropping the antitrust suit against ITT. Interestingly enough, it was the delays granted ITT in its hearings before the Justice Department that enabled Stock Exchange insiders and the heads of ITT to divest themselves of their holdings before public announcment was made of possible action against ITT. It was subsequent to these distributions of stock that, despite the favorable Justice Department decision toward ITT, the stock inevitably declined.

Under pressure from Truman the SEC capitulated. A press release was issued announcing that the Commission was once again willing to help Stock Exchange members with administrative procedures that allowed them to help themselves:

> The New York Stock Exchange has urged us, in lieu of abolishing floor trading at this time, to afford it the opportunity to apply certain regulations which it believes will minimize the undesirable features of floor trading, yet preserve certain asserted benefits. The New York Curb Exchange has expressed its desire to put similar rules into effect.
>
> The proposed rules would generally require floor traders who have acquired a position by purchasing stock on a price rise or selling on a decline to hold that position until the beginning of the second succeeding trading day; they would prohibit members on the floor from availing themselves of the privilege of "stopping" stock unless the stock is "stopped" against the order of another member; and they would terminate the existing privilege of members on the floor, while acquiring a position in a security, of claiming priority over a public order at the same price either by the toss of a coin or by reason of the greater size of his order. . . .
>
> If at any time it becomes evident to us that the Exchange's rules, either in the form now proposed, or as they may be modified, are inadequate for the effective regulation of floor trading, we shall reconsider the recommendations of our staff, or any appropriate modification of those recommendations, and take such action as, in our opinion, will provide an adequate solution of the problems created by floor trading.

Upon release of the Commission's decision the Exchange introduced three of the rules previously turned down by Purcell. If the experience teaches us anything, it is that the SEC is no match, under existing circumstances, for Wall Street's daintily nurtured goons.

It is not stretching a point to say that the Exchange's ability to mock the regulatory agency's authority goes to the heart of the problems surrounding the Exchange's life or death power over investors. As former Chairman of the SEC William Casey stated in his book *Politics and the Regulatory Agencies,* "if anything was to be done, particularly if legislation was needed, we needed support from some of the leaders in the industry." It is fair to ask why do they need this support?

Millions of investors are persuaded to believe the Commission has resolved outstanding problems with the Exchange and that the market merits their confidence. For example, because of the complaints of thousands of investors who had been turned into terminal cases by the practices of floor traders, the Commission conducted more than fifteen studies of floor-trading malpractice. On all these occasions, it pointed out to the Exchange that the energies of the floor traders were ruining investors. The Exchange, on each occasion, protested. It advised the SEC that its members' floor practices were the raw material of a healthy auction market. In 1964 the SEC adopted new rules. The floor-trading rules of both 1945 and 1964 could be seen to be the same old rubber bands capable of being stretched to serve any expedient. The financial press, however, always referred to the SEC's "tough new enforcement" procedures, thereby generating public confidence in the market.

In each instance it was after a series of secret meetings with Exchange officials that the SEC staff made public the new floor-trading rules that the Exchange had agreed to adopt. Yet silence and secrecy are characteristic of the SEC's negotiations with the Exchange. In 1945 the fact that the Exchange had retained the management consultant firm of Cresap, McCormick, and Paget to conduct a study of floor trading was kept secret. The reason for this secrecy was because conclusions of these outside experts reflected unfavorably on floor trading. In fact, their conclusions stated that floor trading did "irreparable harm" to investors. In its unwillingness to disclose information potentially embarrassing to the New York Stock Exchange, the SEC is participating in a cover-up costlier to investors (and the economy) than Watergate.

Eisenhower's interventions at the SEC occurred through his Chief of Staff, Sherman Adams, who was finally forced to resign for his attempts to halt an SEC investigation of his friend Bernard Goldfine, a textile manufacturer.

Concerning the meetings that occurred between President Eisenhower and the high priests of Wall Street, Victor Perlo has this to say in his book *The Empire of High Finance:*

U.S. News and World Report listed 474 non-governmental visitors at 38 White House "stag dinners" during 1953 and 1954. The magazine conservatively classified 294 as businessmen. . . . These informal meetings have a definite role in policy formation. . . . Most of the guests are the really top men of the main financial group. Wall Street influence is shown by the New York addresses of 161, or over one-third of the guests; others reside in New York City suburbs or manage Wall Street-controlled corporate affairs from other home addresses. Four Rockefeller brothers are on the list, and the fifth was seeing Eisenhower as a government official. The Morgans matched this with 5 directors of J. P. Morgan and Company. Also present were the chief executives of the financial and industrial corporations of the Rockefeller and Morgan empires.

Like Truman, Eisenhower was an easy mark for Wall Street since he knew nothing about its practices and relied heavily on the expertise of Wall Street advisers. He too appointed to the regulatory agencies only those who would rubber-stamp Wall Street directives.

Vice-President Nixon, with an eye to the future, used the opportunities presented by his position to become Wall Street's man in the White House.

In his book, Louis Kohlmeier, Jr., has this to say:

> Taken together, the known evidence of interventions from Wilson to Nixon demonstrates that Presidents, Democratic or Republican, have not disassociated themselves from the substance of regulation. Contemporary regulation, in form and substance, also is influenced by a more or less constant application of patronage politics.[1]

This was best expressed by Nixon himself when, on September 25, 1968, as a candidate for the Presidency, he sent a letter to the leaders of the securities industry in which he denounced Democrats for "heavy-handed bureaucratic regulatory schemes." He promised that, if elected, he would ease regulatory controls.

Referring to Nixon's pre-election letter, the *Wall Street Journal* of September 25, 1969, remarked:

> When the letter stirred a political furor some Nixon campaign strategists tried to disavow it. But now President Nixon is making good on last September's pledge—and not just for the securities industry but for business in general.
>
> As appointees of his democratic predecessor resign or their terms expire, Mr. Nixon is filling the "independent" regulatory agencies with men (and one woman) who are generally regarded as friendly to private enterprise and adverse to stiff government regulation. Reaction in the business world is a discreetly voiced approval. Other interested bystanders, including some agencies' staff members, are less happy. "What a crowd. It's the most amazing bunch ever assembled," derisively says a Senate staff official.

In May, 1970, leaders of the financial community decided to form a special delegation to visit Nixon. According to Don Regan, in his book *A View from the Street,* this decision came out of conversations held with

> Louis Lundborg, then Chairman of the Bank of America; George Champion, retired Chairman of Chase Manhattan; Henry Kauf-

[1] Louis Kohlmeier, *The Regulators: Watchdog Agencies and the Public Interest* (New York: Harper & Row, 1969), p. 46.

man, a partner and the chief economist at Saloman Brothers, the largest bond firm and a leading institutional brokerage house and [himself].

It was decided Bernie Lasker, chairman of the New York Stock Exchange, would precede them as their spokesman and arrange the details of the meeting. The benefits to Wall Street gained by Lasker's entree to the White House had been so conspicuous and so subject to public comment that others on the Street had from time to time sought to put a lid on the public relations problem caused by the relationship. In the present instance Lasker talked Nixon into hosting a dinner party at the White House that initially was meant to be exclusively attended only by a select number of Wall Street tycoons. The *New York Times* got wind of the story, and the embarrassed groans from Wall Street caused a change in plan. Accordingly, in order to discourage any thought of financial hanky panky, it was decided to include businessmen outside the Wall Street community. Lasker settled on May 26 as the date for the dinner. The Dow reversed the December, 1968, decline in the market on May 27. Lasker's timing for the dinner therefore warrants a certain amount of speculation. Obviously, he knew when he made the arrangements with Nixon that everyone present would be in a festive mood the following day. Of all those present no one knew better that he and the other specialists on the floor of the Exchange would have just about completed their accumulations of stock and would be ready to launch a bull raid on the market, which, of course, was just what happened on the 27th. The Dow closed up 32.03 points. The Stock Exchange News Bureau attributed the rise to the optimism generated by the Nixon-Lasker dinner party. It should be recorded that the guests, along with the thirty-five from Wall Street, the fourteen industrialists, the seven bankers, the five heads of mutual and pension funds, and the two from insurance companies, included Attorney General John N. Mitchell, Secretary of Commerce Maurice Stans, and, last but not least, Peter Flanigan.

Lyndon Johnson was another Wall Street lobbyist who employed low-pressure get-togethers for the Street's high-pressure causes. In private conversations with members of the regulatory agencies, Johnson left not the slightest doubt that, although their public statements of policy must have public support, they should feel under no obligation to deal with the public truthfully or responsibly. He told them he wanted them to observe a spirit of "cooperation" with big business rather than lay out "new areas of control" over big business. Nixon carried this policy one step further. In Jack Anderson's column of September 1, 1973, we learn: NIXON DEMANDS REGULATORS' LOYALTY.

> President Nixon has suddenly informed the regulators he picks to protect consumers that he is far more concerned about their loyalty to him than he is about their freedom of judgment. . . . Even though [these regulators] are Presidential appointees, they are supposed to act independently of the White House. Several months ago, concerned over too much democratic-type thinking by his regulators and administrators, Mr. Nixon had his chief of staff, H. R. Haldeman, send a private memo to all the new appointees.
>
> A copy of the terse memorandum has reached us, attached to a column by a pro-Nixon writer, Ray Cromley, in which Haldeman says, ". . . The President has read this and feels it is important that you have a copy." The column so endorsed by the President says, "A relatively small group of willful men scattered in key positions throughout the government have for almost four years actively sabotaged the program sponsored by their President." It goes on to say that "the President now aims at weeding out" these dissenters.
>
> Haldeman, still quoting the President's views, said Mr. Nixon wanted the regulators and the appointees to read the column "so that you will thoroughly understand the basis for Nixon's concern regarding the necessity of avoiding having his policies sabotaged by hold-overs in the bureaucracy."
>
> Then, like a grammar-school teacher admonishing an eraser-throwing child, Haldeman said, "It is of course your responsibility to see that this doesn't happen."

Kohlmeier's reflections on this aspect of political theory as it relates to Wall Street is also suggestive of the manner in which Presidents attend to Wall Street's hugging and hoarding instincts:

> All Presidents have run checks with industry before picking regulators, fundamentally because all have looked on regulators more or less as industry's preserve.
>
> Another reason for the checkouts is that all Presidents, Democrats as well as Republicans, number leading industrialists among their personal friends and political contributors.[2]

Congress was fully aware that the Exchange regarded *any* regulation as inconsistent with its license to steal. It therefore imposed on the SEC the role of policeman. To make sure the policeman went fully armed, the Exchange Act gave the SEC authority to prescribe whatever protective measures were needed to guard

2 *Ibid*, p. 49.

against the practices of broker-dealers, specialists, and floor traders —their short sales, stop loss orders, and other manipulative devices. Since its formation the Commission has ignored this mandate.

According to the *Yale Law Review,* the "rule-making authority" provided for under the law

> has been used not as a procedure for the SEC to find the best regulations . . . but as a bargaining threat and then as a formal means of announcing a closed-door bargaining outcome.
>
> [It is also] a formal announcement procedure which is used by the Exchange to shift pressure from itself to the SEC by making it appear that the SEC is forcing Exchange reform.

The reason this process did not have the rule-making authority it should have was that

> the close relationships [that] developed between Commission and Exchange officials inevitably limit the agency's perspective. The essence of the bargaining process is compromise; men constantly involved in that process begin to share viewpoints with those on the other side of the table, and they are almost always Exchange officials.[3]

The collaborative nature of the relationship got a brisk airing when Morris Schapiro, a third-market dealer in bank stocks, sued the SEC (*M. A. Schapiro and Co.* v. *SEC*). He feared, quite rightly as it turned out, that the secret negotiations between the SEC and the NYSE were intended to drive him and other third market-makers out of business. He saw the listing of the common stock of Chase Manhattan as the possible forerunner of a situation in which the Exchange would prohibit members from trading with him in Chase stock.

The meaningful pattern into which the relationship between the SEC and the NYSE had been organized was revealed in a series of fifteen letters that were turned over to Schapiro by the courts—eight from the SEC to the Exchange and seven from the Exchange to the SEC. Mr. Schapiro was kind enough, in his turn, to hand them over to me. Limitations of space allow us to include only one full letter. What these letters reveal, however, is not only that the Chairman of the SEC is not about to back any losers, but that his relationship to the Exchange is that of a team player whom the Exchange has now sent in to make the winning touchdown.

[3] *Yale Law Review* 80 (1971):811.

EXHIBIT "H"

NEW YORK STOCK EXCHANGE
ELEVEN WALL STREET
NEW YORK 5, N. Y.

O. KEITH FUNSTON
PRESIDENT

November 29, 1965

The Honorable Manuel F. Cohen
Chairman
Securities and Exchange Commission
425 Second Street, N.W.
Washington, D.C. 20549

Dear Manny:

As you know I am going into the hospital today for ten days to have a hernia operation. I regret that I have to be away at this time but I guess one can't pick and choose when one goes to the hospital.

As I understand it, the ball rests with you as far as the current thinking of the Cost and Revenue Committee. That committee can not go much further until we have gotten some sort of an indication from the SEC as to your thinking.

As I understand it, the ball also rests with you with respect to Rule 394, inasmuch as the Exchange has given you our views on that subject. As you also know, there have been recent staff to staff discussions on odd lots and we are actively pursuing that subject here. It is expected that the Odd-Lot Committee will be meeting at the end of next week. We, of course, still have our over-riding odd lot anti-trust problem of which you are well aware. We also have other important discussions going on.

If you have any questions about any of these matters during my absence, I would appreciate it if you would take them up with either Duke Chapman or Ed Gray who are following these matters for the Exchange and who will keep me in touch.

I hope that your speech goes well tomorrow and I am sorry that I won't be there to hear it.

Sincerely yours,

Keith

Quarterback Cohen summarizes the game plan for the winning touchdown in his letter of December 22, 1965, to Funston, the head of his no-stone-unturned coaching staff:

As you know, these matters have been considered by the Exchange and the Commission for many months and though we expect ultimate implementation *may* require communication with other self-regulatory institutions and other affected parties, we hope that these matters can be moved forward to their resolution within a reasonably short period of time. [Emphasis added.]

Imagine how the scrawny, pigeon-chested investor must feel when he discovers in the final seconds of the game that his guards and tackles are also playing for the other team.

In 1972, Chairman Casey formalized this game plan with the establishment of advisory committees. In reporting this union between the SEC and the NYSE, one newspaper, *The Sunday Star and Washington Daily News,* headlined its article: "SEC Letting Industry Help Shape Policies."

Ten committees of members of the securities and allied industries had been formed to advise the SEC on the matters pertaining to SEC regulation of the securities industry! In other words, a major financial conspiracy had been laid by the SEC to hand over the regulation of the securities industry to the securities industry. The heads of the stock exchanges and brokerage firms and their lawyers are being asked to establish guidelines that will determine how the Commission should enforce federal securities laws, compliance with those laws, the structure of future securities markets, and the regulations the industry wants (and doesn't want) to see employed to deal with real estate and investment advisory services. During the single month of October, 1972, Casey filled the vacancies in five of those committees.

The SEC release announcing the formation of one committee stated that it would consider the applicability of the Investment Company Act of 1940 and the Securities and Exchange Act of 1933 to investment advisory services. The release stated that

> there is a great deal of uncertainty about the applicability of the Investment Co. Act of 1940 and the Securities Act of 1933 in this area. An advisory service which makes large scale solicitations of relatively small accounts and provides substantially the same advice to clients can become fundamentally indistinguishable from an investment company. Representations as to "individualized" treatment of clients may in such a case also raise questions under the anti-fraud provisions of the Investment Co. Act of 1940.

In point of fact, there was *no* uncertainty. On February 6, 1970, Merrill Lynch and the First National City Bank of New York were charged by the SEC with "operating an unregistered investment company in violation of federal law." A column by Philip Greer in the *Washington Post* of January 17, 1974, discussing the Ralph Nader–sponsored book on First National City Bank, states that the bank

> practically ignores the needs of its trust customers, takes in high fees for its service and uses cash belonging to the trust funds and makes improper use of commercial banking files in making investment decisions.

Citibank had established a subsidiary called the Special Investment Advisory Service, which it advertised as an "advisory service for investors with $25,000 or more, offering personal full-time portfolio management." Under the circumstances, it was inevitable that Merrill Lynch would act as exclusive broker for SIAS. A Merrill Lynch-Citibank combination would be pretty tough competition for any investor. The SEC charged that "facts not disclosed to investors" included:

> Funds were invested in virtually identical manner in one of two groups of securities.
> Approximately 47 per cent of the assets held by SIAS for such investors were invested in securities of companies affiliated or controlled by directors of Citibank.
> After the initial investment, all decisions to buy or sell a security were generally applied uniformly to the entire fund.
> A second count in the complaint . . . charged that SIAS is an investment company within the meaning of section 3(A)(1) of the Investment Company Act of 1940, but has no registration as such.

Merrill Lynch, as might be expected, denied all charges but accepted a consent decree. In addition to agreeing to

> stop offering this service . . . without admitting the commission's charges, Merrill Lynch also agreed to end similar relationships with American Security Bank & Trust Co. of Washington, First National Bank of Minneapolis, Continental Illinois National Bank and Trust Co. of Chicago, and Philadelphia's Girard Trust Bank.

By corralling a few million small investors and getting discretion over their accounts, the firm would be rid of all the hidden annoyances, expense, and litigation caused by brokers obliged to churn their customers' accounts in order to generate the business needed to absorb their institutional customers' big blocks. The plan sanctioned by the SEC would mean they would have to depend less on the efforts of their regional offices, except when the shares being sold were so egregiously bad as to require the small investors in the regional offices to absorb them. In such instances the firm's research analysts could be called on to provide enthusiastic reports.

Chairman Casey's October 12, 1972, announcement was an indication that Merrill Lynch's tribulations with the SEC were coming to an end. The firm would be able once again to employ a sales pitch that, just two years earlier, had been deemed infra dig.

This advisory committee was chaired by Douglas D. Milne,

president of Lionel Edie & Co. Lionel Edie is a Merrill Lynch subsidiary. It was unlikely that the chairman's wishes would encounter any serious resistance from anyone present. As for the conclusions of other members of the advisory committee, a reading of their "Recommendations for Clearer Guidelines and Policies" suggests that the self-serving opinions contained in their report should open up investigation instead of concluding it.

Lawrence Tilton
  Vice President, John P. Chase, Inc.
George A. Blackstone, Esq.
  Heller, Ehrman, White & McAuliffe
John Jansing
  Sr. Vice President, Bache & Co.
William Everdell, Esq.
  Debevoise, Plimpton, McLean & Gates
T. Spencer Everett
  Secretary and General Counsel
Dana H. Danforth
  President, Danforth Associates
Staff member: Alan Rosenblat, Chief Counsel
  Division of Investment Company Regulation

The representative from Bache, Merrill Lynch's strongest competitor, is there to remind the committee that what is good for one must be good for all. The Wall Street lawyers and others on the committee serve to consolidate the grip of Wall Street thinking on the direction of SEC administrative policy.

To convince the small investor that the advisory committee had been formed for his benefit, Chairman Casey's announcement stated:

> Through computer technology it now appears feasible to provide individualized investment advisory services to investors who have relatively small amounts of money to invest. These services can substantially reduce the disparity between research information and investment management available to institutional as opposed to individual investors, by providing the direct investor with continuous account supervision based upon his individual needs.

The quality of the investor's imagination and the quantity of his savings were about to be cruelly tested. In point of fact the commission was about to junk the concept of investment advice based on the "individual needs of the investor" in order to deliver him lock, stock, and barrel to the avant garde bucket shops controlled by the industry's major brokerage firms. The investor's attention would be directed to the ostensible credentials of the brokerage firms' investment advisory subsidiaries. Investors could not be expected to see behind the appearance of things. Their unawareness of who and what these advisory services represented would lead them to assume they were being provided information as sound as that provided to the advisory service's big-fee-paying institutional customers. Machiavelli could not have done better.

But there was one problem that was peculiar to all their enterprises, one barrier that had thrown them on many occasions when in the past they had attempted to hurdle it or go around it. That was the problem of compliance. Compliance with its statutes, with its rules and regulations—all that stood in the way of the infinite and comsummate pleasure potentials of self-regulation.

Thus it came to pass that Casey formed another advisory committee. He had decided that no one knew better than the broker-dealers themselves what their most pressing regulatory problems were, where they were most likely to run afoul of existing securities laws, and what they would like to see done about the Commission's administrative procedures regarding compliance with the securities laws. Accordingly, in discreetly held (nonpublic) meetings with the various Pooh-Bahs and fat cats of the Exchange, Casey delegated the Commission's rule-making authority to an "advisory" committee composed of Wall Street's securities lawyers. The SEC's role in these proceedings would be to implement the new recommendations. The following excerpt from the *SEC News Digest* of October 26, 1972, tells the story:

> Chairman William J. Casey announced on Tuesday the formation of an advisory committee to assist in developing a model compliance program to serve as an industry guide for the broker-dealer community. Assisted by this Committee's work the Commission plans to publish a guide to broker-dealer compliance under the Securities Acts in order to advise broker-dealers of the standards to which they adhere if investor confidence in the fairness of the market place is to be warranted and sustained.
>
> The members of the advisory committee are listed below:
>
> Howard T. Sprow—Chairman
> 　　General Counsel, Vice President and Secretary
> 　　Merrill Lynch, Pierce, Fenner & Smith, Inc.
> Frank J. Wilson
> 　　Senior Vice President (Compliance Regulation)
> 　　National Association of Security Dealers, Inc.
> Bryan P. Coughlin, Jr.—Vice President
> 　　Midwest Stock Exchange

Earl J. McHugh—Senior Vice President
  American Stock Exchange
Stuart K. Malcolm
  Department of Member Firms
  New York Stock Exchange
John A. Wing, Vice President and Assistant Secretary
  A.G. Becker & Co., Inc.
  Robert G. Cronson
  Senior Vice President and Secretary
  The Chicago Corporation
Jon J. Masters
  Secretary and General Counsel
  Baker, Weeks & Co., Inc.
C. Rader McCulley
  First Southwest Company
Ms. Judith G. Shepard
  Associate House Counsel
  Goldman, Sachs & Co.

For the Staff—Sydney T. Bernstein—Secretary
  Attorney Advisor, Division of Market Regulation

Scanning the chairman's list of names his message came in loud and clear. He was not seeking the arbitrament of impartial outsiders. He had gathered together some of the Street's best hit men and kidney-busters.

The human ends the existence of the committee might best serve were foretold by no less an authority than the committee chairman himself, Howard Sprow, vice-president and special counsel to Merrill Lynch. In a compliance memo to his firm's stockbrokers, he had stated earlier that year:

> Although profits in themselves . . . are no defense [against churning], it is rare that a customer who is making money will complain. *The time to slow down an overactive customer* [a euphemism for an account that is being churned—R.N.] *is while he is making money and not after his capital has been wiped out.* [Emphasis added.]

The legitimacy of the premise that it is permissible to "wipe out" a customer does not detain Sprow. His concern is for his stockbrokers; he suggests they "slow down" accounts now being churned so that by the time the customer's "capital has been wiped out," he cannot single them out for fraud.

An update on Casey's plans and recommendations was included in a release dated January 23, 1973. It suggested the advisory committee was about to chloroform the Investment Company Act of 1940 and the Securities Act of 1933 as they applied to investment advisory services.

The Commission recommended that "small account investment management services (controlled by Bache, Merrill Lynch, etc.) should no longer be treated as investment companies and

> the Commission should take appropriate action to institute standards for professional qualifications and financial responsibility of investment advisers and a system of self-regulation of investment advisers.

And who would see to that self-regulation? Why, stockbrokers and their investment advisers! This meant, of course, that advisers like myself had to pledge themselves to the Exchange's policies, or they could not be registered with the SEC. I dispatched the following letter:

RICHARD NEY & ASSOCIATES
INCORPORATED
Investment Counsellors
BOX H
BEVERLY HILLS, CALIFORNIA 90213

January 29, 1973

Mr. William J. Casey, Chairman
Securities and Exchange Commission
Washington, D.C. 20549

Dear Chairman Casey:

I would like to comment on the information included in the SEC News Digest of January 23, 1973 regarding the investment management advisory report. I would like to point out that many members of your advisory committee are stockbroker oriented and in direct competition with the consumer interests of investors. Indeed the firms of some of the members mentioned have already been cited by the SEC and in the courts for fraud against investors.

Yet these are the advisors selected by the Commission that are also being asked to determine the qualifications and financial responsibility of investment advisors and a system of self-regulation of investment advisors. In other words—the regulation of persons like myself who are opposed to the conflicts of interest and low standards of the very persons who are being allowed by the SEC to determine rules of conduct which would serve to inspire further confidence in an industry that should be required to let in the sunlight and fresh air that would be forthcoming with viable information concerning the daily activities of Stock Exchange insiders.

May I also suggest the imperative need to have persons like myself, and Mr. Reuben Robertson of Mr. Nader's staff on such advisory committees. As they now stand they are merely devices to further implement the status, power and authority of the Stock Exchange and its stockbroker affiliates.

Sincerely,

Richard Ney

Within a month a letter arrived from the director of the Division of Investment Management Regulation. In part, it stated that

> of the eight members of the Advisory Committee on Investment Management Services, only three members are employed by broker-dealers or affiliates of broker-dealers; two are affiliated with investment advisers which have no broker affiliation; two are attorneys engaged in private corporate-securities law practice; and one is the Chief Counsel of this division. . . .
>
> The industry members of the Advisory Committee are highly qualified people and gave freely of their time and expertise at great personal expense and inconvenience to themselves. While it is true that the firms of some members may have been cited at one time or another for violations of the federal securities laws, I am not aware that any of the Committee members were ever personally named in any of these actions, nor do I believe that any of these matters reflected adversely on the character, integrity or competency of these individuals.

Obviously, the author of this letter is aware that the expenses of these "highly qualified people" are paid by their companies—and are deductible. But more important than anything else is that any "inconvenience" they suffer is incommensurate with the opportunity provided each of them to put his foot on the investor's neck.

Granted none of the committee members had ever been personally named in any actions, if any of my clients were swindled by one of my employees or a member of my staff, I would expect to hear the Commission's brass knuckles beating at my door. The commonplaces that had been dinned into the ear of Harris-Upham in the Bertha Hecht case and in countless other instances measured the distance between the guilt of the employer and his agent and had concluded it was nonexistent.

The SEC's permissive guidelines would now serve to resolve many of Merrill Lynch's legal problems. Its record is proof that, securities laws notwithstanding, it needs all the help it can get. To mention only a few not previously cited instances: (1) Merrill Lynch was ordered in November, 1968, to close two of its offices (only temporarily) for violating federal securities laws for disclosing nonpublic information on the earnings of Douglas Air-

craft to favored institutional customers. (2) Many law suits against
Merrill Lynch by investors in the stock of Douglas are now in litigation. (3) In April, 1970, a Federal grand jury in Cleveland returned an indictment against a Merrill Lynch official, whose name
(believe it or not) Merrill Lynch was able to have the court with-
hold and keep sealed. (4) On March 12, 1974, it was reported the
SEC had initiated proceedings against Merrill Lynch for causing
up to 10,000 customers to lose between 15 and 20 million dollars
by "pushing them" to buy shares of a Dallas computer company
that its research analysts claimed they had investigated and were
able to recommend when, in fact, their analysts had merely published the computer company's handouts. It was alleged the firm's
salesmen were being encouraged by branch managers to sell the
stock to customers, despite the fact that the firm knew of the
computer company's problems; that Merrill Lynch even solicited
a 200 share order one hour before the firm filed for bankruptcy.
(Note: According to Merrill Lynch's attorney, the brokerage
firm has already won two civil suits that alleged the same charges
as in the SEC case and he fully expected to win this case.) (5) On
December 13, 1973, a class action was filed against Merrill Lynch
charging usury on margin loans to its customers.

As for the "competency" of the members of this advisory committee, President Truman, with a supreme sense of the practical,
long ago disposed of the subject: "You don't set a fox to watching
the chickens just because he has had a lot of experience in the
hen house."

The Commission's failure to disclose the substance of its meetings with these advisory committees, its desire to keep these proceedings secret, raises another problem.

Congressman Moss (D.-Calif.) asserted that if the Commission
continued to refuse disclosing what went on at these meetings, he
would take it upon himself to subpoena the committee's members
and grill them at public hearings.[4] The SEC then placed the proceedings in stark caricature by stating it saw no reason to comply
with the Congressman's request; that if it did it was *"a little
worried . . . some of the members might wish to resign if they
faced the prospect of being questioned by members of Congress
on their positions and recommendations."* (Emphasis added.)

Senator Harrison Williams observed that the SEC was allowing
its "secret dealings" with Wall Street to prepare a machine for the
total annihilation of investors. He took exception, he said, to the
manner in which the Commission had "delegated its initial and

4 *New York Times,* April 25, 1972.

crucial job of policy formulation" to committees, which "meet in secret and are subject to no public accountability." His aide was even more forthcoming. When asked why the members of the committees were unwilling to respond to questions by the press about their activities, he replied, "Casey has sworn them to secrecy in writing."

Yet, this essential characteristic of these advisory committees now places them in direct violation of Federal law. Most regulatory agencies are, like the SEC, captives of the industries they regulate. They too create business-oriented advisory committees similar to those ordained by the SEC for Wall Street. Senator Metcalf watched all this activity behind closed doors for a while and then decided something should be done about it. Having worked for the passage of the Federal Advisory Committee Act, he found it extraordinary that so many agencies, like the SEC, refuse to comply with the Act. On November 7, 1973, he called attention to the problem on the floor of the Senate. The following excerpt is from that speech:

> The Federal Advisory Committee Act was a year old last month. The law, a useful part of the effort to shed more light on the processes of government, requires, among other things, that almost all of the meetings of federal advisory panels must be public. Many committees have opened their doors quite willingly, with substantial gains in public understanding of whatever work they do. But some have resisted reforms, forcing the advocates of openness to engage in a series of skirmishes with those who keep trying to function in the old secretive style.

In *The Regulators,* Louis Kohlmeier came to the conclusion that "independent regulatory agencies like the SEC are not independent and should be abolished." He found them to be the nemesis of competition as spelled out by the antitrust laws and suggested they were instruments meant to serve not the consumer but competing business interests.

Yet, for all that, the SEC regulators are simple people who bless God as well as the Stock Exchange for their bizarre success. When they take to the road we learn that they actually think of themselves as dedicated public servants. That they have convinced so many they are is doubtless the most striking proof of their genius.

6. The Myths and Techniques Surrounding the Specialist's Use of the Short Sale

In which it is shown that the investor doesn't know where his future ends and the specialist's begins until he understands the short sale.

Most investors are aware that the theory, advanced by the Stock Exchange, is that specialists act as agents for their public customers on the one hand and on the other as dealers for themselves. When acting as agents, they employ their trading accounts, and when acting as dealers, they employ not only their trading accounts but also personal investment and omnibus accounts which can be held by brokerage firms or banks. Ignoring an inherently irreconcilable conflict of interest, the Exchange insists that, since definite actions produce definite results, when the specialist takes off one hat and puts on the other, although he may look like the same man, sound like the same man, even tell the same jokes, he is nonetheless behaving as an entirely different creature. Function A, in other words, is never, under any circumstances, allowed to interfere with Function B.

This conclusion, easily arrived at by the Exchange, is quite simple to dispense with once we gain insight into the strategies the specialist employs as a *merchandiser of stock*. As a dealer for his own account, he must operate according to certain principles to set in motion the chain of events that enable him to distribute or accumulate stock. He cannot do so without totally disregarding the standards of behavior befitting an agent acting for others. That investors have, for so long, failed to perceive this disconcerting fact accounts for the Exchange's ability to found a system upon the ignorance of the many and the cleverness of the few.

To understand the specialists' practices, the investor must learn to think of specialists as *merchants* who want to sell an *inventory of stock* at *retail* price levels. When they *clear their shelves* of their inventory they will seek to *employ their profits* to buy *more merchandise* at *wholesale price levels*. Once we grasp this concept we are ready to posit eight laws:

(1) As merchants, specialists will expect to sell at retail what they have bought at wholesale.
(2) The longer specialists remain in business, the more money they will accumulate to buy stock at wholesale, which they will then want to sell at retail.
(3) The expansion of communications media will bring more people into the market, tending to increase volatility of stock prices as they increase elements of demand-supply.
(4) In order to buy and sell huge quantities of stock, Exchange members will seek new ways to enhance their sales techniques through use of the mass media.
(5) In order to employ ever increasing financial resources, specialists will have to effect price declines of ever increasing dimensions in order to shake out enough stock.
(6) Advances will have to be more dramatic on the upside to attract public interest in order to distribute the ever increasing accumulated inventories.
(7) The most active stocks will require longer periods of time for their distribution.
(8) The economy will be subjected to increasingly dramatic breakdowns causing inflation, unemployment, high interest rates, and shortages of raw materials.

The deluded investor spends his days seeking stocks with sound growth prospects while the specialist, operating less like a human brain than like a human machine, is able to devote himself solely to the solution of his complex merchandising problems—all of which are dependent on the simple fact that day in and day out he is concerned only with adding to or distributing his inventory in each of the stocks in which he is registered. This, in essence, is the problem of all specialists. It is also the problem of all investors.

The Stock Exchange abets its specialists' merchandising strategies by training investors to address their attention to business statistics, economic data, and other concepts that have but limited relevance for investment purposes. It does this because investor thinking along these lines enables specialists to predetermine their own activities on the basis of the investor's misdirected behavioral attitudes. Furthermore, it understands that, however much of a chucklehead the investor may be, he is not going to plunk down his life's savings without being given *something* in the way of theory that allows him to assume he is using his brain. The investor is provided, therefore, with market terminology that purposely blurs perception, making it next to impossible to make intelligent decisions or to recognize or create values.

The term "auction market," for example, has a great pull on the public's imagination. Investors have been led to believe that demand sends prices up and supply sends them down. Yet, since great demand for stock by the public causes prices to decline instead of advance, it can be seen that the market provided by the New York Stock Exchange is not consistent in any respect with the notions of a legitimate auction market. In fact, it is exactly the reverse. Most investors bypass the fundamental fact that big block selling by insiders at the *top* of the market can, of necessity, only be in response to public demand—just as big block purchases at *bottom* prices by insiders can take place only if the public sells everything in the fear stock prices are going lower.

For example, when a corporation like Occidental Petroleum negotiates a $3 billion deal with the Soviets, the investor assumes that the company's earnings will skyrocket. That being so, he assumes the stock's price will advance to reflect this gain in earnings. However, as Stock Exchange insiders and individuals like the chairman of Occidental Petroleum knew, the public's demand for this stock would not cause the stock's price to advance, as many expected, to $100 or more per share. Thus, on the announcement of the agreement or shortly thereafter, we find corporate and Exchange insiders selling (and selling short into the bargain) in response to public demand. The stock advanced to 18¼ and went no higher. It then declined, despite the fact that demand for Occidental Petroleum stock broke all records for a single day's trading in a stock listed on the New York Stock Exchange. In a true auction market such demand would have sent the stock's price on a long upward advance. In the case of Occidental Petroleum, however, the stock declined from 18¼ to 7¾ a number of months later.

The manifestation of characteristically limited public understanding can be attributed in large part to the daily bombardment of false assumptions and pseudo-knowledge by the media. This fact was brought home to me in the course of a luncheon at the home of Lawrence Spivak, producer of "Meet the Press," and his wife in Washington, D.C., on July 8, 1970. I had appeared before

Congressman Moss's subcommittee that morning to speak against the Investor Protection Bill. I had told the Spivaks that the purpose underlying my appearance before the subcommittee involved a continuing effort to expose the public's false assumptions about the market, such as the traditional theory of supply and demand. In response to their questions about the future course of the market, I told them I expected a bull market of dramatic proportions extending over at least the next six months.

"Do you think most people should stay out of the market?" I was asked.

"Yes," I said.

"But, didn't you just say we were now going to witness a bull market?"

"Yes, but by the time most of the public returns to the market, prices will be at their highs."

"But, if everyone listened to you and stayed out of the market, what would happen to it?"

"Just what will happen to it now," I told him. "Prices will advance sharply for at least the next six months."

The thinking of the Spivaks reveals that the thoughts of even the most brilliant political analysts, like those of investors, are cemented to false assumptions about the market.

Obviously the investor's insights into the market and the motivation underlying the specialists' practices are inadequate. His mistakes are attributable to the propositions he is compelled to entertain. When he is persuaded to read books by authors who are supposedly eminent market experts, who preach methodologies that have nothing to do with the premises upon which the market operates, he cannot help but make mistakes. For example, I fail to see where the thoughts of two of the market's most celebrated academic authorities have any relevance to the immediate needs of investors. On the first page of their book *Security Analysis,* Benjamin Graham and David Dodd say:

> The analyst needs a wide equipment. He must understand security forms, corporate accounting, the basic elements that make for the success or failure of various kinds of businesses, the general workings of our economy, and finally the characteristics of our security markets. He must be able to dig for facts, to evaluate them critically, and to apply his conclusions with good judgment and a fair amount of imagination.

It is not possible for the investor to make decisions that can stand up against the substantial reality of the specialist system on the basis of these high-level abstractions. That is not to say there are not viable alternatives. By scrapping traditional theory it becomes possible to discover the true order of things, to show how the aspirations of investors can be linked to the aspirations of the specialist as he proceeds to merchandise his stock. With that in mind, I shall describe the workings of an instrument that, more than any other, sustains the privileges and power of the specialist system. It will be disturbing to learn about it. It should be. Its impact upon the market as the specialist's chief merchandising instrument is contrary to everything investors have believed about the way the laws of supply and demand operate in the market. I am referring to the short sale. The Exchange defines it as follows:

> A short sale is made by an investor when he sells stock he does not own. He borrows the stock to make delivery and expects the price of the stock will be lower when he buys later to return the borrowed stock.[1]

There's a saying, "A little truth helps the lie go down." While the specialist's constant preoccupation with the short sale as an indispensable adjunct to his power is a matter of common knowledge on the floor of the Exchange, its utility to him is all but unknown to the public. That is because investors have been conditioned to think of the short sale in terms of their own short-sale transactions rather than the specialist's. An understanding of the specialist's use of the short sale can yield tremendous insights into the principal processes of the Exchange. For this reason I shall provide theory that connects the term with the events it really represents. This will enable investors to think realistically about the events and situations that are a by-product of this instrument's use by the specialist.

In order to put the short sale into proper perspective, the investor must first realize that, according to the *NYSE:*[2]

> Well over half of all short selling is done by specialists carrying out their functions of maintaining markets. [The figure is approximately 75 per cent at market highs.] A heavy influx of buy orders is usually met by the specialists initially from their inventories or with short selling.

The importance of the short sale is in terms of the advantages it affords the specialist rather than the investor. To understand the range and scope of these advantages, we must understand the setting that sustains them. An example perfectly suited to this purpose is close at hand.

1 *NYSE Fact Book,* 1969, p. 42.
2 Ibid.

As of August 4, 1973, the losses sustained by investors because of a two-year decline in stock prices were compounded by the rally in the Dow Industrial Average that began on July 9 and lasted until Friday, July 27. During this period the Dow advanced from 870 to approximately 940. A state of euphoria invaded the market. It brought with it the thought that the long-term decline had come to an end. Although the rally began on July 9, the bright effulgence of the Exchange's most powerful rhetorical devices did not make their critical appearance until precisely the right moment— at the end of the rally on July 26. At that time specialists were able to establish massive short positions as the public rushed to buy stock at the top of the rally.

According to the comments in the *Wall Street Journal,* the rally was caused by circumstances that served to hypodermic the market. This is profoundly significant, for it can be assumed that without these events the earlier decline in stock prices would have continued. This idea carries with it the assumption that the events taking place from July 9 were quite distinct from and without relationship to the events that had precipitated the earlier decline. Implicit in this is the further assumption that market trends are caused by events that bear no relationship to the market's past or future. Since Exchange insiders are at the center of things, however, it can be demonstrated that there is no watertight compartment that separates today from tomorrow, or tomorrow from yesterday. We must not dissociate the specialist's critical judgments involving the short term from the larger context of his long-term objectives. The "short term," "intermediate term," and "long term" are not three different realities but three aspects of the same reality. The long term is predetermined by the specialist. The fluctuations he creates in his particular stock to achieve his goal determine what the short and intermediate movements will be within his major blueprint. This type of control over price movement is made possible by the magic of the short sale.

How, it may be asked, does the July rally fit into all this? Dow specialists had been intent on taking prices down so that they could make major accumulations of stock for themselves. As specialists executed the sell orders on their books (as they lowered prices), they acquired substantial inventories of stock. They therefore created rallies in order to divest themselves of these shares before taking stock prices lower.

Chart 6–1, from Trendline Daily Basic Stock Charts, provides the reader with a conceptual view of the setting in which the July rally occurred. It also provides a bird's-eye view of the extent of

CHART 6–1

DOW-JONES AVERAGE OF 30 INDUSTRIALS

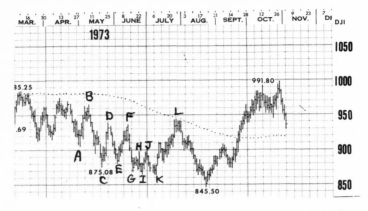

the rally and the series of fluctuations that preceded the rally. The rallies that culminated at points B, D, F, H, and J not only enabled specialists to liquidate inventories acquired in the earlier declines *but also allowed specialists to establish short sales. When they initiated their short sales, they halted the advance; this gradually reduced public demand, which then enabled specialists in the Dow stocks to drop prices again below the 900 level.* In each instance stock accumulated by specialists in the course of each decline necessitated a rally so that they could divest themselves of stock before proceeding to lower price levels.

The July rally was an echo of what had already taken place in April, May, and June. Examining the logic underlying these rallies, it becomes immediately apparent that, had specialists intended to conduct a long-term rally in July, they would not have diminished their stock inventories by conducting the five earlier (short-term) rallies and distributing their inventories at the tops. Instead, they would have accumulated as much stock as possible under the 900 level for their investment and trading accounts. Under these circumstances, the profit incentives would have existed for a major bull raid on the market. The absence of such accumulation before July made it a simple matter for a competent analyst to anticipate no more than another short-term rally in July.

Some of the circumstances surrounding the July rally, however, had been absent from the earlier rallies. Because of the new intermediate low that had been established prior to the July rally, specialists had accumulated larger inventories than during the earlier declines. They therefore needed a sharper and longer rally with greater volume at the top to divest themselves of these shares. Hence, at the beginning of the rally insiders made a greater effort to "sneak" prices up so that demand for stock would not enter the market until prices were at their highs.

On Monday and Tuesday, July 9 and 10, the Dow advanced +7.15 and +11.06, respectively. The *Journal* quoted brokers as saying the rally was "technical." On July 11, the Dow advanced +19.87. The *Journal* commented: "Helping to support the rally, brokers said [the *Journal*'s hedge clause] was the testimony yesterday of former Attorney General John Mitchell before the Senate Watergate committee in which he said President Nixon was unaware of the coverup effort." On succeeding days, investors were advised that the rally was being "fueled by continuing improvement in the dollar abroad," that "brokers were encouraged by the way the market held its ground in the face of negative news such as rising interest rates" and attributed it to the "sloughing off of uneasiness about what Phase 4 would contain."

Monday and Tuesday, July 23 and 24, began a week in which the *Journal* would launch a propaganda barrage. On Monday investors were brought into contact with the subtle commerce of big money: "Some money managers think they detect a few signs of improvement in the stock market." Tuesday was more of the the same. On Wednesday the 25th, like *Playboy* laboring to present in one transcendental centerfold the sum total of joy that had been displayed in all earlier centerfolds, the *Journal* produced an image of such unprecedented technical authority and opportunity that, like crazed lemmings, investors leaped into the market. Volume was 22.2 million Wednesday and 18.4 million Thursday.

The piece on July 25, I noticed, was written by Charles Elia, former financial editor of the New York *Daily News*. We'd met on several occasions in 1970 and 1971 while I was touring, trying to bring the ideas in *The Wall Street Jungle* to the attention of investors. I had found him personable. He was the American idea of what a journalist should look like; lean, oval-faced, Van Dyke beard, and a warm, amiable smile. A refined model of the Hemingway prototype, he had a recognizable aura that distinguished him from most financial editors. We'd talk, he would take voluminous notes, but nothing ever appeared in his column to indicate we'd met. At first I didn't understand why he didn't bewail the corruption of ideas that had taken place in the market.

He began his "Abreast of the Market" column on Wednesday on a high note of optimism. Using the same language that had been employed in that space for decades, he attributed Tuesday's rise in the Dow of +5.57 "to the partial defusing of the potential constitutional crisis that developed Monday in the Watergate affair." There followed a comment on the White House statement that it was studying "appropriate action" to take in replying to subpoenas of tape recordings and documents. He concluded his comments by emphasizing that "analysts saw the day's action as further evidence that the upward momentum . . . hasn't yet been broken." Following Wednesday's advance of +14.30 in the Dow, from top to bottom his column provided the eclectic chitchat that investors always regard as the real inside stuff:

> Stock prices rolled forward on a broad front in the heaviest trading on the NYSE in more than six months. . . . "Once the tide turns you get the bandwagon syndrome," said one broker. . . . Analysts said investor sentiment also was apparently encouraged by news from Washington.

On Thursday the Dow advanced +1.51. On Friday, July 27, it was up +2.18. In a bear market specialists will invariably advance the Dow on a Friday in order not to allow pessimism to build over a weekend—thereby causing heavy volume selling on the following Monday, which would then necessitate a rally before proceeding lower thereby interfering with their timetable.

Beginning on Monday, July 30, the decline was begun that would carry the Dow from 936.71 to its August low of 851.90 in the course of eighteen trading days. The lofty cynicism used to alibi the decline was as traditional as the Wodehouse rationale that alibied the earlier caper to the 936 level.

The calculable result of the advance to the July high is that specialists' shelves were cleared of their inventories, short positions were established so that prices could once again resume their decline to levels where large accumulations of stock could be made and then sold in the course of *another* highly profitable rally. Thus, such is the power of the short sale that it enables the specialist to have control when he needs it most in the framework of a declining market. It thereby eliminates the risk factors inherent in a decline. In this setting, and with an exact apprehension of the factors of demand versus supply made possible by the gathered insights of his "book" and incoming orders, the tactical control granted the specialist by the short sale enables him to define the future trends of stock prices.

These tactics may be taken by some as proof of the specialist's ability to maintain a "fair and orderly market" as an "agent" on behalf of his public customers. It seems to me, however, that anyone still inclined to this assumption has missed the whole point of the specialist's merchandising strategies, and what it means to be the obsessive proprietor of an instrument like the short sale.

Implicit in the use of the short sale by specialists is the principle at the root of the investor's problems: the relationship between what the Exchange insider wants the public to do at the top of the market and what he wants him to do at the bottom. As I have already suggested, the insider cannot successfully maximize his profits if the investor buys at the bottom (along with other Stock Exchange insiders) and sells at the top. What is good for the public is bad for the insider. For this reason insiders have devised a number of expedients to neutralize the effects of such public buying and selling. As I have tried to indicate, the most important expedient is centered upon the specialist's unique short-selling privileges. Once the investor understands the relationship between the short sale and the specialist, he will be on the way to solving many of his investment problems.

For example, when the Dow average advances after a major bottom has been established in the market and then moves back down to that bottom for a second (or third) time, the investor is always told that "the market is testing its bottom." This is an absurd euphemism for an operation in which the short sale has been employed to halt an advance caused by public demand for stock at wholesale price levels. The public, in other words, had moved into the market too soon and had acquired stock that, in the opinion of the Exchange, "rightfully" belonged to insiders. As prices rise, the advance is halted by selling short to supply public demand. Then, once demand falls off, prices are pulled back down to wholesale price levels and investors are told "the market is testing its bottom." In the course of this decline specialists are able (1) to shake out investors who fear the market may again go lower and (2) to accumulate additional inventories of stock for a second set of investment accounts.

Anyone who wishes to extract all the venom from this instrument's deadly bite must also recognize that public selling at the bottom is what enables the specialist to employ his short covering operations. These transactions then serve to halt the decline. Thus we see that another major function of the short sale is that it enables specialists to absorb public selling in the course of a decline and to halt it at a predetermined price level. When public selling has exhausted the covering potentials of the specialists' short sales, the specialists purchase the additional stock being sold by the public for their own accounts before taking prices up. Thus, the short sale instrument allows the specialist to control stock prices in much the same way as you control an elevator; advances can be halted and declines begun with short-selling, while declines can be halted and advances begun with short covering.

Unfortunately, the SEC does not provide information about the specialist's short sales until a month or more after his short-selling has taken place. This is still important information, but it is provided too late to be of any use to the average investor. Regarding the specialist's short covering transactions, nothing at all is published. Yet, they signal the specialist system's decision to reverse a market downtrend in order to inaugurate a bull raid on the market.

On too many occasions, my analysis of specialist short selling indicated that the amount of short sales attributed to them on high volume days occurring at market highs had to be in error. The amounts of short-selling attributed to specialists in SEC bulletins seemed always to be much less than I had expected to see published. Either that or stock was being supplied by the specialists' investment accounts in greater amounts than seemed possible, which of course was also a disconcerting possibility. I suspected, however, that at the top of every rally specialists were hauling in enormous amounts of ammunition (in terms of short sales) that they would subsequently use to destroy an army of investors. I was soon to have my suspicions confirmed.

I had written the SEC to ask what I thought at the time might be considered a manifestly ludicrous question: Was there a rule that allowed specialists not to disclose their short sales? It seemed unlikely that such a rule existed, yet my researches had disclosed disturbing evidence of a possible loophole. The wording in one section of the Special Study Report suggested that, despite the intent of the securities acts and the proscriptions of earlier SEC rulings, something might have happened in the interim that under the cover of broad generalizations allowed specialists an exemption from the short sale rule.

I was aware that in 1935 the SEC had requested Stock Exchanges to initiate controls over the short-selling practices of Stock Exchange insiders. It had come upon conclusive evidence that Exchange members were conducting massive short-selling operations that served to "demoralize the market." In the early and middle 1930's, over the violent opposition of the heads of the Stock Exchange, evidence came to light that short selling by Stock Exchange members at prices lower than the last sale exerted a highly depressing effect on the market. In 1935, therefore, although short sales were permitted at the last sale price, a rule was promulgated that prohibited short-selling at a price *below* the last sale price. At the time the SEC voiced the hope that the rule would "preserve those features of short-selling which are in the public interest." Since there is nothing about short-selling that is in the public interest, the SEC was employing a euphemism which suggested that if the Exchange was going to guillotine the public it shouldn't do it in broad daylight.

In the fall of 1937 there was a sharp drop in the market, and the Commission began a "study of the market decline" with a view to reassessing the Exchange's short selling rules. The hearings produced rules that supposedly corrected the limitations of the 1935 rule. They also defined a short sale as "any sale of a security which the seller does not own or any sale which is consummated by the delivery of a security borrowed by, or for the account of, the seller." The important part of this new set of rules, however, was contained in paragraph (A) of the second rule, which stated: "No person shall . . . effect a short sale of any security *at* or below the price at which the last sale thereof, regular way, was effected on such exchange." This meant that all short sales were prohibited unless they occurred at a price above the last sale price, usually at least an eighth of a point. The principal purpose of this rule, of course, was to prevent short selling at successively lower prices thereby eliminating the use of this instrument by the Stock Exchange "bear raider" to drive the market down. Such short-selling was effected on "minus ticks" when all public offers to buy stock at a specific price level were exhausted by the short-selling of insiders. Invariably, however, there were buy orders entered on the specialist's book at lower price levels. Specialists then dropped prices and sold short to these orders. Obviously the short sale uptick rule was aimed at eliminating this use by specialists of the orders entered on their books.

Another provision of the same rule stated that all sales were to be marked either "long" or "short." Paragraph (D) provided exceptions that were supposedly only meant to include any sale of an odd lot and certain off-setting transactions by the odd lot dealer. Then, from the Special Study Report of 1963 (Part 2, Page 252), I learned that "the third rule related to the conditions under which a broker could borrow securities for a long account."

This, I thought, could very well be another clear demonstration of what a loophole looked like and how the whole loophole process operated. For want of a better term, I thought of it as the use of "protective coloration" by the SEC. Obviously it was as illogical and as unethical to allow insiders to borrow stock for what was called a "long," instead of a "short," account as it was to call a rattlesnake a lizard.

The same section of the SSR contained the following statement:

> In the months after adoption of the Commission's rules, the total short interest on the New York Stock Exchange declined more than 50 per cent, and Exchange officials suggested, and had extensive discussions with the Commission about, modification of the rules. In March 1939 the Commission promulgated what is now the main portion of rule 10a-1(a). Whereas the 1938 rule had prohibited all short-selling at the last long sale price, the new rule permitted it at such price if that was higher than the last different price. On several other occasions the New York Stock Exchange has urged the Commission to modify the existing rules, usually suggesting that short sales should be permitted without restriction at any price above the security's closing price on the preceding day. The Commission, however, has indicated that it did not believe such modification to be in the public interest.

The new rule was apparently having a great effect on profits. Under these circumstances, the NYSE makes the fact known to the SEC that its rule is serving to limit the great and exclusive privileges of Exchange members. Ultimately an SEC Commissioner is found who is willing to implement the Exchange's suggested course of action to remedy this problem. Thus, as I was about to learn in the response to my letter to the commission, rule 10a-1(a) was modified and the Exchange was provided with rule 10a-1(d)(1). There is no information published anywhere, however, of any permission having been granted by the SEC that tells the public that specialists can sell short without disclosing the fact that they are doing so, or sell short on "minus ticks." For the SEC to publish this information would be to admit that it is allowing Stock Exchange insiders to exploit the existence of the auction market in a way that Congress had sought to prevent. Yet that is the whole plot of the rule. But, as I indicated earlier, I was not positive about the existence of such exemptions, and it was in this context that I then received the accompanying letter from the Commission regarding the possibility of an exemption from the short sale rule.

SECURITIES AND EXCHANGE COMMISSION
WASHINGTON, D.C. 20549

DIVISION OF
Market Regulation

October 11, 1972

Dear Mr. Ney:

This is in reply to your letter of August 29, 1972, in which you inquire whether SEC Rule 10a-1(d)(1) grants a specialist who has an investment account an exemption from the Commission's short sale rule, and whether the rule permits a specialist to sell short on a minus tick.

Rule 10a-1(d)(1) states that the provisions of paragraph (a), the short sale rule, shall not apply to any sale by *any* person, for an account in which he has an interest, if such person owns the security sold and intends to deliver such security as soon as is possible without undue inconvenience or expense. Therefore, where a specialist owns the stock, in an investment account or otherwise, and intends to deliver it as soon as possible without undue inconvenience or expense, a sale by him of that stock is a long sale and is not subject to the restrictions set forth in paragraph (a). I would expect, however, that where the specialist is selling stock which he owns, he would usually sell stock from, and make delivery from, his dealer account rather than his investment account.

With regard to your second question, the exemptions from the short sale rule are enumerated in sub-paragraphs (1) through (9) of Rule 10a-1(d). In order for any person to effect a short sale which is exempt from the restrictions of the short sale rule, that person and short sale must come within one of these exemptions. Thus, as noted above, if a specialist, or anyone else, owns the stock to be sold and intends to deliver that stock as soon as possible without undue inconvenience or expense, the sale of that stock is a long sale not subject to the short sale rule of paragraph (a), and the sale may be effected on a minus tick. Of course, there must be compliance with all other applicable exchange rules and securities laws.

Sincerely,

Harry F. Day, Acting Chief
Branch of Regulation & Inspections

I had to look again to see if the letter was indeed from the SEC or from the New York Stock Exchange! This was an essentially humorless situation in which the specialist was being allowed to act as king because the SEC had agreed to serve as court jester. Certainly investors have never been told—even when they sell short against the box—that they can make a "long sale not subject to the short sale rule," so long as they intend to deliver stock they already own "as soon as possible without undue inconvenience or expense." Nor are they advised they can effect the sale "on a minus tick." Now that the public *does* know about this exemption it will be interesting to see what is done to make it impossible for the public to use it.

Among a number of other disillusioning consequences, the rule enables Stock Exchange specialists to prevent disclosure of the information surrounding their short sales at the very time the public should have it. When specialists have a loophole provided by the SEC's exemption, they can sell short to their heart's content and then cover these short sales at the end of a sharp decline, and no one is the wiser. All the specialist need do is deliver the stock from his investment account that he borrowed, and no one—certainly not the public—is aware of just how the pressure of events precipitated by the specialist, who is *supposed* to be working as an agent on their behalf, is about to force them to choose some method for dealing with their problems in a context of total crisis. By allowing specialists to ignore the "up-tick" rule, the SEC defeats the purpose of the legislation enacted to protect the public from the tremendous losses occasioned by insider short-selling.

Equally interesting about the Commission's letter is this statement that

> where a specialist owns the stock, in an investment account, or otherwise, and intends to deliver it as soon as possible *without undue inconvenience or expense,* a sale by him of that stock is a *long sale and is not subject to the restrictions set forth in paragraph (a).*

And here we come to the tortured phrase:

> I would expect, however, that where the specialist is selling the stock which he owns, he would usually sell stock from and make delivery from his dealer account rather than his investment account.

Who, one wonders, is trying to pull whose leg? Why would the specialist sell short from his trading (dealer) account under the special exemption if he already had the stock in his trading account? *Obviously,* if he avails himself of the exemption it is to make delivery *from his investment account!* Furthermore, I would advise the SEC that there is an SEC rule that prohibits specialists from being simultaneously long and short in their trading accounts.

The SEC Special Study Report of 1963 (4:785) described how specialists use their trading accounts: "The specialist's trading account distributed large blocks of stock to the public by selling short. The account then covered by transferring stock from specialists' long term investment accounts."

Having whipped up public demand for their stocks, specialists build up enormous short positions in their trading accounts. They subsequently cover these short sales by delivering their investment accounts over to their trading accounts for long-term capital gain purposes. But here is one of the heads of the SEC suggesting just the opposite of the information provided by his agency's most important staff study. The same Special Study group also pointed out the inadequacy of the information supplied the public about member short sales (Part 2, pp. 252–53):

> The drawback common to most of the short selling information on file with the commission is that it does not provide, with respect to either round lots or odd lots, the total volume of short selling occurring in single issues over continuous periods of time. . . .
> The only data regularly compiled and published concerning short sales are daily aggregate figures for all stocks on the New York and American Stock Exchanges and monthly figures on the short positions in certain stocks on the NYSE and in all securities on the Amex. Analysis of such data permits only broad conclusions about short selling practices.

Thus the SEC concedes that the public is provided with only a partial abstract of the information it should have about Stock Exchange member short sales.

Corporation insiders must disclose their investment holdings. Regrettably, the SEC makes no such demand of Stock Exchange insiders. Lack of disclosure has but one purpose: to make it possible for Stock Exchange insiders to confiscate investor capital with the use of any one of a hundred alibis. Although I recognized it was not realistic to suppose the SEC might want to see investors participate in some of the easy affluence enjoyed by Exchange insiders, I wrote the Commission in May, 1971, to try to persuade it to release information pertaining to specialists' short sales. I received a reply that same month. I quote part of one paragraph:

> You suggested in your letter that short sales by specialists, identified by stock, be made public daily. We appreciate your suggestion but we cannot ignore the possible adverse effect of such immediate release of these figures on the specialist's ability and statutory obligation to maintain a fair and orderly market.

I've never encountered an SEC official who could not bear the investor's bad fortune like a good Christian.

Few investors realize how much they are deceived by their senses. I have been trying to make clear the fact that their inclination to favor one stock instead of another is based not on free choice or a personal sense of value but on what they are being made to think, feel, and want in accordance with the wishes of Exchange insiders. While investors tend to have an animal faith in their own freedom, their intellectual convictions about the market are determined for them by the specialist's plans to maximize profits. The insider's dramatic use of the short sale in a specific situation can circumscribe the investors' actions, so that their most important decisions are directed by emotional experiences caused by forces operating on the floor of the Exchange. Investors may believe they are exercising their powers of choice when they buy and sell stock, but in fact the *timing* of their investment decisions is largely determined for them by specialists as they raise and lower stock prices.

One of the best instances of how investors are cajoled and hypnotized into making their investment decisions at precisely the *wrong* time can be found in the events leading up to and following President Nixon's announcement on August 15, 1971, of his New Economic Policy. Investors were unaware that the economic decision about which they had such an eager and legitimate interest was about to provide insiders with a gadget they could use to trigger investors into the market.

For anyone who has paid the least bit of attention to Richard Nixon's career, it is reasonably safe to assume he would allow his friends on the Stock Exchange to determine something as financially important as the date of the economic announcement. As the ordained representative in the White House of Wall Street's main temple, he would be more than willing to take his place at the mighty Wurlitzer and call the market's disciples into their place of worship at the proper time. Nor is this difficult to imagine when one considers the relaxed way the SEC, at his direction, allows the Exchange to formulate Commission policy. There is no sure way of knowing whether he timed his announcement at the Stock Exchange's signal or whether the Exchange scheduled its drop to the August low to conform to Nixon's schedule. But that there was conspiring between the White House and the Stock Exchange, I have not the slightest doubt. In looking for evidence bearing on the authenticity of this proposition, we have only to consider the October 15, 1971, *Washington Post* column of Jack Anderson:

Treasury Secretary John Connally met privately in a secluded Smokey Mountains lodge with some of America's most potent corporate panjandrums exactly one week before President Nixon's wage-price freeze.

Connally landed secretly at McGee Tyson Air National Guard Base outside Knoxville on Aug. 7. About the same time several sleek Gulfstream IIs rolled in at Cherokee Aviation, the civilian facility just across the airport from the base.

From these carpeted executive jets stepped John Harper, the folksy, capable boss of Alcoa, one of America's industrial giants. Another arrival was Baxter Goodrich, the new chairman of Texas Eastern Pipeline. Still other titans of industry stepped from their gleaming jets parked at Cherokee Aviation.

Connally and the moguls climbed into expensive cars and sped southward toward the dusky smokies near Chilhowee, Tenn., where Alcoa maintains a richly paneled "rustic" lodge for secret discussions.

So carefully concealed from the public was the conference and its guest list that Alcoa spokesman H. T. McDade refused to say where the lodge was located.

"I don't think Alcoa would want these men's names bandied about," huffed McDade, who then refused even to spell his own name.

At Cherokee Aviation, manager Don Strunk had also been struck dumb. "It's none of my business who files in and out of this airport. I was told to hush up," he said nervously. Strunk wouldn't say who silenced him.

Throughout the weekend, Connally talked earnestly with the industrialists. One report has it that he briefed them on the forthcoming wage-price freeze, information worth countless millions to their corporations.

In the poker game of politics, Nixon is not the kind of dealer to deny his friends on the floor of the Exchange the same trump cards in time for them to profit from the announcement.

It is not difficult to guess precisely when Nixon held his secret meetings with Exchange insiders to acquaint them in advance with his economic plans. I place it during what was intended to be a secret dinner with members of the New York Stock Exchange in April, 1971, which, because of the investigative reporting of *New York Times* correspondent Terry Robards, was made public. I would suppose the information was divulged and plans were made for the timing of the announcement in meetings held with important specialists before or after the dinner. Thus, we note that most stocks in the Dow and on the New York Stock Exchange were launched on major downtrends in April (see Chart 6–2).

CHART 6–2

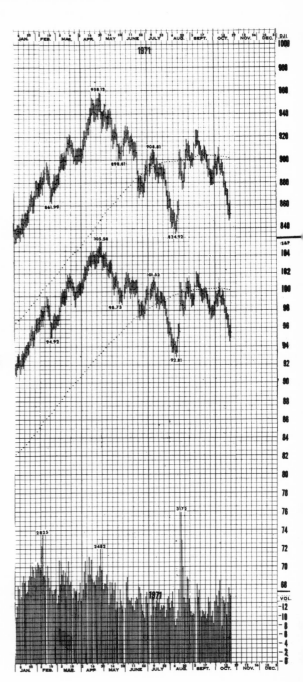

It is typical of the specialist's *modus operandi,* however, that, regardless of the trend then under way, specialist merchandising strategies will adapt themselves to exploit the profit potentials of bullish or bearish announcements. In the present instance, it was apparent that, regardless of whether a stock was in an uptrend or a downtrend prior to the announcement, if stock prices were dropped one to two weeks prior to the announcement, thereby allowing specialists to clean out their books and acquire an inventory of stock, this stock could then be sold at a handsome profit and shorts could be established once the announcement was made public.

On August 15, 1971, President Nixon, employing the statesman's ostensible credentials, announced his New Economic Plan. On Monday, August 16, like an armada launched on deep waters bound for a distant territory, investors moved into the market. To their surprise and chagrin, they were halted by the vast power in the hands of the force that opposed them. The next day they again launched a tremendous demand for stock, and again they were stopped by the overwhelming power embodied in the specialist's short sale.

We can begin to recognize the autonomy of specialists' thoughts, preferences, and value judgments when we examine the Charts 6–3 through 6–14. Here we see how, on August 16 and 17, they were able to leap over the logical difficulties created by the greatest demand for stock in the market's history simply by neutralizing the situation with their short sales. The tremendous impact of their short sales served to completely halt the further advance of stock prices, which then retreated, enabling specialists to cover their short sales (in many instances in a matter of days) prior to resuming their major trends.

The short selling of August 16 and 17 discloses a situation that investors always confront and that has never been clearly defined: Specialists have virtually unlimited credit for emergency situations and, equally important, access to as much borrowed stock as they may need. On the rare occasions when the claims made on available supplies of stock are temporarily too great, trading is halted until specialists are able to locate more stock to borrow.

Firms like Merrill Lynch are always anxious to loan stock for which they receive 100% cash collateral. The cash will then be invented.

CHART 6–3

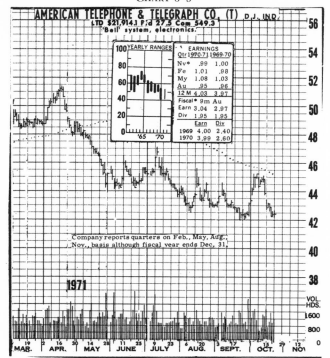

CHART 6–4

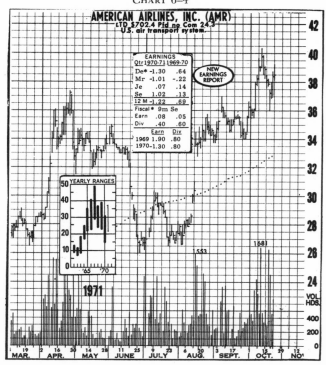

CHART 6–5

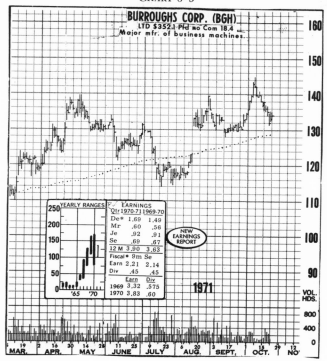

CHART 6–6

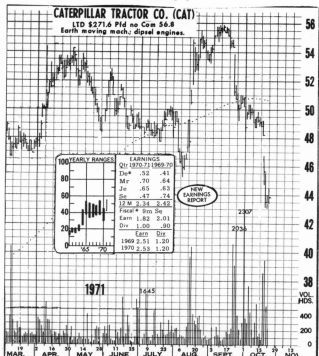

CHART 6–7

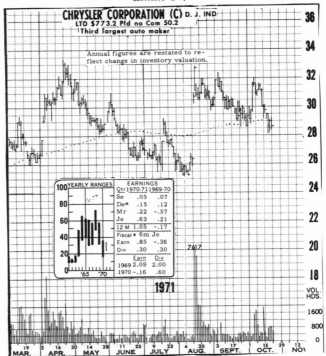

CHART 6–8

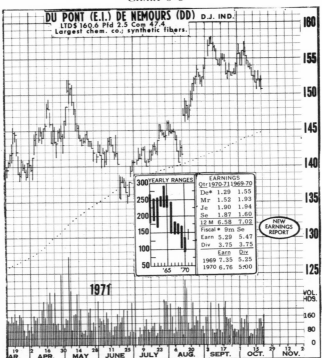

CHART 6–9

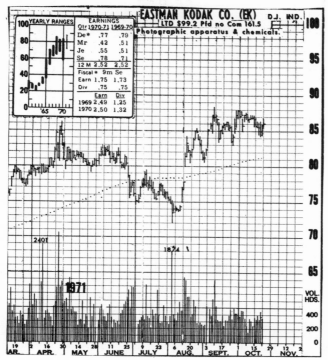

CHART 6–10

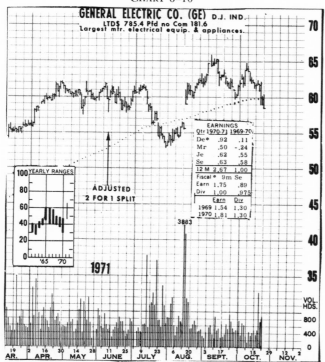

CHART 6–11

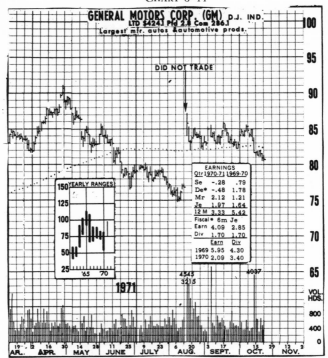

CHART 6–12

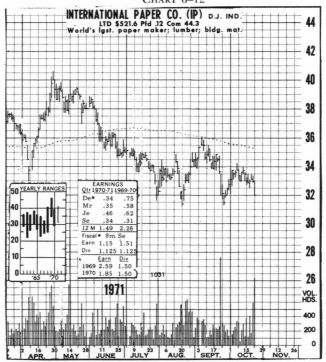

CHART 6–13

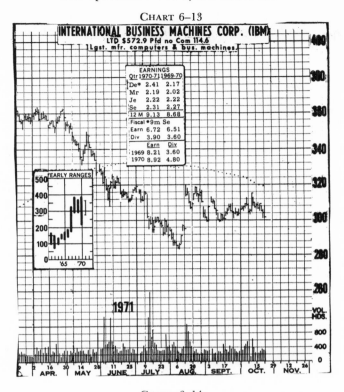

CHART 6–14

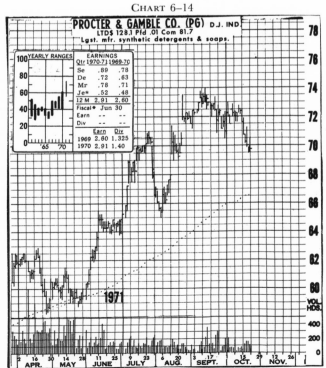

UNITED STATES
SECURITIES AND EXCHANGE COMMISSION
WASHINGTON, D.C. 20549

For Release August 31, 1971

STATISTICAL SERIES   Release No. 2540

ROUND-LOT STOCK TRANSACTIONS ON THE
NEW YORK STOCK EXCHANGE (SHARES)

Week Ended August 13, 1971

Trade Date		Total Reported Volume	Transactions of Members for Own Account, Except as Odd-Lot Dealers		
			As Specialists	As Floor Traders	Others
Mon.	Purchases	8,116,800	1,298,360	15,200	605,357
	Sales–Total	8,116,800	1,157,550	21,100	662,690
	–Short	553,600	243,960	2,200	129,500
Tues.	Purchases	9,469,380	1,469,730	55,200	703,720
	Sales–Total	9,469,380	1,385,590	38,700	679,050
	–Short	644,360	326,490	7,200	114,120
Wed.	Purchases	11,368,930	1,442,950	52,800	1,598,265
	Sales–Total	11,368,930	1,852,580	42,700	1,097,402
	–Short	986,320	440,280	4,700	326,800
Thurs.	Purchases	15,914,330	2,181,000	37,500	1,419,676
	Sales–Total	15,914,330	2,820,120	88,200	1,409,606
	–Short	1,370,310	768,460	16,600	291,800
Fri.	Purchases	9,963,750	1,383,910	27,000	1,042,630
	Sales–Total	9,963,750	1,464,280	34,800	1,076,249
	–Short	886,210	408,690	14,200	259,100
WEEK	Purchases	54,833,190	7,775,950	187,700	5,369,648
	Sales–Total	54,833,190	8,680,120	225,500	4,924,997
	–Short	4,440,800	2,187,880	44,900	1,121,320

NOTE: The term "members" includes regular Exchange members, Exchange allied members and Exchange member organizations. Transactions for the odd-lot account of odd-lot dealers are reported separately. All sales totals include short sales.

The statistics provided by the SEC enable us to visualize the manner in which the specialists' trap was sprung. Note that they sold short 4,269,400 shares on the 16th and 1,774,960 shares on the 17th. For comparison, the reader should note that the figures for Monday and Tuesday of the previous week were 243,960 and 326,490 shares.

UNITED STATES
SECURITIES AND EXCHANGE COMMISSION
WASHINGTON, D.C. 20549

For Release September 8, 1971

STATISTICAL SERIES   Release No. 2542

ROUND-LOT STOCK TRANSACTIONS ON THE
NEW YORK STOCK EXCHANGE (SHARES)

Week Ended August 20, 1971

Trade Date		Total Reported Volume	Transactions of Members for Own Account, Except as Odd-Lot Dealers		
			As Specialists	As Floor Traders	Others
Mon.	Purchases	31,730,960	5,111,230	130,400	2,020,560
	Sales–Total	31,730,960	8,001,830	304,000	2,390,407
	–Short	5,391,510	4,269,400	159,400	498,500
Tues.	Purchases	26,793,630	4,367,350	148,100	2,293,149
	Sales–Total	26,793,630	4,168,760	229,000	1,946,360
	–Short	3,029,820	1,774,960	149,700	564,600
Wed.	Purchases	20,675,570	3,546,720	159,750	1,663,497
	Sales–Total	20,675,570	3,003,320	105,670	1,702,200
	–Short	1,850,040	1,162,640	23,800	388,200
Thurs.	Purchases	14,189,860	2,469,950	87,600	1,712,065
	Sales–Total	14,189,860	2,058,250	82,800	1,353,705
	–Short	1,159,700	675,000	17,100	253,200
Fri.	Purchases	11,899,550	1,996,760	50,600	936,837
	Sales–Total	11,899,550	1,702,270	26,500	1,034,194
	–Short	854,950	549,520	2,900	155,790
WEEK	Purchases	105,289,570	17,492,010	576,450	8,626,108
	Sales–Total	105,289,570	18,934,430	747,970	8,426,866
	–Short	12,286,020	8,431,520	352,900	1,860,290

NOTE: The term "members" includes regular Exchange members, Exchange allied members and Exchange member organizations. Transactions for the odd-lot account of odd-lot dealers are reported separately. All sales totals include short sales.

In an effort to warn investors of what was about to take place, I sent telegrams to all the major wire services and newspapers on August 16. I also appeared on local television and by telephone on Jerry Williams's radio program on WBZ in Boston. The situation, however, was irreversible. The press could have defined for its readers the singular eminence of the specialist's imperial axe—the

short sale—and the manner in which its blade was about to mur-
der the rally. The media could have focused attention on the specialist, as he employed his short sale to set effect before cause,
knowing full well that the rally would have to be followed by a
sharp decline—that *only* after a sharp decline in stock prices
would the specialist cover his short sales. Instead, financial editors
across the country applauded rapturously. When prices declined
on Wednesday, August 19, the headline from the *Los Angeles
Times* read, "MARKET BEATEN DOWN BY PROFIT TAK-
ING TO END 2-DAY RALLY; DOW OFF 13.73." This was
followed by the Associated Press's forgettable fairy tale: "Profit
taking hammered stock prices Wednesday bringing the two day
rally to a sudden stop."

As is customary, the Associated Press neglected to tell investors
who was taking profits. It was a sticky scene, one that called for
the Alice in Wonderland storytellers of the Stock Exchange News
Bureau. Skilled in the use of language, committed to the belief
that the investor is essentially a mechanism whose behavior is
capable of conditioning, the Exchange's propaganda machine
went to work. Having persuaded investors to buy on command
and now employing the machinery of acquiescence, they would
provide specialists with a sympathetic audience. Accordingly, as
the public's losses began to mount, stories about the specialist
began to appear in the financial press.

The following excerpts appeared in the Allentown, Pennsyl-
vania, *Morning Call* on September 8, 1971:

Even on the biggest day in New York Stock Exchange history . . .
even with the buy orders flooding in, outstripping sell orders by the
hundreds of thousands—Wall Street's specialists have to stay cool,
to keep the excitement on the floor under control. Here's the inside
story of how they handled the record-breaking trade on August
16. . . .

The pressure on the specialists on August 16 came not only from
the record volume. At the 10 a.m. opening of the Exchange, there
was an avalanche of orders on the buy side to cope with.

For example, in Chrysler, buy orders stood at more than 600,000
shares, with sell orders less than 300,000.

In General Electric, there was an imbalance on the buy side of
195,000 shares—worth almost $11 million.

In U.S. Steel, public demand exceeded public supply by more
than $3.4 million worth of stock.

Just how well the specialists performed under this "acid test" is
pointed up by the day's statistics:

—Just to help open the market that day, specialists risked $142 million of their own capital by providing 3.6 million of the 10 million shares in opening trades.

—In 10 issues alone, specialists risked $24 million of their own capital to help trading open.

—*During the day, specialists sold 4.3 million shares short,* selling another 3.7 million long for their own accounts. In addition, they also bought 5.1 million shares during the day.

—Selling from their own accounts when investors wanted stock and buying when investors were selling, *specialists participated as dealers in 41 per cent of the day's 32 million share volume.*

—*More than 97 per cent of their purchases and sales were stabilizing for the market.* That is, 97 per cent of all specialist's dealings were sales at prices above [almost always—R.N.] and purchases at prices below [almost always—R.N.] the last different price.

During the day, Exchange specialists made the thousands of decisions necessary, and risked millions of their own capital, to make sure the primary market could cope with the huge flow of orders from investors. [Their profits were guaranteed.]

The demand for stocks by buyers was so great that trading in more than 200 issues of the more than 1,300 common stocks listed on the Exchange had to be delayed beyond the time they would normally have opened. [And some weren't opened until the next day.—R.N.]

"Many of these issues could have opened around 10 a.m., but the Exchange delays trading when there is a heavy preponderance of buy or sell orders," explains Stephen M. Peck, Exchange vice chairman, who was in the thick of the trading all day.

"In this case, the delay gave potential buyers sufficient time to see that opening prices might be considerably different than the previous close. This then permitted them to change their orders if they cared to, at the same time assuring sellers a fair price [the sellers for the most part being specialists].

"Our job," said Mr. Peck, "was to try and create a balance in the supply and demand situation *at a price as near the last sale price as possible.*

"We later learned that 87 per cent of the stocks that opened a point or more above the previous close continued to go up, stayed the same or declined a half-point or less from the opening price," Mr. Peck noted.

"This is testimony to the specialists' unique ability and responsibility to judge and reflect the market appropriately."

A floor broker summed it up this way: "We gave the public a minimum of an hour—and in some cases several hours—to form decisions on whether to buy or sell a particular stock. In my opinion, the specialist system was tested, met the challenge, and passed with flying colors."

Typical of the hectic problems that specialists faced in opening their stocks was the experience of Zuckerman, Smith & Co., the specialist firm handling Chrysler. The automaker stock was one of the most sought after issues that day, a result of the President's statement of his plan to lower the price of autos by repealing the federal excise tax.

In the morning, orders to buy Chrysler as high as $31 totaled 670,000 shares. These orders, based on Friday's closing price of $26⅜, were worth some $18 million.

Zuckerman had only a small inventory of its own in Chrysler stock. And during the morning public investors had come up with offers to sell only 269,000 shares at prices between 26⅝ and $31.

That meant somebody had to come up with another 400,000 shares.

"We circulated the situation to the Street," a Zuckerman official explained. "This resulted in brokerage houses around the country telling holders of Chrysler that more shares were sought in the primary market and that this demand would increase the selling price."

"About 3 p.m., we received orders to sell about 325,000 shares," the specialist firm official said.

The specialist then put his money on the line. At his own risk he went short and supplied *75,000 shares worth 2.3 million,* selling the shares to the public and matching up the other public orders to make an opening block of 670,000 shares at $31, up $4⅝ from the previous session's closing price. This same specialist, moreover, risked additional capital to help open his other stocks, including 1.3 million to open Chrysler warrants.

Equally pressured that Monday were floor officials. "I had to make several hundred decisions that day on whether to open a particular stock," commented Albert B. Tompane, managing partner of Benton, Tompane & Co., and the senior floor governor. The Exchange requires a floor governor's approval before a specialist can open a stock more than two points higher than the previous closing price, or one point higher on issues below $20.

By the end of the day's 5½ hour trading session, the Exchange ticker had recorded 60,600 transactions, triple the pace of the previous trading day.

"It was busy, all right," said one of the younger specialists as he left the trading floor for his office at the end of the day, "and my legs feel it.

"But it could happen any day and we'd be ready for it."

And they were. The very next day, almost 27 million shares were traded—the third largest day in Exchange history. [Emphasis added.]

Again, on August 17, my analysis suggested that the specialist in Chrysler had established major short positions with one block for 90,600 shares at 32¾ at 3:10 and another big block for 9,000 shares at 32⅞—none of which, according to special SEC exemptions, he would be obliged to record as short sales.

By the time the Exchange News Bureau covered its typewriters, it was thumbs up for the specialists, the Exchange, and the comprehensive syntax of total confiscation.

This, then, is the picture of the ultimate workings of the short sale. It is also another indication of the great extent of the specialist's freedom and the limited nature of the investor's. We see not only that investor demand is unable to advance prices but also that investors must buy when and at whatever prices specialists choose.

The impasse reached by society when a small, select group of Exchange insiders is allowed to exploit the human nature and ignorance of the rest of society could not be more concisely summarized.

7. The Secondary Offering:
An Examination of Legalized Larceny

Blessed is he who expects nothing, for he shall never be disappointed by the stockbroker who sells him into a secondary offering.

The Stock Exchange is forever putting forth one deceptive practice or another to score over investors. Always there is a twist given to the element of rationality to turn the investor's blind endeavors against him. This is particularly true in the underwritings of the great bulk of big block offerings.

In this sense, the emergence of the "secondary distribution" constitutes a clear victory over investors. The cumulative impact of secondary offerings tends to run counter to the expectations of those who invest in them.

As Stock Exchange members employ the term, a secondary distribution means the offering of a block of stock by a group or syndicate of Stock Exchange members. The offering takes place after the close of the market at a fixed price, not exceeding the last sale price on the floor.

Many big block distributions take place entirely through the selling efforts of a firm that has many retail outlets. It is a simple matter for a firm like Merrill Lynch, utilizing only its own network brokers, to unload blocks of stock worth hundreds of millions of dollars. This in fact is why "the little investor is king at Merrill Lynch." Because Merrill Lynch has in excess of 20 million customers, the firm is able to handle by itself more than five times as many big block distributions for its fee-paying institutional customers as any other brokerage firm.

In such transactions, brokers are supposed to tell their customers that the stock they are being asked to purchase is part of a specified number of shares being offered; that they and their firm are serving as agents for the seller; what the special commission is that they receive; and whether investors are paying a regular commission for receiving the stocks "net." This of course is rarely done.

The methods involved in big block offers involve what the Exchange refers to as "stabilizing operations." Concerning these practices, the Securities Exchange Act of 1934 held that a series of transactions in a stock effected for the purpose of maintaining its price at or above the level to which it had been artificially raised so as to induce purchases and sales by others violates the provisions of Sections 9 (a) (2) of the 1934 act. In a number of suits concerning this provision that the Commission instituted and helped prosecute, the offense charged was that the defendant established artificial market prices and solicited orders for the stock without disclosing that the price on the Exchange was an artificial one resulting from the seller's activities on the Exchange. The issue of artificially *maintaining* a price did not seem to disturb the Commission. In fact, by 1940 a new rule, X-9A6, was adopted that permitted the pegging, fixing, or stabilizing of security prices on stock exchanges "to facilitate an offering at the market of any registered security."

In 1940, Judge Robert Healy, a commissioner on the SEC, held that the new rule introduced by the Commission permitting price pegging and stabilizing was logically inconsistent with the posture taken by the Commission in the past. He stated that, in the cases brought by the Commission, brokers

> were found guilty of *raising* prices by manipulation to assist them in distributing securities; whereas the present rule permits not the raising of prices but the preventing of price declines. I can see no differences in substance between manipulation that causes a rise in price and a manipulation that prevents a fall in price.

As might be expected, most investors assume the price has been established by the free play of supply and demand in a fair and unmanipulated market. Commissioner Healy points out that, when investors are allowed to assume the offering price is "at the market,"

> the possibilities of deception and injury to investors are immeasurably increased. Securities issued "at the market" are issued on the theory that the price is set not by the underwriter but by the interplay of the forces of supply and demand.

He viewed the Commission's new rule as a deception:

> Yet the regulation by permitting stabilizing of such securities permits an interference with the free forces of supply and demand and thereby tolerates the creation of a price mirage and the distortion of the price which would be set by the market if it were to function without artificial support.

The process of distributing "at the market" where the market is controlled by the distributors has in the past caused public investors losses amounting to many tens of millions of dollars.

He wrote those comments in 1940. Since then investor losses have run into the billions of dollars.

With the foregoing in mind, let us now proceed to a consideration of some of the more important aspects—from the investor's viewpoint—of the secondary offering.

Although there are variations (always to accomplish a particular objective) there are twelve basic functions that take place in the complex of manipulations surrounding these offerings:

(1) *The shakeout.* This is a decline that takes place in a stock that is meant to frighten investors into selling their shares to insiders prior to

(2) *the run-up in prices* that almost always occurs prior to the offering. This allows insiders to sell profitably the stock they acquired during the shakeout. It also enables insiders to

(3) *liquidate their trading and/or investment accounts* as the run-up phase is completed. The sale of these accounts is then almost always followed by

(4) *the establishment of short sales* by the underwriting group. These short sales are then used to "peg" the stock at the offering price by "covering" any public selling that might occur in the course of

(5) *the offering,* the occasion when investors purchase the stock, having had their attention called to it by their brokers. This is almost always followed by

(6) *the shakeout in the "aftermarket."* in which stock prices are carried below the offering price by the specialist, which enables the managing underwriters (and the specialist) to

(7) *complete short covering* and

(8) *add to inventories* prior to the advance in price that will allow insiders to

(9) *sell out their trading and/or investment accounts* prior to

(10) *again establishing short positions* in order to profit from

(11) *a decline in prices* that will culminate in

(12) *new accumulations for investment accounts,* etc., etc.

The writing of this chapter was begun in 1972. The examples of secondary distributions provided below are therefore from 1971 and 1972. If the reader wishes further confirmation of the principles outlined here, he can easily obtain them from the countless examples that occurred in 1973, almost all of which have caused unprecedented losses to investors.

The examples chosen are from the SEC's statistical bulletin. The particulars surrounding the offerings were as on the accompanying table. There were many additional secondaries at this time. Space limitations allow us to include only a small percentage.

The secondary in Clark Oil provides a characteristic example of the worst kind of secondary for investors. At no time were they given the opportunity to sell for more than a one-point profit. The shakeout in the stock occurred during the month of January, 1971. That was followed by a 21 per cent run-up in price prior to the offering on March 9.

Twice after the launching of the secondary at 22.75 the stock dropped below 22 and then advanced to 24, where it was sold short each time by its specialist and other Stock Exchange insiders. Short selling in the "aftermarket" needs to be emphasized since it is public demand for stock at these highs that enables insiders to sell short. It is this short selling that lays the foundation for a decline in the stock's price.

Note in Chart 7–1 that the stock sold at the highs (C and D) is stock that is generally acquired by members who participate in the offering (A) and who in the aftermarket continue to absorb what-

CHART 7–1

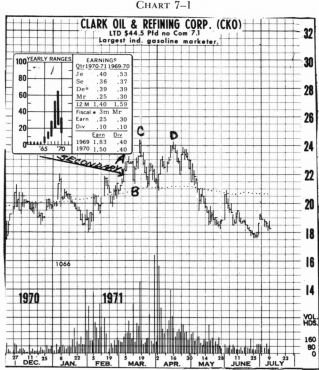

BLOCK DISTRIBUTIONS OF STOCKS
Three Months Ended June 30, 1971 (2nd Quarter)

	Distribution		Number of Shares		Offering Price per Share (Dollars)	Value of Shares Sold (Dollars)	Type of Vendor
	Began	Ended	In Original Offer	Sold			
Secondary Distributions NEW YORK STOCK EXCHANGE							
Clark Oil & Refining Corp.	3-9	3-11	502,640	515,470	22.75	11,726,943	Various
The Singer Company	4-15	4-16	238,250	240,520	72.625	17,467,765	Indivs., Trs., & Insts.
Aileen Incorporated	5-3	5-12	300,850	309,750	49.00	15,177,750	Offs. & Dirs.
Cummins Engine Company, Inc.	5-6	5-11	800,000	810,350	48.50	39,301,975	Foundation
Simplicity Pattern Company, Inc.	5-26	6-2	162,805	167,605	117.50	19,693,588	Various
Bunker Ramo Corporation	6-30	7-1	2,339,410	2,378,330	11.25	26,756,213	Corporation

CHART 7–2

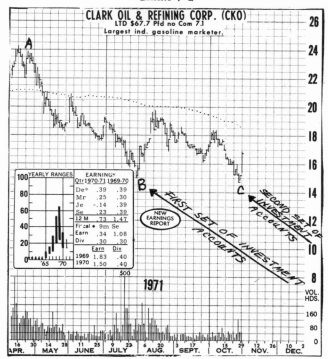

ever stock is sold by the public at ever lower prices (B). The buying at the lows is done in the almost certain knowledge that the specialist will soon enable them to unload their shares at top prices (C and D).

Charts 7–2 and 7–3 of Clark Oil illustrate the dictates of long-term specialist planning in stocks that have had a large secondary offering.

An attempt is almost always made to persuade investors who bought at the offering price to then *sell back to the specialist* the same stock when it moves down to wholesale price levels. In the present instance, this carried the price of Clark Oil to its July and October, 1971, lows (B and C). The stock was not, as brokers maintained, "testing its support" at the 15 level. The specialist was "cleaning out" his books by purchasing all the limit orders that had been placed with him down to 15. It should also be noted that these purchases enabled him to cover previously established short positions and then, in addition, acquire inventories of stock for his investment accounts (B and C). These inventories created the built-in incentives for another bull raid in the stock to January and March, 1972, highs (D and E).

CHART 7–3

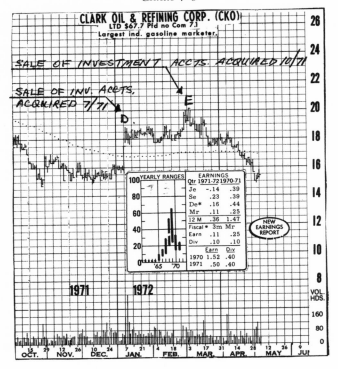

Note that in terms of both public selling (he accumulates in order to prepare for a bull raid) and public demand (during which he sells short and prepares for a decline), the specialist in Clark Oil shows us he is able to totally reject the economic impact of supply and demand. It is this ability that enables him to establish long-term capital gains (for his July investment accounts) in January and (for his October accumulations) in March.

The underwriters require much information from the corporation, from the Stock Exchange, and from the underwriter's analysts to determine the best time to launch the secondary, as well as information from the specialists registered in the stock, with whom the underwriters are always in close touch. The example provided by the Singer Company is typical. The probability is that, although the secondary was on April 15, 1971, discussions concerning the offering in Singer were conducted by the managing underwriters no later than the third or fourth quarter of 1970.

Note the shakeout that took place in Singer in the October through November, 1970, period (from A to B). This was followed by the familiar run-up in price (to C). The decision to shake out investors (in the decline A to B) meant that plans for the insider

CHART 7–4

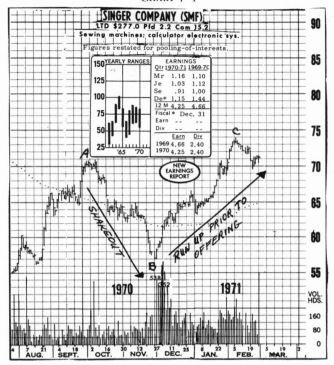

short-selling that precipitated the decline from point A would have necessitated a blueprint for the launching of the secondary (in April, 1971) to be produced as early as August or September, 1970! The success of the shakeout can be determined by the increase in public selling that occurred at the November bottom (note volume). The run-up in price covers a long-term capital gain period of six months. The volume characteristics beginning in early April show that, as the stock moved to its high (D), it was possible for its specialist to sell it short and then a few days later, as his investment accounts matured (for long-term capital gains purposes) to deliver his investment accounts to his trading accounts.

Note on Chart 7–5 how the secondary is timed to coincide with a drop from the March, 1971, high. The high prior to the offering enables underwriters, specialists, and other insiders to sell short and then profit from the subsequent decline in price by

(1) pegging prices at the offering by "covering" public selling with their short sales and

(2) adding to inventory with further buying in order to

(3) maximize profits further by taking the price up 2 points

and launching massive short sales at the top (note the volume at F), which are

(4) then covered at the aftermarket low (note the volume at G).

It is possible to trace a causal link between the amount of the overallotment and the nature of the stock's price movements in the offering's aftermarket.

In the Singer offering of 238,520 shares of stock, the difference between the number of shares in the secondary and the number of shares sold (240,520) shows us that the "overalloting" (that is, the number of shares sold short) performed by the underwriters to cover stock sold by the public in the course of the offering was only 2,000 shares. In this case it meant conditions had been created prior to the offering that would make it profitable for specialists to be in a position to absorb as much public selling in the aftermarket as possible. Of necessity, underwriters would have had to conduct a major short selling operation before the date of the offering. Although the extent of this short selling is far from clear, by looking at Chart 7–5 we are able to determine that it was consummated at the stock's March high at the 77 level (D). In substantiation, there is the increase in volume noted at the time of the offering.

In the Singer offering insiders knew they could depend on a large quantity of stocks being sold by the public if the price was dropped below the 70 level, since 70 is an important psychological price level. By dropping the stock's price below 70, insiders were not only able to cover short sales established at the 74 level (F) but were also able to accumulate enough stock to create the built-in incentives for another bull raid.

Given this perspective, we see why the bull raid in Singer from the 67 to the 77 level (G to H) during the May–July period was inevitable. Obviously, if the specialist's plans for this stock ultimately called for a decline below the earlier low at the 67 level (G), insiders would not want to carry this stock in inventory as they moved it down to wholesale price levels. The strategy they employed against this contingency was to conduct a rally in the stock (to 77½ in Singer), in the course of which they then divested themselves of their inventories to an unsuspecting public (G to H). Only after the rally has made it possible for them to sell all their stock to the public (and sell short) are prices then taken down to the 63 level (I). Note that these prices were taken down so fast on large gaps that investors would have had difficulty selling. The secondary in Aileen is the same mixture as before (Charts 7–7 and 7–8). The secondary offering was timed so that officers and directors were able to sell their holdings (in this instance $15,-

CHART 7-5

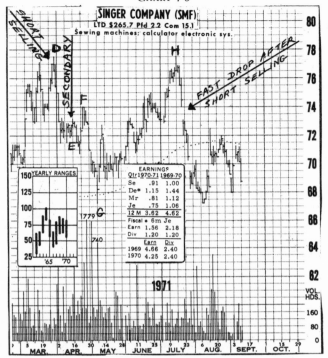

CHART 7–6

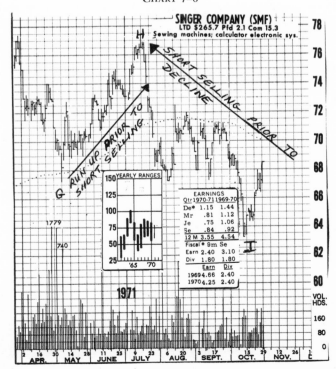

CHART 7–7

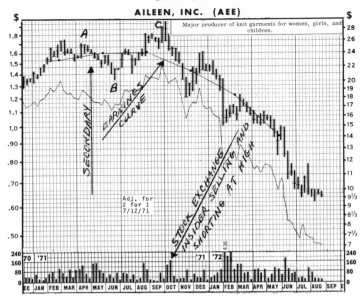

AILEEN, INC. (AEE)

Major producer of knit garments for women, girls, and children.

CHART 7–8

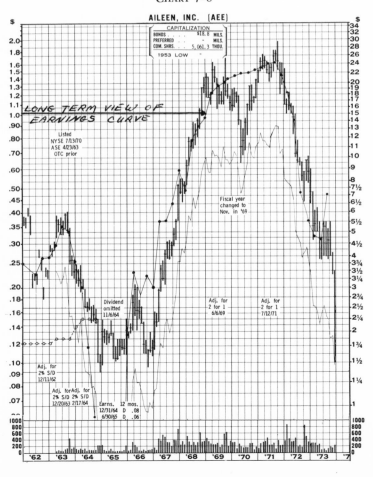

AILEEN, INC. (AEE)

CHART 7–9

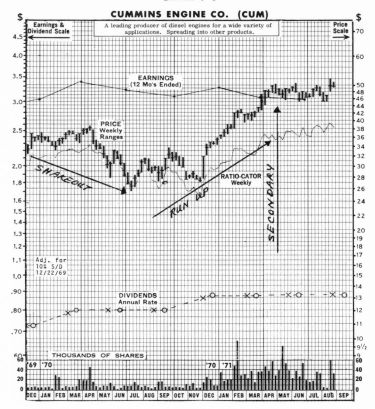

CUMMINS ENGINE CO. (CUM)

A leading producer of diesel engines for a wide variety of applications. Spreading into other products.

177,000) while earnings were still trending upward. In fact, the bad earnings announcement was postponed not only until after the offering had been completed (at point A) but until the underwriters had sold out the stock they acquired in the aftermarket (at point B) at the October high (point C). To further excite interest in a stock that is destined to decline after insiders have sold out at the highs, a stock split was announced for July 12.

During the same period secondaries also occurred in Cummins Engine (Chart 7–9), Simplicity Pattern (7–10), and Bunker-Ramo (7–11). If the charts of these stocks do anything they show that the financial philosophy which is extemporized to justify such offerings have no bearing on the growth of free enterprise or the needs of industry.

AMP (Charts 7–12 and 7–13) presents us with an even more complex example of the peculiar circumstances involved in the launching of a secondary.

Note that the offering occurred at point D after the usual shake-

CHART 7–10

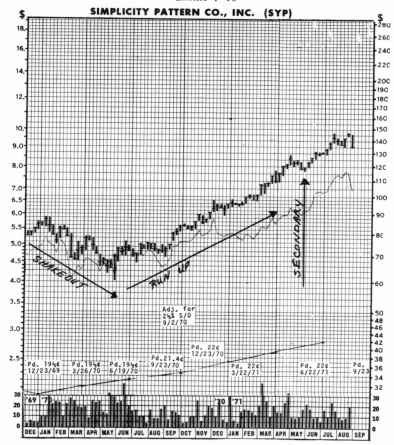

SIMPLICITY PATTERN CO., INC. (SYP)

out from A to B and the run-up from B to C. Looking at the
Trendline chart we note that point D occurred at the May low
of 64. It took six days to close the books on the offering of 225,000
shares; there was an overallotment of only 300 shares; and the
stock subsequently advanced to 72. For practical purposes we can
say that the amount ultimately sold during the offering was the
same as the amount in the original offering. What is the significance
of these facts?

To answer this question, you should ask yourself under what
circumstances underwriters would not wish to employ short covering transactions to buy stock sold by the public during the offering.
Obviously that would occur only if they were not worried about
public selling but in fact *welcomed* it. An overallot in order to
be on the short side of a forthcoming offering would be absurd
only if they were certain the stock's price was going to advance

CHART 7–11

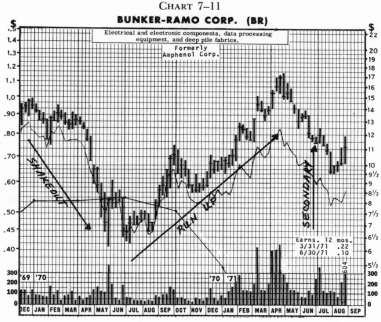

BUNKER-RAMO CORP. (BR)

Electrical and electronic components, data processing equipment, and deep pile fabrics.

Formerly Amphenol Corp.

immediately after the offering. Under these circumstances, the underwriters would accumulate as much stock as possible for their trading accounts. This explains why only 300 shares of stock were overalloted. It also explains why the stock advanced from 64 to 72 soon after the offering. But more important than anything else, it means the underwriters had to be in close touch with the stock's specialists.

We will now consider the secondaries in General Mills (Chart 7–14) and Gulf Oil (Charts 7–15 and 7–16) that occurred in the last quarter of 1972. General Mills provides another example of the type of collaboration seen in the AMP secondary. The reader will note that an offering was made of 529,759 shares on October 3 at a price of 51.75 and that exactly the same amount of shares were sold in the course of the offering. This then is another instance in which no overallotment was made by the underwriters of an offering.

Note that the low in General Mills occurred just two trading days prior to the offering. Presuming the specialist in General Mills had conferred with the underwriters just two trading days before the offering and advised them the stock had established its low, the underwriters would want to accumulate as much stock as possible. Obviously, they would not want to be on the short side of the market in the stock. The advance that took place from its October low to its January high helps us to understand why.

CHART 7–12

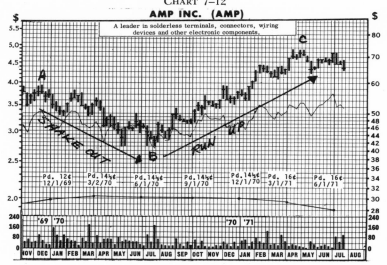

CHART 7–13

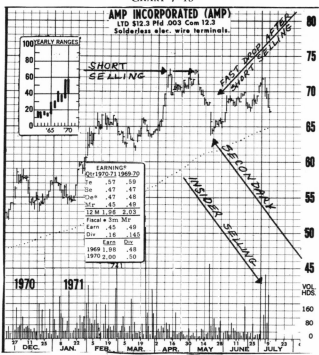

CHART 7–14

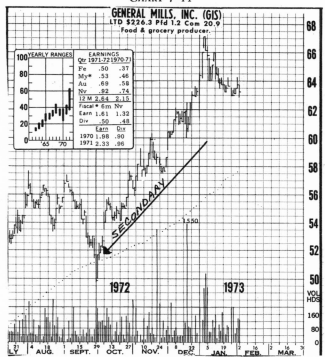

CHART 7–15

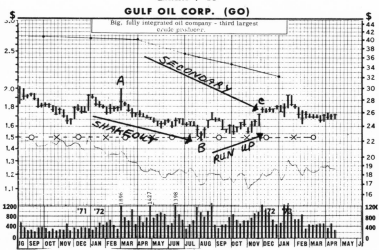

BLOCK DISTRIBUTIONS OF STOCK
THREE MONTHS ENDED DECEMBER 31, 1972 (4th QUARTER)

	Distribution		Number of Shares		Offering Price Per Share (Dollars)	Value of Shares Sold (Dollars)	Type of Vendor
	Began	Ended	In Original Offer	Sold			
SECONDARY DISTRIBUTION NYSE							
General Mills Inc.	10-3	10-5	529,759	529,759	51.750	27,415,028	Corporat
Gulf Oil Corp.	12-5	12-12	9,225,000	9,459,783	26.000	245,954,358	Various

The secondary in Gulf Oil was for the sale of a block in excess of 9.25 million shares. With a cash value of almost $246 million, it took six days to complete and was the largest secondary in Stock Exchange history. There was an overallotment of 234,783 shares.

The size of the overallotment leads us to assume that the underwriting team did not want to be heavily on the long side after the completion of the offering. The reason for this is obvious. They anticipated an important drop in price below the offering price of 26. The drop in price that occurred in Gulf Oil subsequent to the termination of stabilizing operations conforms to the standard formula. So, too, was the subsequent advance to the 29 price level, which was then followed by the usual decline.

Of far greater significance to the investor is the fact that if one is willing to pay him for protection, the Stock Exchange member can dump more than 9.25 million shares of stock into the auction market without dropping the price one-eighth of a point. All too often, however, the ordinary investor will enter an order to sell 100 shares of a stock "at the market," only to see the price drop a full point for his execution. During the six days it took to unload this block of stock, most investors who were persuaded to purchase it did not realize that the price was "pegged" at 26 but bought it under the assumption that the price being quoted for Gulf Oil was representative of the continuing tug between auction market buyers and sellers. What we are witnessing in the Gulf Oil secondary is a typical instance of discrimination in restraint of trade.

The technique employed by the Exchange to corral investors into secondaries like Gulf Oil is comparable to a side show shell game.

The brochure "Marketing Methods for Your Block of Stock: An Investment Manager's Handbook" (published by the New York Stock Exchange) states on page 16:

CHART 7–16

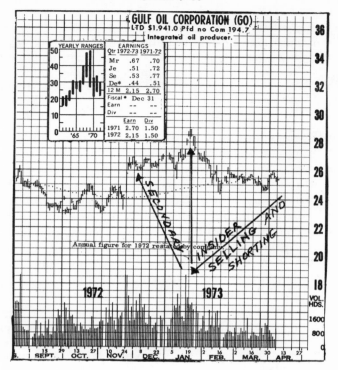

... the special offering [a big block] method is an efficient procedure whereby the investment manager and his member firm may command the aid of the entire Exchange community in achieving a large block distribution. Buyers, . . . are attracted by the net price offering [no commission—R.N.]. *The incentive commission (the special bonus) invites special brokerage efforts* [emphasis added].

The incentive commission paid to brokers can be as much as $1.00 a share or more, which would be $100 or more on the sale of 100 shares. The Gulf Oil secondary offering of 9,225,000 shares was offered at 26 "net." The incentive commission was 55 cents. It was possible to keep the bonus low since a favorable climate had been created for oil stocks. Thus it was possible, with the help of the bait offered both customer and broker, for brokers to sell not merely 100 shares of stock to three or four customers, as might be the case in an ordinary day's trading, but hundreds of shares to a large percentage of their customers. An event like the secondary in Gulf Oil might make it possible for brokers to earn in one day more than they would make in an ordinary month.

Brokers all over the country circumvented whatever pessimistic attitudes investors might have had toward this offering by a period of pre-offering human engineering. Thus the Blyth, Eastman, Dillon & Company Bulletin of November 24, 1972, had this to say:

Gulf Oil is selling near 1972 low. Nine million shares of the Mellon family interests is being sold to public on December 12 [the correct date was December 5]. . . . Closing down of unprofitable retail stations has kept the stock from advancing with the rest of the oils. Gulf's 1973 earnings estimate is $2.90 per share—at 15 times multiple it should sell at 43½. Energy crisis is here, oil stocks after three years of relatively flat performance should lead the market in 1973.

The stock was selling at 24½ at the time of this bulletin. This kind of propaganda made it easier for stockbrokers to persuade their customers to buy the stock when it was offered on December 5. Interestingly enough, while oil stocks did advance, the direction of Gulf Oil was down. Not for a moment would Exchange members tolerate the idea of placing the public in a position where they could sell 9 million shares of stock at a profit.

The SEC Special Study Report had several observations on secondaries that are worthy of note. Concerning the speed with which some secondaries are dumped into the market the Special Study report had this to say (Part 1, Page 567):

> The speed with which these distributions occur is evidence of the efficiency of the marketing facilities of the financial community, but rapid distribution may not be conducive to an unhurried, informed, and careful consideration of the investment factors applicable to the securities involved. Representatives of one member firm stated to the study that "flash" secondary distributions, occurring on the same day they were announced, were sold by salesmen who had little time to inform themselves about the securities being offered and who, under the incentive of extra compensation, told the customers of "a wonderful opportunity" without disclosing the fact of the distribution and the payment of a higher than normal rate of compensation.

In the same section of the report an official of a large mutual fund selling organization is quoted as telling us that "the funds sponsored by it sometimes used secondary distributions to dispose of sick situations rapidly."

The Special Study report also comments on the way stock brokerage firms wholesale stock to other brokers or to institutions while conducting retail business with the public (Part 2, Page 578):

> The integrated firm [like Merrill Lynch] combines wholesaling and retailing activities. Its trading activities may be primarily an adjunct of its retailing activities, although in certain securities the integrated firm may conduct its trading activities like the wholesale dealer. . . . *The integrated firm may use its trading department to accumulate inventories for retailing to its customers.* . . . It would appear that the trading activities of the integrated firm have become of increasing importance in the wholesale markets.

Charting is the language of financial crisis. **Above:** *When the protractor's vertical track describes the angle from General Motors's major low in 1938 back up to its 1936 high we obtain its principal angle of 74°. The horizontal track is then automatically set on the 16° complementary angle.* **Below:** *The 74° angle on the protractor head and the manner in which it aligns the vertical and horizontal tracks on the General Motors Chart.*

All photos, except the one of Senator Metcalf, by Suzy Koniecy.

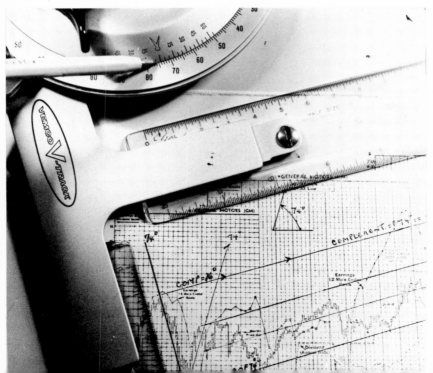

At twenty-seven, Mei-Lee finds everything useful and nothing indispensable. Having joined my organization in April, 1973, in my opinion she already knows more about the movement of stock prices than 99 per cent of the market's professionals.

Senator Lee Metcalf: His way of life suggests that great things are not so much accomplished by a man's special exertions as by his habitual acts.

In my cubicle at the UCLA Research Library stacks. Below: With an immense understanding of my research needs, Mei-Lee locates a Senate Subcommittee's comments on the SEC.

One leaves the library with an awareness that even reading has become
a financial speculation. For while books on the stock market may inspire
great hopes in men, they prevent them from achieving them.

*Mei-Lee tapewatching: I think we have something to learn from China.
I think we shall never learn it.*

The affection of animals is not limited, only their vocabularies. Mei-Lee brings my Afghans, Pavo and Raindrop, to meet me on my return to Los Angeles.

The true test of a profession is the love of the drudgery it involves.

The study group quotes a large managing underwriter who made substantial purchases in the aftermarket: "We either retail it out through our retail department or we will make a market between brokers." The testimony continued:

QUESTION: Which of the two procedures was followed most often?
ANSWER: I would say the former.
QUESTION: Retailed out to your customers?
ANSWER: Yes.

As for the manner in which underwriters work with specialists, an SEC staff study of the American Stock Exchange stated:

> Wycliff Shrieve, senior partner of Hayden Stone & Co., has testified that it was his practice with regard to secondaries on both the American and New York Stock Exchanges to inquire of the specialists directly, a day or more prior to the date of the offering, as to the aggregate bids on the book between the market price and the estimated offering price. . . . He asserted that it was necessary for Hayden, Stone to have this information prior to the offering so that it would have some idea as to how much stock had to be allocated to the book and how much would be available for allocation among the members of the underwriting group.

The staff study added this:

> More, *the possibility of abuse in connection with the disclosure of non-public information on the specialist book in secondary offering as revealed by the instant investigation is substantial.* While Reilly [a governor on the Exchange] and other exchange officials have indicated that they concur in these views, it is evident that the principles have not been made sufficiently clear to the exchange staff and member underwriting houses. [Emphasis added.]

Thus we see that as stocks move to their highs big blocks are sold in a highly deceptive manner to the public. Despite the fact that transactions raising prices for the purpose of inducing purchases violate Section 9(a) (2) of the act and result in jail sentences, injunctions, and disbarment of brokers from exchanges, the SEC sees fit to sanction transactions designed to prevent or retard a decline in the price of a security in order to facilitate its distribution to the public.

The layman's mind is made to assume that managed big block offerings solve the problem of liquidity. Someone, it is argued, must make it possible for institutions to sell one hundred thousand or a million shares of stock. The trouble with this theory is that it ignores the fact that big block offerings are profitable for the sellers, the underwriters, the stockbrokers, and the specialists —for everyone, indeed, except the investors who buy them. The truth is if institutions were forced to sell stock in the same manner as the average investor, they would plan ahead before buying big blocks and would plan to feed big blocks out slowly so as not to depress the market for themselves.

Recognition of the truth about secondaries was detected long ago by most people in the business. Every attempt to get the heads of the Exchange or the SEC to legitimately comment on them is doomed at the outset. Because of the bonanza they provide the securities industry, we are faced with the irreducible fact that it is allowed to pursue profits in this way without any real resistance from anyone. And, as usual, this is not because there is no one empowered to halt such practices. According to Commissioner Healy:

> "Practices such as pegging, fixing, or stabilizing the price of a security are subjected to regulation by the *Commission, which is authorized to prescribe such rules as may be necessary or appropriate to protect investors and the public from the vicious and unsocial aspects of these practices.*"
>
> If this Commission took the view which I take, that so-called stabilization in connection with offering "at the market" is not in the public interest and that *prohibiting it is necessary for the protection of investors,* it would be at liberty to say so and to make its view effective by enacting a rule forbidding it.

With Healy's indictment looking it right in the eye, the government nonetheless allows the congealed power of irresponsible authority to behave as if no one else exists. The fundamental reason for this can be attributed to pragmatic bureaucrats who know in their bones what is meant when they are told "the ball rests with you."

8. How Insiders Use the Boomerang Power of Demand

In which it is shown that investors are ruined as easily by businessmen who operate like Exchange insiders as they are by Exchange insiders who operate like businessmen.

Trading on the basis of inside information, whether by Stock Exchange or by corporate insiders, is a form of militancy which serves to further define the efficacy of means and the choice of ends not traditionally available to investors at large. Investor trading on the basis of inside information is proscribed by the SEC. There are, of course, logical as well as legal scruples which should, but don't, cause the SEC to prohibit the use of such practices by all insiders.

Stock Exchange members are more eligible for the epithet "insider" than the officers and directors of any company, if they work within the inner councils of the Exchange and are able to collaborate closely with specialists.

Admittance into this paradise of anarchy is also accorded, however, to important corporate officials. One way they gain "insider" status is when, either directly or indirectly through the Stock Exchange member on their board of directors, they acquire a link to the specialist in their company's stock. Thus, while anarchy may be further compounded for the stockholders of a corporation, the opportunities for insider trading provided its chairman can be considerably increased.

Although many corporation executives lack the ability to look beyond their own ideas in order to determine when to buy and sell company stock, we find others whose insider status enables them to anonymously fleece their stockholders. Hidden behind a mask of virtue, this group is able to exercise its predatory instincts just as ruthlessly as the Exchange insider. One of the ways they accomplish this is by conferring with the specialist beforehand concerning corporate developments. This, incidentally is encouraged by the Exchange. It then becomes a simple matter for both men to lay their plans for maximizing profits when an announcement of major proportions is planned. We will examine one such instance. Here we see the head of a major corporation employing the opportunity provided by a run-up in the price of his stock to sell his stock near its high. In another instance I shall show how an important stockbroker, while serving on a corporation's board of directors, is able to exploit his insider status to his advantage. The point of this will be to show that having stockbrokers or their lawyers on a corporation's board of directors introduces a middle man pregnant with danger for the corporation's stockholders.

Before attempting to enumerate the advantages provided these insiders when they can bargain to their benefit at both ends of the market or to describe the manner in which their merchandising strategies introduce a large element of inequality into the market, I will touch briefly on the regulatory attitude that prevails toward these routine by-products of "high finance" and commercial enterprise.

Law enforcement for the protection of investors is important in this area. The existence of these practices is, in my view, a reflection of callous SEC indifference about a matter that is affected with the gravest implications for both investors and the structure and purposes of the auction market.

At present the SEC requires that officers and directors of companies and members of their families make public any and all trading in the shares of their company's stock, but it does not require the same of Stock Exchange members trading in the shares of such companies on the basis of inside information.

A member of the Stock Exchange sitting on a company's board of directors can not only collaborate with the specialist on important announcements, he can advise other members of his own brokerage firm of impending events. This enables this group to acquire financial benefits for themselves to which they are not legitimately entitled. Just what services these stockbrokers render the stockholders of the companies they serve as directors can best be learned from the transactions of Howard Butcher, who, as the senior partner in the Philadelphia brokerage firm of Butcher and Sherrard, was at one time a director of more than seventy different corporations.

As our account begins, we find Butcher employing the services of the *New York Times* to persuade investors to buy Penn Central Railroad stock. He was a director of Penn Central until 1969 when awkward revelations suggested a resignation was in order. Then, on January 9, 1970, we have the *New York Times*'s financial columnist Robert Metz devoting his space to the details of a telephone conversation with Mr. Butcher: "When Howard Butcher 3d–that anomaly of anomalies, an outspoken Philadelphia financier—rattles off a story about the Penn Central Company, even Wall Street listens." He is quoted as saying: "Penn Central has the greatest prospects of any stock I know about. I don't know of any other stock that could go to five times what it's selling at now." The column concluded with Mr. Butcher's final words, "Oddly enough, you're talking to a broker who knows what he's talking about." The public scrambled to buy the stock.

At the time Penn Central was selling at approximately 29. After the appearance of this column in the *Times* the stock advanced to the low 30s and, subsequently, declined to below 2. As the *Times* well knew Butcher was even then embroiled in court cases launched by investors who had alleged they had suffered from a bewildering series of conjuring tricks at his hands. Curiously, no investigation has been made to determine what shares might have been sold directly or indirectly by Butcher or his firm during that period and as a result of his and his firm's public recommendations.

On December 11, 1972, however, the SEC maintained that Butcher and Sherrard's research department, which had been recommending Penn Central stock since 1960, reversed its position on May 11, 1972. In its settlement agreement with the SEC, the firm agreed to provide a fund of $350,000 to reimburse those of its clients who suffered losses as a result of not selling their shares between May 11 and May 22, the period when the firm's partners and "preferred" customers liquidated their holdings. Nothing is said in the SEC's charges about any losses that might have been suffered by the public during that period or earlier because of Butcher's or his firm's recommendations, which appeared in the press and which made it possible for the firm to distribute shares through the years.

Mr. Butcher's activities when he served as director of one corporation and chairman of the board of another illustrate perfectly the power of insiders over the destiny of investors. Note the fastidiousness with which he pinpointed his transactions in order to maximize his trading profits. In a manner of speaking, it was like playing tennis with the net down.

In the following example Butcher was a director of the Walworth Company. Observe the manner in which he sold its stock at its high (Chart 8–1).

In the example provided by International Utilities, Butcher was the chairman of the company and had, again, demonstrated an enviable ability to sell his stock at its intermediate high and then, three months later, move in and, with his entire family and several friends, purchase this stock at its March 1, 1968, low (Chart 8–2).

On the very day Butcher sold all his preferred shares of International Utilities, John Dale, another director, bought 550 shares of the common stock—which moved synchronously with the preferred. This is of interest since it shows how the Exchange insider can exercise the advantages of insider knowledge and relationships in order to benefit himself in ways not accessible to others who may sit on the same board. Imagine, then, how far removed the shareholders must be who, like the director, bought when Mr. Butcher sold. Having been persuaded to buy, it is their demand that makes it possible for the Stock Exchange's Butchers to sell.

The problem presented by Butcher as a stockbroker-director is typical of a situation that exists in almost every major American corporation. The Exchange has steadfastly preached to the nation's corporate hierarchy that in their own and their companies' best interests such a liaison between the Exchange and the corporation provides the best means for everyone to become richer and richer. Hence, heads of these corporations are indifferent to the implications for their stockholders of having Stock Exchange members on their boards.

An equally dramatic illustration of the kind of inside activity conducted by corporate insiders in conjunction with Stock Exchange insiders is the case of Occidental Petroleum.

On July 18, 1972, headlines in the *Wall Street Journal,* the *New York Times,* and hundreds of other newspapers announced a major agreement between Occidental Petroleum and the Soviet Union. The *Journal's* headline read: "OCCIDENTAL PETROLEUM EXPECTED TO DISCLOSE RECORD $3 BILLION PACT WITH SOVIETS TODAY." The editorial cheers for the head of Occidental, Armand Hammer, were deafening.

Sensitive to the potential this would have for OXY's earnings, investors charged into the market to create a record for one day's trading in a stock on the New York Stock Exchange.

Yet on the very day the public was buying as a result of his announcements to the press, insider Armand Hammer sold 20,000 shares of Occidental Petroleum. It was a beautiful execution.

CHART 8–1

SEC Official Summary of Stock Transactions (January, 1968)

ISSUER / SECURITY / REPORTING PERSON / INDIRECT ACCOUNT	DATE (or month) of Trans-action	TRANSACTIONS Bought or Otherwise Acquired	Sold or Otherwise Disposed of	Month-End Holdings of Security Traded
WALWORTH COMPANY Common Howard Butcher III	D 12-28-67		5000	0

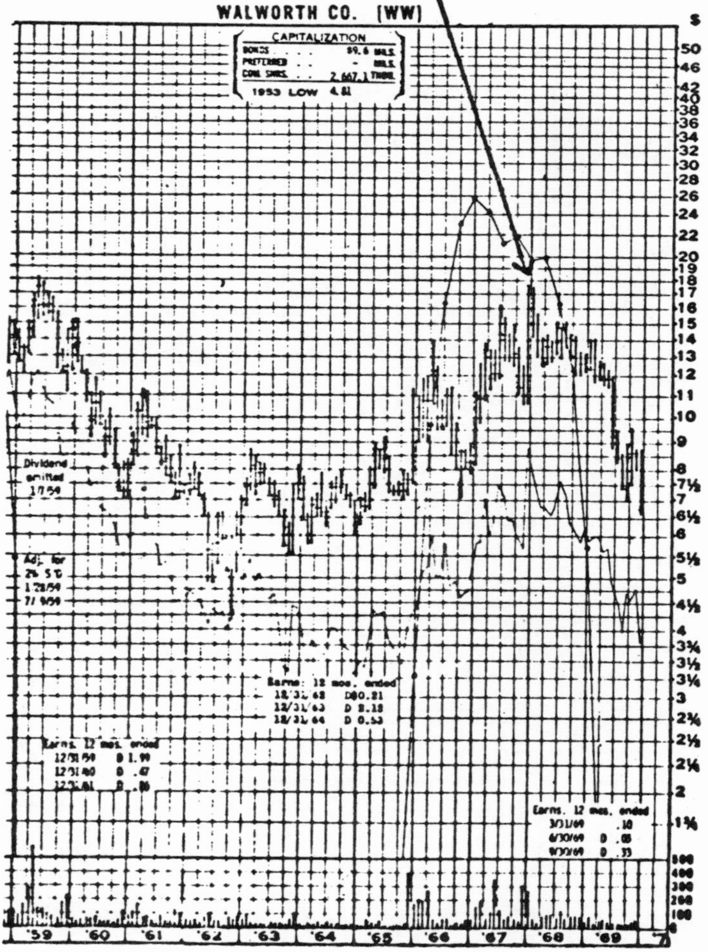

CHART 8–2

SEC SUMMARY (January, 1968)

ISSUER
  SECURITY
    REPORTING PERSON
      INDIRECT ACCOUNT
	MONTH	Transactions and Ownership Symbol	TRANSACTIONS		Month-End Holdings of Securities Traded

			Bought or Otherwise Acquired	Sold or Otherwise Disposed of	
INTL UTILITIES CORP					
Common					
John C Dale	OD 12-18-67	x	550		2550
Preferred					
Howard Butcher III	D				0
Trusts	12-18-67	2		7000	0

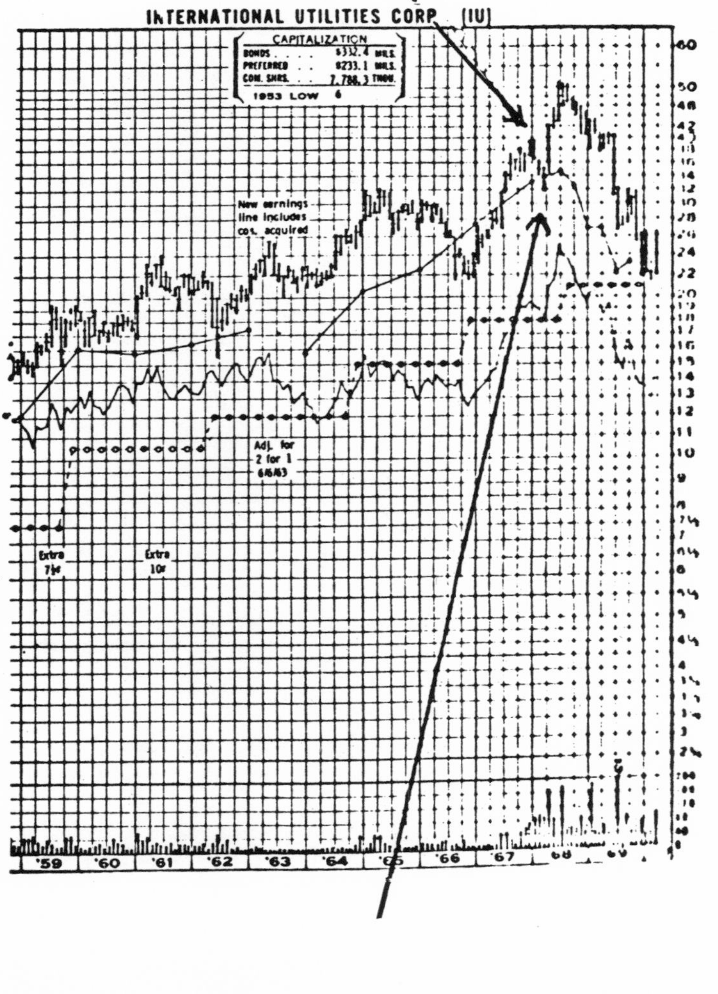

SEC SUMMARY (May, 1968)

ISSUER / SECURITY / REPORTING PERSON / INDIRECT ACCOUNT		MONTH	Transactions and Ownership Symbol	TRANSACTIONS Bought or Otherwise Acquired	Sold or Otherwise Disposed of	Month-End Holdings of Securities Traded
INTL UTILITIES CORP						
Common						
Howard Butcher III	D	3-1-68		135145		145145
Wife		3-1-68	3	131250		131250
Trusts		3-1-68	2	71375		71375
Series A Preferred						
W W Keen Butcher	D	3-1-68	*	14095		14095
Wife		3-1-68	* 2	3861		3861
Trust #1		3-1-68	* 2	50625		50625
Trust #10		3-1-68	* 2	3000		3000
As guardian		3-1-68	* 2	1409		1409
Trust		3-1-68	* 2	807		807
As custodian		3-1-68	* 2	1216		1216

*Acqd in exchange for shs of Genl Waterwork Common stock as a result of the acquisition of said co

Aware of the impact his announcement would have, he entered his order to sell on the day the story broke. That was Tuesday, July 18. On Friday Occidental began a major decline in price.

The recent accounts of Occidental's good fortune were in marked contrast to the news stories published about the company in December, 1971. Implicit in the news media's stories at that time was the idea that Armand Hammer was the cause of OXY's problems. Articles describing the slump in the company's fortunes followed one another with mathematical precision. *Business Week* stated on December 18, 1971: "OCCIDENTAL PETROLEUM'S UNHAPPY VENTURES," then added that, "this year, Hammer's magic seems to be fading. The company has run into a wall of problems that have stopped its spectacular earnings growth."

What investors consider bad news is really good news for insiders. Not recognizing this, however, investors had difficulty in bringing the bad news about OXY into proper focus. The continuing reports of bad earnings and worse prospects caused heavy selling in the stock. A glance at Chart 8–3 shows that the timing of the bad earnings announcements terminated the decline that was begun in the stock in 1969.

AUGUST 1972

OFFICIAL SUMMARY OF SECURITY TRANSACTIONS AND HOLDINGS

ISSUER SECURITY REPORTING NATURE OF OWNERSHIP	Relationship	Date of transaction	Character	Late, amended or inconsistent	TRANSACTIONS				Month end holdings of securities	Option reported
					Bought or otherwise acquired		Sold or otherwise disposed of			
					Amount	Price	Amount	Price		
OCCIDENTAL PETE CORP.										
SUB DEB CONV										
HAMMER ARMAND	H	07/18/72								
INDIRECT		07/18/72	H						$ 100,000	
DIRECT	H	07/18/72					20,000		1,135,368	
INDIRECT		07/18/72							7,649	
INDIRECT									153	

The propaganda barrage in December, 1971, concerning OXY's bleak prospects had caused public selling that again enabled Stock Exchange insiders to accumulate shares in anticipation of another bull raid on the stock's price structure.

What the investor must understand, therefore, is that the events being described by the media in July, 1972, were embedded in an

CHART 8–3

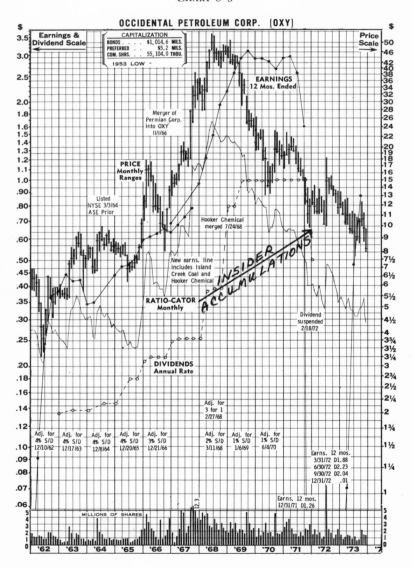

event of much longer duration; that, in fact a whole series of events had to be integrated to form the whole that was now ready for exploitation.

An investigation of the events surrounding the announcements on July 18 would show they were timed so that the Stock Exchange insiders who had acquired this stock at its low (9+) in December and at 11+ in January, 1972, could now claim long-term capital gains. More than that, it would show that, just a week before the press announcements heralded the Soviet pact, insiders were able to pause long enough to accumulate another bundle of stock at its new low for the year (10) prior to the bull raid that would guarantee short- and long-term gains.

OXY had closed on Monday, July 17, at 12¾. Following the announcement on the 18th, and after a halt in trading, it opened that afternoon at 15½. Those who'd bought at the opening paid 2¾ points more than the previous day's close. The volume in OXY that day was 1,118,900 shares.

Another front-page article on Occidental appeared in the *New York Times* on Wednesday the 19th, under the headline "Broad Trade Deal with Soviet Is Set by Occidental Petroleum." On the first page of the financial section the *Times* presented a biographical sketch of the chairman of Occidental, Armand Hammer. The stock opened that day at 16⅝ (up 1⅛ points from its Tuesday close) and closed at 18¼ for a gain of 2¾ points on the unbelievably high volume of 1,411,300 shares; 18¼ was to be the high in Occidental.

It may be asked why the stock only went to 18¼ instead of 100 or 200 with that much public demand. Certainly the public had a right to assume that an influx of more than 3 million shares in two days' trading would send the stock higher.

To understand what halted the advance at 18¼ one must understand that the probability existed that specialists in this stock were able to obtain only a small fraction of the amounts that would be needed to supply demand. Once this is understood it becomes apparent why their inventory became exhausted at 18¼, and why they then had to begin borrowing at 18¼. This also serves to clarify why, after the market's close on Wednesday, the Exchange imposed the 100 per cent margin rule for trading in Occidental. This naturally limited further purchases by the public. The Exchange knew that if public speculation was not reduced the specialist might find it difficult to expeditiously borrow more stock to sell short. Under such circumstances specialists and other Exchange insiders who'd sold the stock short at 18¼ would be in for big losses as the stock rose to higher levels. The fact that the specialist was having difficulty borrowing stock was evidenced by the numerous times trading was halted during the day.

It is of interest to note the comments from the *Commercial and Financial Chronicle* of July 27, 1972, which states that "in contrast to the NYSE's difficulties, other market makers were able to maintain orderly, continuous trading in Occidental's stock." Although the NYSE informed the public that the halt in trading was due to an "enormous influx of orders," trading in OXY on the Philadelphia Baltimore and Washington Stock Exchange, for example, jumped from 85,000 shares on Monday the 17th to 302,000 on Wednesday the 18th without necessitating a halt in trading. Similar examples could be given for both the Pacific Coast and Midwest exchanges. But it was the NASDAQ market that truly showed up by contrast the poor performance of NYSE specialists. NASDAQ records show that Occidental volume jumped fivefold from Monday to Tuesday, with another increase on Wednesday, all without any halts in trading.

Since Occidental rose no higher than 18¼, there was no question but that the specialist on the NYSE was again selling enormous blocks of stocks short at the 18¼ level and had halted trading in order to locate more shares.

The stock opened Thursday morning on high volume at 18¼, the same price it had closed at on Wednesday afternoon. The fact that the stock never went higher than this told me the specialist had indeed sold massive amounts of stock short on Wednesday and again Thursday morning at 18¼.

On Thursday the specialist handled the stock according to formula. Shortly after the opening the price dropped. Speculators who had been counting their profits while they waited for the market to open now began to sweat. Occidental closed Thursday afternoon at 17⅞, down ⅜ for the day (the stock had made an intraday low of 16½) on a volume of 2,330,100 shares. This was the largest volume for a single stock ever traded in one day on the floor of the New York Stock Exchange.

Again it was all according to formula. The rationale existed for a bull raid to 18¼, now the rationale was provided that would make the public willing to accept a decline in the price of the stock. The *Wall Street Journal* advised its readers on Friday, July 21st, that "Commerce Secretary Peterson said the accord was prematurely regarded as a commercial transaction." This then provided the specialist in OXY with the perfect alibi to rationalize taking the stock down—which he did by executing the sell orders entered on his book.

In case any investors were still uninformed concerning the reasons for the decline, financial editors across the country proceeded to publish the party line. The financial page of the *Washington Post* quoted the customary stockbrokers:

> A number of analysts said the unusual activity in the issue was unwarranted. The company has many problems in Libya and elsewhere, Monte Gordon, analyst for Sartorious and Company said. "The trading has been emotional. On sober reflection, I think you'll see a reverse trend."

The *New York Times* reported the comments of the OXY specialist:

> "When the Secretary of Commerce made his statement, Mr. Romano said, 'Bango,' it was the wildest scene you ever saw in your life." The specialist declined to evaluate the investment potentials for OXY, but he noted that the vast majority of the orders were for 100 shares, pointing to great interest by small investors. "It's strictly emotional," he said.

How fitting that it was the specialist in OXY who revealed that investors were pitchforked into his stock by financial propaganda. Naturally neither the *Times* nor the OXY specialist referred to the advantages the investor's emotions afforded Exchange insiders.

On August 7, 1972, I appeared before Senator Gaylord Nelson's (D.-Wisconsin) subcommittee investigating corporate secrecy.

I used the OXY example to show that demand by the public creates a tool, like an ax, which the public hands the specialist to cut off its head. I stated that due to short selling the stock would decline below 10. OXY was then trading between 15½ and 16. As of this writing the stock has dropped to a low of 7¾. More than a month later aggregate short sales by specialists for the week ending July 21 were published in the SEC Statistical Bulletin as follows: Monday, the 17th, 405,070; Tuesday the 18th, 494,600; Wednesday the 19th, 619,000; Thursday the 20th, 617,520; Friday the 21st, 497,510 (total: 2,633,700). Thus, although the OXY specialist may have availed himself of the privilege of not recording all his short sales (see p. 97), we nonetheless note a jump of more than 200,000 shares for the 19th and 20th over Monday's figures which can be attributed to his short selling.

It is distressing to learn that those we turn to for assistance serve themselves by betraying our trust. By the same token, it should please us to learn that we hold the trump cards; that by scrapping traditional approaches to the market and by timing our transactions to coincide with the transactions of the specialist, we can beat him at his own game.

9. Buying and Selling

In which it is shown that the "theory of numbers"
provides a major key to gaining a sense of "timing."

Conditioned to confidence by his culture, the investor enters a boardroom with a life supply of money, which he spends in six months. His investment decisions lacked the direction provided by proper timing. Yet through an understanding of the relationship of interacting price and volume patterns to the specialist's inventory—all of which is revealed by the ticker tape—the investor can acquire the central insights necessary to achieve a sense of timing. This is a precondition of survival in the stock market.

The essential difficulty in dealing with this subject is that, if one is to be perfectly honest, no chapter (or book), however full of data or autobiographical experience of the market, can do any more than provide the investor with the necessary information about the market. For this information to have value the investor must, to some extent, fit himself into the personal drama and struggle that exists within the market. Unless he tests his knowledge, and with it the restrictions that surround his vision, against the competitive forces of Stock Exchange insiders, there is no way to measure his competence or to assess how well he has educated his intuitions.

I should point out that, because the process dramatically involves the emotions, entry into the market without sufficient preparation can result in disappointments, which can create so many negative moods and fears that one loses the objectivity needed to effectively employ the techniques. For this reason, before attempting to solve the problems contingent on the actual commitment of capital, I recommend the investor begin with a model portfolio. Although working with a model is not a true test of one's competence since the investor does not have to deal with his emotions as he does when risking his capital, beginning with a model will enable him to gain a working knowledge of my methods. This will help him gain control over his emotions when trying to convert his knowledge into actual experience. I would start my model portfolio with three stocks—General Motors, Eastman Kodak, and Dupont. I select these stocks because they are among the most actively traded stocks in the Dow Jones Industrial average. In working with them the investor not only can gain the insight needed to predict the direction of the Dow average but also can begin to develop—and think in terms of—a usable technology that enables him to distinguish between propitious and unpropitious circumstances. When the results of his efforts begin to show a history of fairly consistent accuracy, he will then be ready for the real test: working with his own money in competition against the forces of the specialist system.

Many investors may assume the strategies I shall outline are easy to master. They are not. As I have implied, understanding is grounded only in experience. It is, moreover, an experience that does not correspond to anything in the investor's earlier experiences of the market.

The cultural response of most investors is based on the assumption that "if somebody is buying, somebody is selling"; not for a moment is it recognized that, in most cases, "if somebody is buying," it's the specialist who is selling; and if "somebody is selling," it's the specialist who is buying. Add to this the fact that investors assume that what happens in the economy or to the corporation in terms of earnings or sales determines the trend of stock prices, and you have the basis for a fallacious theory in which events in the market exist independent of each other.

On the basis of this fundamentalist approach, the investor is obliged to memorize countless formulas that have no common bond, root basis, or theory to which everything that happens in the market can be linked. The most misleading element in this type of analysis is that it ignores the basic needs and motivations of the specialist system. This, then, is one of the essential distinctions between my approach to the market and that of most others. I align myself with the specialist as he seeks to solve his inventory problems. The thrust of all my efforts is to buy when he buys and to sell when he sells.

My assumptions about the value of tape-watching also run contrary to the point of view that assumes "a stock is worth what it's selling for." In my opinion the purpose of the tape is not merely to tell us what a stock is worth now, but rather, and in a very special sense, to define ultimate values by telling us what it will probably be selling for one week, one month, or a year from now. Only when one can define ultimate values can one hope to move successfully into and out of the market.

To illustrate how the specialists' motives and habits of mind are brought into play and how their motives are at the heart of the Exchange technology, I will provide insights into three areas of enormous importance:

(1) how an analysis of a stock's short, intermediate, and long term trends combine to reveal the specialists' future objectives

(2) how the theory of numbers and the dynamically new concepts involved in this theory provide the investor with a key to the operation of the specialists' merchandising strategies

(3) how an analysis of specific Dow stocks enables us to predict the trend of the Dow

It is impossible to look solely at the tape as it passes in review and hope to determine longer-term trends in the market. One can understand the tape and decipher its code of communication only when experience is shaped through memory—or through the use of charts. In a manner of speaking short and long term charts provide both a microscopic and a telescopic view of what has happened. In the final analysis, we need both in order to make financially rational decisions.

Most chartists believe it is possible to take a stock's price trend and project it into the future. This is dangerous since the need to use existing investor techniques to mislead compels the specialist to change the trend in some way if he is to gain the element of surprise needed to make his manipulations "pay off." As he moves from one phase or price level to another, however, his inventory objectives begin to reveal themselves in terms of specific trends. Since the chart is merely the linear history drawn from information provided by the ticker tape, the combination of the two can reveal the specialist's merchandising objectives.

For insights into the market's short-term trend, I would recommend Trendline's "Daily Basis Stock Charts," published by Standard and Poor's. In my opinion, the charts that best describe the picture of the long and intermediate trend are the semi-logarithmic charts of Securities Research Company, 208 Newbury Street, Boston, Massachusetts 02110. I also believe that the book by William Jiler, *How Charts Can Help You in the Stock Market,* is a good introduction to standard charting techniques. I should point out that, while I disagree with the manner in which Mr. Jiler perceives and experiences the market and the reasons he gives for the chart formations in his book, his illustrations of these formations are, in my view, among the best now available.

The specialist's objectives can be classified in terms of the short, intermediate, and long term. Thus we see that there are three broad classifications into which we can place the market's price movements.

1. *The long term trend:* This is the major movement of stock prices in which are contained the intermediate and short term trends. It can last anywhere from ten months to four years or longer. The downtrend from the 1971 high, for example, is already well into its third year.

Major trends have their origins in the specialist's desire to accumulate and distribute stock profitably over the long term for accounts in which he is directly or indirectly interested. To do this he must keep stocks at price ranges that are attractive to investors. *Since the specialist profits as much in a declining market because of his short sales as he does in an advancing market, there is no financial disadvantage to him in a major downtrend.* Viewed practically, unless inflation of stock prices is continually followed by deflation it would be impossible for many investors to gather the cash needed to buy 100 shares of a $150 or $200 stock. This, then, enables the specialist to distribute larger amounts of stock to the public after a 50 per cent to a 100 per cent or more rise in the price of his stock, and subsequently to accumulate more stock for his investment accounts than would otherwise be the case. This should be of interest to investors who have been conditioned to believe that fundamental economic conditions are the cause of the market's trends.

The decline from the December, 1968, high in the market to the May, 1970, low is an instance of a major trend; the advance from the May, 1970, low to the April, 1971, high is typical of another major trend.

2. *The intermediate term trend:* This is an important merchandising trend operating within the major trends and can last from weeks to approximately six months or more. Both short and intermediate-term trends are created by the specialist as he solves his inventory problems in the course of moving stock prices in the direction of his major trend.

Two examples of important intermediate term trends are the

movements from April, 1971, to November, 1971 (downtrend), and from January, 1973, to August, 1973 (downtrend).

3. *The short term trend.* This can last from two days to two months. Within this trend there can be even shorter term trends lasting no more than several hours. The importance of the short term trend is that it is within this context that the specialist resolves his day-to-day inventory problems with his intermediate and long term objectives always in view. It is as though the short term trend is the spade with which the specialist digs the investor's intermediate and long term grave.

Big blocks form the major boundaries both at the top and at the bottom of the market's intermediate, long, and some short-term trends. They are the prime stuff of the Stock Exchange. While the influence of big block activity becomes more diluted the farther one moves from the stock's highs and lows, the moving spirit of big block activity, although on a smaller scale, is a fact of enormous consequence. It makes its appearance at all stages in the development of a stock's trend and is cumulative in its effect on the thinking of the specialist. As such, it provides the signal for a reversal of trend from the trend then under way.

The ticker tape provides us with a microscopic view of the techniques of big block distribution at the top and big block accumulation at the bottom on behalf of the specialist's inventory. We will show examples from the transactions of May 26, 1970, showing accumulation at the bottom, and August 16 and 17, 1971, showing distribution at the top.

On May 26, 1970, the Dow Jones established both its intermediate and long term low in the market. An analysis of the ticker tape of American Telephone & Telegraph, Bulova, City Stores, and Honeywell, for example, reveals the big blocks with which specialists covered their short positions and/or accumulated stock in preparation for a bull raid. Following are excerpts from the transactions of that day which show some of these big blocks.

American Telephone & Telegraph	*Bulova Watch*
Opened at 43 on 5/26/70	Opened (on 200 shs!) at 15 7/8 on 5/26/70
300 at 42 7/8 at 10:23	200 at 14 at 3:02
100 at 43 at 10:23	200 at 14 at 3:07
100 at 42 7/8 at 10:23	1200 at 14 at 3:24
3200 at 42 3/4 at 10:23	128800 at 13 1/4 at 3:24
200 at 42 3/4 at 10:24	200 at 13 1/4 at 3:26
700 at 42 3/4 at 10:24	200 at 13 1/4 at 3:26
100 at 42 7/8 at 10:24	200 at 13 1/2 at 3:27
100 at 43 at 10:24	
Closed at 44 on 5/27/70	Closed at 15 3/4 on 5/27/70

City Stores	Honeywell
Opened at 8 1/4 on 5/26/70	Opened at 83 3/4 on 5/26/70

	City Stores				Honeywell	
100 at	8	at 12:42		200 at 85 3/4 at	10:46
100 at	7 1/4 at	1:36		100 at 85 3/4 at	10:46
100 at	6 3/4 at	1:41		100 at 85 1/4 at	10:47
114800 at	5	at 1:42		2100 at 83 1/2 at	10:48
300 at	5 1/8 at	1:45		100 at 84	at 10:51
200 at	5 1/8 at	1:45		100 at 83 3/4 at	10:51
200 at	5 1/4 at	1:48		200 at 83 3/4 at	10:53

City Stores	Honeywell
Closed at 5 7/8 on 5/27/70	Closed at 88 7/8 on 5/27/70

	DOW	
May 25th	−20.81	(641.36)
26th	−10.21	(631.16)
27th	+32.14	(663.20)

On the other hand, the following figures illustrate the manner in which big blocks make their appearance and call at least a temporary halt to the advance of a stock's price structure. They are excerpted from the transactions that occurred on August 16 and 17, 1971—the days after President Nixon's New Economic Policy announcement of August 15, 1971.

Chrysler Aug. 17	*Disney August. 16*
Opened at 31 3/4 on 81,500 shs. @ 11:21	14300 at 112 at 10:32 (Opening)

	Chrysler				Disney	
100 at	32	at 12:58		500 at 112 1/4 at	10:32
2000 at	32	at 12:59		200 at 112	at 10:37
90600 at	32 3/4 at	3:10		100 at 112	at 10:37
200 at	32 3/4 at	3:12		100 at 111 7/8 at	10:39
1000 at	32 3/4 at	3:12			
9000 at	32 7/8 at	3:12		Closed at 108 3/8	
100 at	32 3/4 at	3:13			
400 at	32 3/4 at	3:13			

Closed at 30 3/4

Eastman Kodak Aug. 17	*Ford Aug. 17*
Opened at 81 1/4 on 3700 shs. @ 10:12	Opened at 67 on 185,000 shs. @ 12:03

	Eastman Kodak				Ford	
1500 at	83 1/4 at	1:53		200 at 70 7/8 at	2:04
3000 at	83 1/4 at	1:56		200 at 70 3/4 at	2:04
100 at	83 1/2 at	2:01		28000 at 71	at 2:04
100 at	83 3/4 at	2:06		1000 at 70 3/4 at	2:06
3600 at	84	at 2:08		200 at 70 5/8 at	2:07
500 at	83 3/4 at	2:08			
100 at	83 3/4 at	2:17		Closed at 69	

Closed at 83 1/4

General Motors Aug. 17			
Opened at 85 on 183,800 shs.			
@ 11:39			
200	at 86 7/8	at	2:10
2000	at 87	at	2:10
100	at 87	at	2:10
3800	at 87	at	2:10
100	at 87	at	2:11
200	at 87	at	2:11
100	at 87	at	2:11
1400	at 87	at	2:11
2700	at 87	at	2:12
100	at 88	at	2:12
200	at 87	at	2:12
100	at 86 7/8	at	2:13
Closed at 85 3/4			

IBM Aug. 17			
Opened at 314 3/4 on 4,300 shs.			
@ 10:05			
69000	at 320	at	2:38
500	at 320	at	2:38
100	at 319 1/2	at	2:38
200	at 319 1/2	at	2:38
300	at 319 1/4	at	2:38
Closed at 314			

As volume picks up, big block activity increases as a stock approaches or penetrates an important price level. In terms of what I call the "theory of numbers" this activity provides us with a key to understanding specialist intent. The specialist's ability to control price, to choose between raising or lowering it in order to execute the orders on his book, or to invalidate with his invisible short sales the laws of supply and demand, are all functions of numbers.

To understand the concepts that follow, one must understand that a specific set of psychological conventions and subconscious reflexes hover around the reality of numbers. The public has been conditioned to respond to numbers in powers of ten. The principal forms of the normal child's attention is on his ten fingers. In the theory of numbers, 100 would represent the exponential epitome of the number 10. Ovid's comments are particularly instructive:

> Ten cycles of the moon the Roman year comprised:
> This number then was held in high esteem,
> Because, perhaps, on fingers we are wont to count,
> Or that a woman in twice five months brings forth,
> Or else that numbers wax till ten they reach
> And then from one begin their rhythm anew.

Nor is there any question but that the investor is the mute servant of such numbers as 40, 60, and 80. The vital resonance of the number 40 in the investor's subjective reality can be traced, among other sources, to the Bible. The rains that caused the great deluge lasted 40 days and 40 nights. Moses spent 40 days and 40 nights on Mount Sinai. The Jews wandered through the wilderness for 40 years.

A specialist in an active stock cannot drop his price to 300, 100,

80, 60, or 40 unless he has enormous financial resources available to absorb the public selling and stop loss orders that have accumulated on his book. Nor can he penetrate these price levels with impunity. For amid the general exodus of investors out of his stock above the critical price level, by carelessly moving so much as a point under it, he could precipitate a wave of selling that would send him scurrying for emergency credit.

His use of the psychology surrounding numbers forms the corpus of the specialist's presumptions as he launches a major rally or decline in the price of his stock. This is a part of the pact of common awareness that he shares with other specialists; this is knowledge that has been shaped into an intense and highly specialized, secret idiom which is guarded by technical jargon.

In the following charts the reader is asked to observe the deliberate and carefully calculated manner in which specialists approach (either from the downside or the upside) a critical price level.

If it is the specialist's intention to take his stock's price below 10, 20, 30, 40, 60, etc., in order to accumulate big blocks of stock for his investment accounts, he will consult his book. More often than not, there will be more sell orders than buy orders. In these instances he may decide to penetrate the price level. Note the increase in volume as the specialist lowers his stock's price to 300 (or 100, 80, 60, 40). (See pages 157–62.) This is public selling, which is then taken into inventory. His harvest of stock is then sold back to the public in the course of a rally. Having acquired the needed cash and, for practical purposes, having cleaned out his book on the previous decline to the critical price level, the specialist is then able to lower prices *through* the critical price level. The fluctuations in the price levels of IBM, for instance, are seen to be characteristic of a stock that is destined for a dramatic penetration of the important 300 level. It is quite obvious, in fact, that IBM is being set up like a clay pigeon for the shot that will knock it off its perch. What then remains is merely the pretext that will provide the specialist in IBM with a seemingly legitimate rationale for taking it down (to the 260 level) and, once having acquired an enormous inventory, the pretext that will allow him again to raise prices in order to liquidate the inventory. In this instance, since the courts were used to alibi a decline, it is reasonable to suppose the courts will be used to alibi a rally.

On the other hand, situations exist in which buy orders placed by sophisticated Wall Street traders *and* insiders (not the public who will be selling) can serve to create a situation for the specialist in which the buy orders on his book, below the critical level,

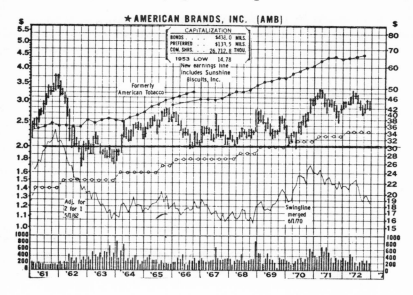

★AMERICAN BRANDS, INC. (AMB)

CAPITALIZATION
BONDS . . . . $438.0 MILS.
PREFERRED . . . $133.5 MILS.
COM. SHRS. . . . 26,712.8 THOU.
1953 LOW 14.78
New earnings line
includes Sunshine
Biscuits, Inc.

Formerly
American Tobacco

Adj. for
2 for 1
5/1/62

Swingline
merged
6/1/70

'61 '62 '63 '64 '65 '66 '67 '68 '69 '70 '71 '72

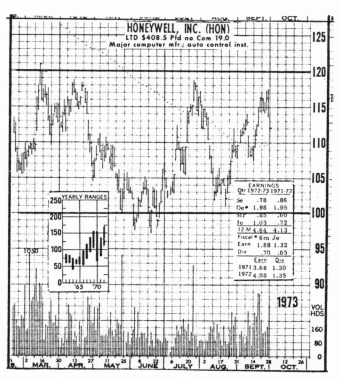

HONEYWELL, INC. (HON)
LTD $408.5 Pfd no Com 19.0
Major computer mfr.; auto control inst.

YEARLY RANGES

'65 '70

EARNINGS
Qtr 1972-73 1971-72
Se   .78   .86
De* 1.98   1.95
Mr   .85   .60
Je   1.03   .72
12 M 4.64   4.13
Fiscal * 6m Je
Earn 1.88 1.32
Div   .70   .65
       Earn   Div
1971 3.68   1.30
1972 4.08   1.35

1973

VOL
HDS

MAR. APR. MAY JUNE JULY AUG. SEPT. OCT.

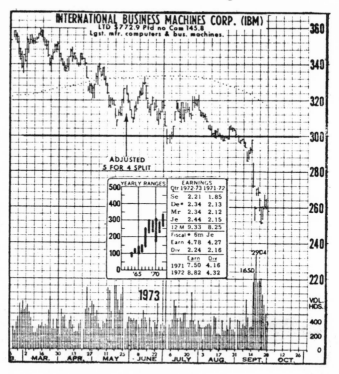

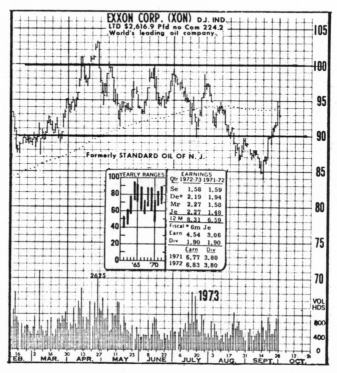

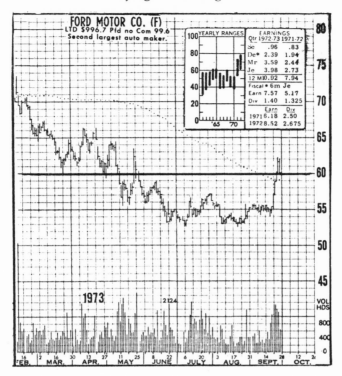

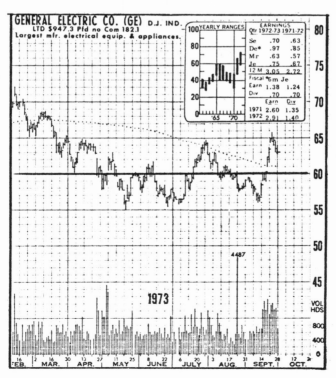

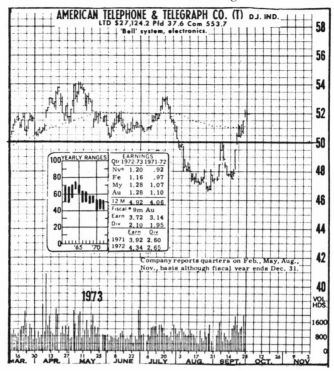

AMERICAN TELEPHONE & TELEGRAPH CO. (T) DJ. IND.
LTD $27,124.2 Pfd 37.6 Com 553.7
'Bell' system, electronics.

EARNINGS		
Qtr	1972-73	1971-72
Nv*	1.20	.92
Fe	1.16	.97
My	1.28	1.07
Au	1.28	1.10
12 M	4.92	4.06
Fiscal * 9m Au		
Earn	3.72	3.14
Div	2.10	1.95
	Earn	Div
1971	3.92	2.60
1972	4.34	2.65

Company reports quarters on Feb., May, Aug., Nov., basis although fiscal year ends Dec. 31.

1973

VOL. HDS.

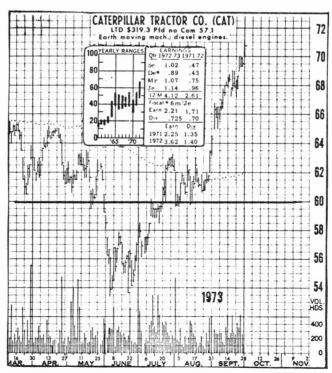

CATERPILLAR TRACTOR CO. (CAT)
LTD $319.3 Pfd no Com 57.1
Earth moving mach.; diesel engines.

EARNINGS		
Qtr	1972 73	1971-72
Se	1.02	.47
De*	.89	.43
Mr	1.07	.75
Je	1.14	.96
12 M	4.12	2.61
Fiscal * 6m 'Je		
Earn	2.21	1.71
Div	.725	.70
	Earn	Div
1971	2.25	1.35
1972	3.62	1.40

1973

VOL. HDS.

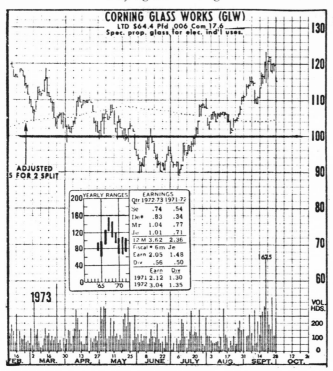

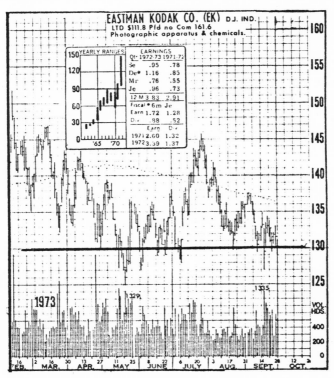

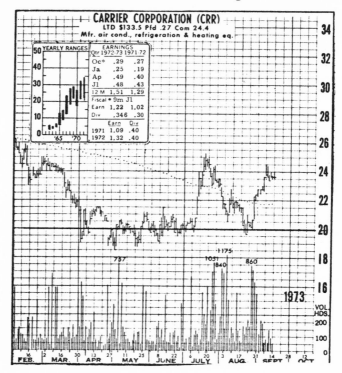

on balance outweigh the sell orders. If the specialist took the price under the critical level he would be filling these orders from his own investment accounts *at wholesale price levels.*

He could, of course, supply demand from his trading account. If he did, and demand was heavy, he would also have to sell short. This would, of course, upset his timing schedule. Under these circumstances, he will halt his decline at the 22 or 21 (or 31, 41, etc.) level. He may even proceed just down to the 20 (or 40, 60, etc.) level, test it to see what additional buying or selling comes into the market when he penetrates it, and then decide his profits are best served not by executing the buy orders that then come on his book but by immediately advancing the price of his stock.

This is also true of higher-priced stocks. In the charts that follow (pages 163–65) I have, therefore, included an example (Polaroid) in which the specialist wishing to add to inventory before advancing it to the next major price level proceeds to manipulate his stock lower. Note that he allows the price to decline only to 61. It is possible his book showed him he would have had to accommodate a waiting bevy of "sophisticated" buyers under 60. In his subsequent advance to the 100 level, he is fully aware from the information provided by his book that sellers will prevail over buyers above the 100 level. Rather than subject his casino to a run on the bank were he obliged to cash in customer's chips, he shoots up to 100 (or just under it), executes his short sales, and then immediately drops his price. This should be of interest to the head of Merrill Lynch, who confesses in his book *View from the Street* (p. 170) that this matter leaves him somewhat confused:

> I noticed . . . when the specialist's book was crowded with orders below the current market for a stock, the price of the stock would go up and the orders would never be executed. Conversely, if orders were bunched above the current level of the market, the market would go down and the stocks would never be sold. . . . *I was never able to determine why this happened and never able to get a specialist to explain it to me.* [Emphasis added.]

Or could it be that the knowledgeable head of the biggest brokerage firm in the world is telling us as much as he ought, not as much as he can?

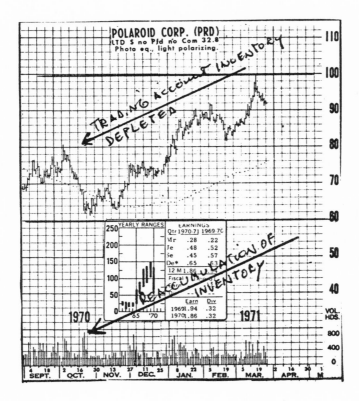

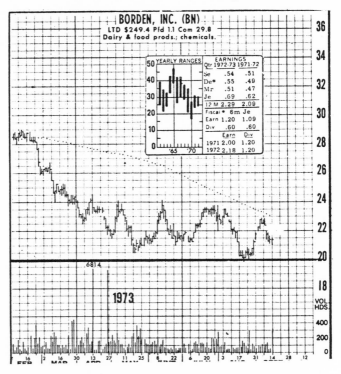

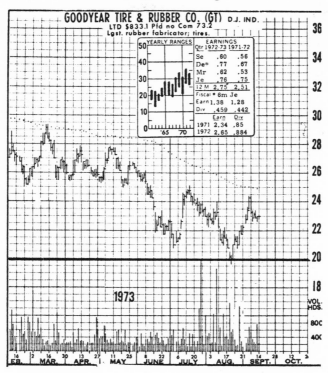

GOODYEAR TIRE & RUBBER CO. (GT) D.J. IND.
LTD $833.1 Pfd no Com 73.2
Lgst. rubber fabricator; tires.

YEARLY RANGES

EARNINGS		
Qtr	1972-73	1971-72
Se	.60	.56
De*	.77	.67
Mr	.62	.53
Je	.76	.75
12 M	2.75	2.51

Fiscal * 6m Je
Earn 1.38 1.28
Div .459 .442

	Earn	Div
1971	2.34	.85
1972	2.65	.884

1973

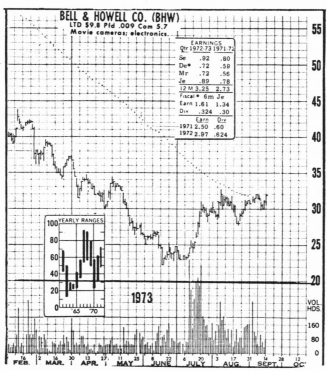

BELL & HOWELL CO. (BHW)
LTD $9.8 Pfd .009 Com 5.7
Movie cameras; electronics.

EARNINGS		
Qtr	1972-73	1971-72
Se	.92	.80
De*	.72	.59
Mr	.72	.56
Je	.89	.78
12 M	3.25	2.73

Fiscal * 6m Je
Earn 1.61 1.34
Div .324 .30

	Earn	Div
1971	2.50	.60
1972	2.97	.624

YEARLY RANGES

1973

Note in Chart 9–17 the decision made by the specialist in Schering-Plough not to advance his price to just under 90. Note, too, that once having penetrated 80 (in August), he encountered major selling, which he had prepared for with his earlier short selling. His decision not to advance his price through 80 could be attributed to his unwillingness to allow customers who had entered sell orders at that price and just above to get out. Proctor & Gamble (Chart 9–18) performs in textbook fashion. Note the decision of the specialist not to advance his price above 120. Apparently his book showed him that had he advanced his price any higher, he would have incurred heavy public selling, which would have made it necessary to postpone his decline until he had disposed of the additional inventory he would have acquired above 120.

The geography of the 100 and 120 price levels is well known to the specialists in Exxon and Sears, Roebuck (Charts 9–19 and 9–20). Hence, if they see that the buy orders are, on balance, greater than the sell orders above these levels, they will, like guerrillas, make a sudden dash into this territory and then immediately withdraw, carrying their prisoners (short sales) with them.

Analyzing these charts, one observes numerous similarities of technique and strategy. What, one may well ask, are the circumstances that distinguish one chart pattern from another? Analysis reveals the primary difference can be located merely in the differences in one specialist's mentality from another's. Note, if you will, the chart patterns of United Aircraft Corporation and UAL, Inc. (Charts 9–21 and 9–22). Here we have two totally different stocks in two totally different industries. Both, however, are under the supervision of Ben Jacobson, one of the cagiest poker players on the Stock Exchange. Note the similarities in the chart patterns and the manner in which his price pattern follows the trajectory of earnings in each instance. Note too his methodology for distribution. He prefers the head and shoulders pattern. The myriad additional similarities can be left to the reader's insights.

Resistance to the imposition of the specialist's arbitrary assumptions and to his power to summarily dismiss the authority of market forces is made possible by a careful analysis of the ticker tape. Despite the shortcomings and limitations of the information made available to investors, the tape-watcher can combine the experiences provided by the ticker tape with the theory of numbers in order to detect the specialist's intentions to lower or advance his stock's price.

I should point out that I use a Trans-Lux "Personal Ticker," which provides information on forty stocks of my choosing.

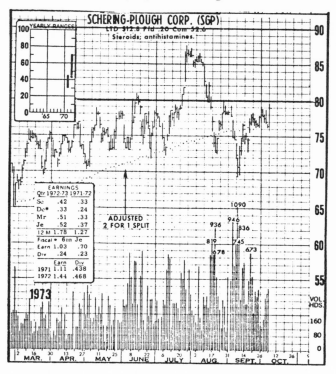

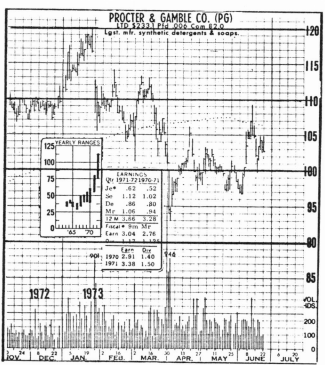

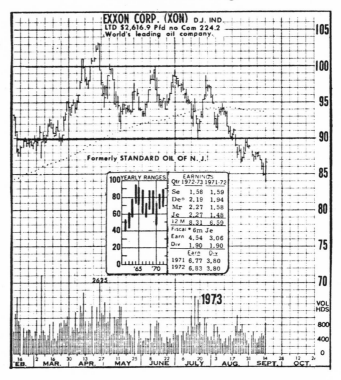

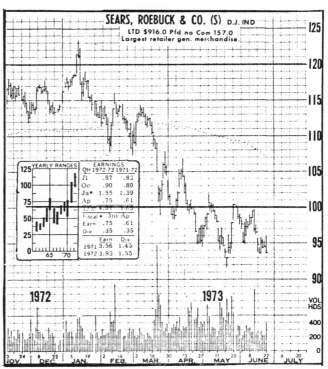

The enormous advantage this provides is that the information is always available for study and does not require my constant presence during market hours. The investor who cannot afford his own ticker, however, or who is unable (or unwilling) to visit a boardroom, can acquire a record of daily transactions of all stocks on the New York and/or American stock exchanges by subscribing to the Francis Emory Fitch Company's service. One thing must be understood, however. The individual who wishes to trade on a daily basis must watch the ticker on a daily basis during market hours. Only the long term investor can afford to study the tape after the close of the market or subscribe to the Fitch sheets.

To begin, the tape watcher must train himself to an awareness of the natural tendencies of the specialists in the thirty Dow Jones Industrial Average stocks. Applying the theory of numbers and big block activity, and price and volume patterns to these stocks, the tape watcher will begin to time his purchases and sales to conform to the way in which the majority of stocks in this average and in the over-all market advance and decline.

I employed this mode of analysis when I appeared on the Lou Gordon program in Detroit in early 1971. General Motors was moving to its high of approximately 90. I commented that major distributions had begun in this stock. I expected to see it decline

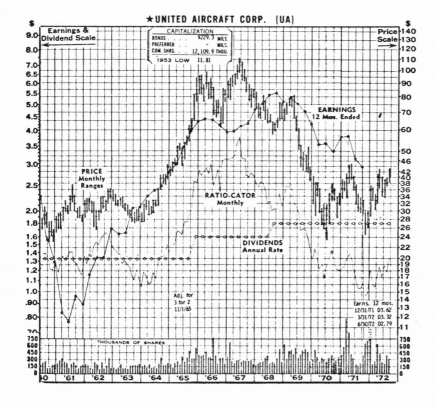

to a level just under 60, where I assumed it would be a bargain. The reason I mention it here is to point out that, as the stock approached the 60 level, the ticker tape informed me that the specialist's ultimate objective had to be at a lower level, possibly in the 50 area; when the price reached the 50 level, the ticker tape's revelations concerning this specialist's habits told me his next objective would be at least at the low 40 to 45 price level. This was further confirmed by aligning the expectations provided by my ticker tape with the expressions of specialist intent revealed by my charts.

By the time the tape watcher has finished the next chapter, he will be able to recognize, as those who purchased General Motors at 60 have, that even a bargain can cost too much.

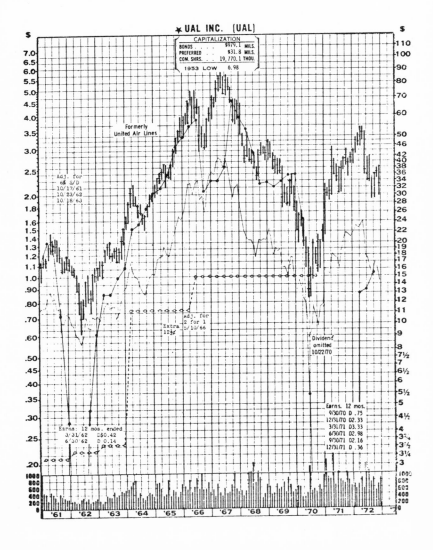

10. The Dirty Thirty

In which it is shown that, with the proper tools, investors can employ a strategy for using the information provided by the Dow stocks to move with the current of the market.

Most investors look at the market in terms of the performance of the Dow Jones Industrial average and, lumping all thought into this complex abstraction, seek to acquire a consciousness of the market's direction. Looking at a chart of the Dow average, for example, the investor is aware that when this index declines below the 900 level the thirty stocks making up this average have, on balance, declined in price. Yet this fact does not tell him which stocks in this average have declined in price, nor does it tell him which stocks may have advanced while the over-all list declined. Nor are most investors aware that, when the average once again rallies back up to the 900 level, the prices of the individual stocks are not the same as they were in the past when it was at that price level.

A sensitive appreciation of the market insists we direct our attention to the specific stocks in this average so that, as their prices change, we become aware of new equilibriums that are established, which in turn indicate the probability of a new direction for the Dow. These equilibriums are, of necessity, transient. They are based on the most volatile of all ingredients, the minds of the specialists registered in these stocks.

Since the specialist's logistical attitudes toward his inventory and price objectives are in a constant state of flux, it can be seen why the material of the market is never quite the same. This also helps us understand what a mistake it is to analyze the Dow average as though it were a single entity and the difficulty we impose on ourselves in seeking to lump thirty logistical attitudes into a

171

single abstraction. The conscientious tape-watcher will keep a careful check of the Dow stocks in order to determine the relation of, say, General Motors, General Electric, and Eastman Kodak to other stocks in the Dow. Since Dow stocks tend to move, on balance, in the same direction, the price and volume characteristics of the more important stocks in this average will tend to move together.

The experienced tape watcher differs from the inexperienced tape watcher in his ability to sense why some specialists in the Dow stocks are rallying prices, while others in this index are dropping prices. In a sense, they are all like a row of horses trying to line up at the starting gate before a race. In the case of Dow Jones specialists, there are many inventory problems that have to be solved for each of the thirty stocks before the index as a whole will be allowed to leave the starting gate. Oftentimes, if a specialist unit is behind schedule in its attempts to move to wholesale levels, trading will be halted in that stock, usually on the pretext of some bad news; quite possibly the price will reopen 5 or more points lower. What the specialist has done is to bypass the time-consuming inventory problems that would have occurred had he proceeded to lower stock prices according to formula.

Always, the basic premise underlying the principles presented in this and the preceding chapter is that the specialist's fundamental rules of conduct can always be studied in terms of the way they integrate with each other in response to the specialist's basic merchandising needs. Never more than among the specialists in the Dow average does the motto "one for all and all for one" hold true. In other words, until each and every specialist in this average has solved his stock's basic inventory problems, all Dow specialists will make whatever adjustments and adaptations are necessary in order to accommodate the specialist who, because of an announcement that might have affected his stock in terms of inventory, must now divest himself of that addition to inventory before proceeding to lower price levels.

It is no exaggeration to say that, by placing the fluctuations of the Dow stocks in the context of the theory of numbers as outlined in the previous chapter, and cultivating an awareness of the manner in which these stocks interact with each other like wheels in a watch, the investor can begin to sense the probable price levels at which specialists will seek to resolve their inventory problems. The value of this insight can be demonstrated in the most concrete of all results—the development of a sense of timing.

This sense of timing, I must reiterate, will come slowly. It is an educated intuition about events, and as such it can be written about and talked about but it must be self-taught. It is my conviction, however, that, by employing the methodology about to be outlined in this chapter, and with the knowledge from the earlier chapters, as the investor comes to discern the manner in which the specialist consciously pursues his objectives, he will event ally be able to anticipate the specialist's behavior patterns. Inevitably the fullness of the investor's intuition will be reflected in the manner in which he times his investment decisions.

In order to bring the investor into imaginative contact with the merchandising strategies outlined in this and the preceding chapter, I will analyze a major instance of inventory distribution, the September–October, 1973, bull raid on the market by Exchange insiders. This event opens the door wide on the way specialists employ price to distribute their accumulated inventories, and then, through the medium of their short sales, establish the ground for a major market decline.

The following portion of a trendline chart of the Dow Jones Industrial average focuses on the price and volume characteristics of the period in question. The vertical line at the September 14 period marks the beginning week of the bull raid. (See page 174.)

The prime purpose of the September rally's complex strategy was to distribute specialist inventory in order to harmonize future price objectives with present inventory requirements. As stated in the previous chapter, a major downtrend had been in operation from the April, 1971, high to the current ('73-'74) lows in the market. In this instance, the specialist's objective is to establish accumulations of stock at wholesale price levels. From the chart, it becomes apparent that specialists must have accumulated large inventories of stock in the course of the decline from the July high to the August low which would have to be disposed of if they were not to be carried to lower levels when the price structure declined further. It was this, of course, that necessitated the rally. There was, however, a more pressing problem facing the specialist system. Short sales would have to be established in sufficiently large quantities to enable specialists to not only absorb whatever selling came into the market as they once again declined through the territory just traversed in the course of the rally, but enough to absorb selling at even lower levels. Otherwise, they would have to conduct an endless series of rallies to divest themselves of accumulated inventory as they proceeded lower. Had specialists intended to establish major accumulations of stock at or near the 800 level in the Dow, as I thought they might when the Dow approximated

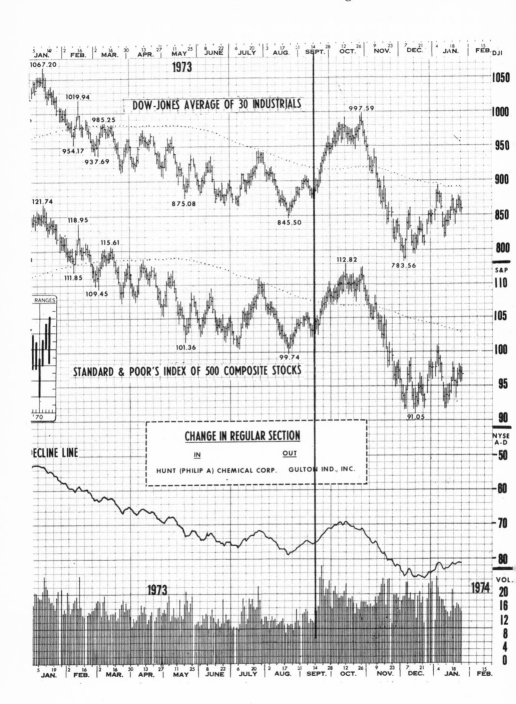

JAN. FEB. MAR. APR. MAY JUNE JULY AUG. SEPT. OCT. NOV. DEC. JAN. FEB. DJI

1067.20

1973

DOW-JONES AVERAGE OF 30 INDUSTRIALS

1019.94

985.25

997.59

954.17

937.69

1050

1000

950

875.08

900

121.74

845.50

850

118.95

115.61

112.82

783.56

800

S&P

111.85

110

109.45

105

RANGES

101.36

99.74

STANDARD & POOR'S INDEX OF 500 COMPOSITE STOCKS

100

95

'70

91.05

90

NYSE
A-D

CHANGE IN REGULAR SECTION

DECLINE LINE

IN   OUT

HUNT (PHILIP A) CHEMICAL CORP.   GULTON IND., INC.

-50

-60

-70

-80

VOL.

1973   1974   20

16

12

8

4

0

JAN. FEB. MAR. APR. MAY JUNE JULY AUG. SEPT. OCT. NOV. DEC. JAN. FEB.

950 in July, the decline would not have halted at the August low but would have gained momentum as specialists made an all-out drive to create panic selling. This could have been accomplished in two days. That they did not do this was an important element in the formulation of my conclusion that the run-up in prices from mid-September would be of short-term duration.

By selecting a representative number of stocks from the Dow average, we can present the hidden reasons underlying the bull raid, along with the reasons why I anticipated a sudden reversal. It will be necessary first, however, to sketch in the background of the rally and the role played by the financial press. Specialists rely on the myths surrounding bull or bear raids, earning announcements and economic movement of stock prices from retail to wholesale levels (or the reverse).[1] The beginning of the September, 1973, rally was dispensed with by the press as a "technical rally." Not surprisingly, few investors placed big orders. The plan called for them to buy at the top of the rally.

As prices moved to their highs, the media focused on institutional buying as the cause of the advance. The *Wall Street Journal's* comments were typical:

Friday, Sept. 21:	Brokers attributed the great bulk of activity to mutual funds hustling to reduce their cash positions in what might be an actual bull market.
Monday, Sept. 24:	The market has "passed through the eye of the storm and the worst is over," in the view of Henry P. Renard, Senior Vice President of Channing Management Corp.
Tuesday, Sept. 25:	Brokers said some mutual funds were scurrying to commit part of their high cash reserves by Friday.
Wednesday, Sept. 26:	Newton K. Zinder of E. F. Hutton stated "some institutions may not want to show large cash holdings in their reports for the period."

[1] There has been widespread questioning by the public concerning the reasons for the sudden announcement of an energy crisis in October, 1973. Certainly, it is maintained, this problem must have been known before then. Why then this sudden impact of escalating prices and fuel shortages? The reasons are obvious once the power of the financial establishment is understood. Had the condition been announced in 1970, when it was known, it would have made it impossible to distribute to the public the countless billions of dollars of stock sold it during the 1971–73 period.

Thursday, Sept. 27:   "There's a change in psychology; banks, mutual funds and other institutions think the market is going higher and there's a buying stampede under way," observed one analyst.

Friday, Sept. 28:   Another factor behind present strength brokers noted was some "window dressing" by mutual funds.

His newspaper's financial page focused the investor's attention on the feverish rise in the Dow Industrial Average instead of the prices of the stocks in that average. The *Los Angeles Times* Sunday, September 30, headline was characteristic: "Feeling Grows on Wall Street that New Bullish Trend Is Under Way." More and more people on Wall Street were becoming convinced that the stock market had embarked on a new bull trend.

The average daily volume on the NYSE for the week ending Sept. 14 was 12.3 million shares. Beginning with the week of September 17 and for the next three weeks, to the close on October 5, the average daily volume increased to in excess of 21 million shares; for the same period the Dow advanced approximately 85 points. Dupont's contribution to this figure went unnoticed by the public. Yet, in point of fact, whereas most stocks in the Dow had failed to gain as much as 5 points for the three week period, Dupont had gained 33¼ points.

By the end of the first week of the rally it had become clear that many specialists had already emptied their trading accounts after the heavy insider selling of Wednesday and Thursday, and that by Friday had begun to establish major short positions. Monday, September 24, would undoubtedly see an increase in this short-selling on higher prices.

Although only the specialists themselves were aware of their exact inventory objectives (in terms of short as well as long sales), it was highly probable some specialists would approximate their short selling price objectives during the forthcoming week or the week after. In any event, the writing was on the wall. Since specialist short selling is the fertilizer to which every decline in the market owes its growth, the evidence of major short selling in the course of the present rally could be seen to have prepared the ground for a decline of dramatic proportions.

It occurred to me my vision of the market might also interest the heads of television network news services. Altogether aware that what I was about to do was an attempt at an imaginative rather than a practical solution to the problems I saw ahead for investors, I sent the following letter to Walter Cronkite of CBS news, John

Chancellor of NBC news, and Howard K. Smith of ABC news service:

RICHARD NEY & ASSOCIATES
INCORPORATED
INVESTMENT COUNSELLORS
BOX H
BEVERLY HILLS, CALIFORNIA 90213

September 22, 1973

Mr. John Chancellor
NBC NEWS
30 Rockefeller Plaza
New York City

Dear Mr. Chancellor:—   For the record:

Stock Exchange insiders have just completed the first phase of a major manipulation of stock prices. The death watch beetles are in the rafters. Beginning this coming week the second phase of this manipulation will be initiated. A major decline in stock prices will be launched by the Exchange. It could be set in motion as early as Monday. It will be rationalized employing an economic, political or monetary alibi.

This is a financial conspiracy with government as accomplice. It is made possible by self regulation and the American people's ignorance of their ignorance. It is merely another in an endless series of such conspiracies against American investors and, because of the impact of this continuum on the economy, against the American people as a whole.

Our sick society is in shock. It must have information about the source and shaping forces underlying its continuing crises. The manner in which everything including taxes and interest rates are subverted to the whims and caprice of the Financial Establishment must be investigated by communicators like yourself and then reported. Nothing else is so vital to the well being of your viewers.

As communicators in service industries our paramount responsibilities as professionals is to inform, not only about the disagreeable personalities of corrupt politicians but about the financial conspiracies this corruption makes possible on Wall Street. We can be of extraordinary use to the community only if, at long last, we serve the brute needs of communication.

Sincerely,

Richard Ney

Their silence (except for the return receipt from my certified letter) made it clear they weren't so much bullish on America as on those who owned it.

As it turned out, events proved to be more dramatic than I had anticipated. The following week, the big blocks going across the tape at or near the highs in individual Dow stocks left no doubt whatever that short selling of truly extraordinary proportions was under way.

By the end of the week, the decline I'd forecast had begun to set in. Eight Dow stocks were lower at the close on Friday the 28th than they had been at the close on the 21st. In the accompanying chart, the second column shows the prices in the Dow stocks at the close on September 28. Column 3 shows the close on October 5 and column 4 the gain or loss for the one week period from September 28 to October 5. Column 5 shows the gain or loss for the three week period. Note in column 4 that eleven stocks were lower on October 5 than they were on September 28. I mentioned earlier that in the course of the September bull raid my analysis of the stocks in the Dow Industrial Average gave me a clear indica-

DOW JONES 30

	Close 9/14/73	Close 9/28/73	Close 10/5/73	Gain/ Loss 9/28-10/5	Gain/ Loss 9/14-10/5
A	22	22½	24	+ 1½	+ 2
AA	71⅜	73½	78	+ 4½	+ 6⅝
AC	29¾	30⅞	30⅜	− ½*	+ ⅝
ACD	36⅛	40	43½	+ 3½	+ 6⅜
AMB	35⅞	37⅞	36⅝	− 1¼*	+ ¾
BS	27¾	32¼	33½	+ 1	+ 6½
C	25½	28⅛	25⅞	− 2¼*	+ ⅜
DD	164¾	183½	198	+14½	+33¼
EK	132⅞	130¼	128⅛	− 2⅛	− 4¾*
ESM	25¼	26¾	28⅝	+ 1⅞	+ 3⅜
GE	58½	63	66⅜	+ 3⅜	+ 7⅞
GF	25⅝	28	27⅞	− ⅛*	+ 2¼
GM	64⅛	67	66½	− ¼*	+ 2⅜
GT	23	24⅞	23⅞	− 1 *	+ ⅞
HR	32½	32½	35	+ 2½	+ 2½
IP	44½	47	50⅛	+ 3⅛	+ 5⅝
JM	19⅞	23	22⅝	− ⅜*	+ 2¾
N	32¼	35¾	37⅛	+ 1⅜	+ 4⅞
OI	35⅝	38	40⅜	+ 2⅜	+ 4¾
PG	96¼	99	95⅞	− 3⅛*	− ⅜*
S	95⅛	97⅞	99⅜	+ 1½	+ 4¼
SD	61¼	69¼	69½	+ ¼	+ 8¼
T	48	52	51¼	− ¾*	+ 3½
TX	30	32⅜	35¼	+ 2⅞	+ 5¼
UA	28¾	32	30¾	− 1¼*	+ 2
UK	35⅞	39¼	41⅛	+ 1⅞	+ 5¼
WX	31½	36¾	38	+ 1	+ 6½
X	29⅞	32½	34	+ 1½	+ 4¼
XON	86⅝	92⅞	96⅛	+ 3¼	+ 9½
Z	21¾	24½	25⅜	+ ⅞	+ 3⅝

tion that the general direction in which the market was moving would soon be dramatically reversed. I have therefore selected five stocks which exhibit the thought processes that led me to that conclusion and caused me to send my letter of warning to the three networks.

In the analysis that follows there are six categories that the activity of the Dow average and the individual stocks in this average will fall into. I will list these categories. The reader can then examine my evaluation of the Dow stocks under review in order to determine the categories that are applicable.

(1) A gradual advance in the Dow average to the accompaniment of low or medium volume, followed by a sharp increase in the Dow and over-all volume. The indication is that the market has become vulnerable due to insider short selling.

(2) A sharp advance in a stock of one or more points on a large increase in volume. Indication: The stock may be highly vulnerable due to insider short selling.

(3) A gradual decline (or sharp decline) in the Dow average to the accompaniment of light volume. This is followed by an important increase in over-all volume to the accompaniment of a sharp decline in the Dow average. Indication: Insiders are accumulating stock for investment and/or trading accounts.

(4) Big blocks at or near a stock's high. Indication: Specialist short-selling is under way.

(5) Volume of Dow Jones Industrial Average stocks on upside and downside in excess of 1,400,000. Indication: possibility of a reversal of trend over the near term. As over-all volume increases in the next few years, the figure of 1,400,000 will become inoperative.

(6) Important increase in volume as a stock penetrates an important downside price level like 60, 80, 100, etc. (the reverse is also true on the upside). Indication: Over the short term a rally (or decline) will occur so that specialists can dispose of (or reaccumulate) inventory. Rally (decline) can be for short or intermediate terms.

The week of Monday, September 17, began quietly enough. The Dow advanced +6.62. The following day it declined −1.73. The volume of the Dow Industrials was only 968,000 on Monday and 1,129,000 on Tuesday.

On Wednesday the high volume (24,570,000) and the sharp advance in the Dow (+19.11) clearly established the probability of insider distribution and/or short selling. The Dow stocks in our examples then performed as follows:

	Cl. 17th	Vol.	Cl. 18th	Vol.	Cl. 19th	Vol.
C	26^1	98,500	26^2	70,400	25^5	43,000
DD	165^4	6,300	162^5	17,900	166^4	11,800
EK	133^2	43,600	129^4	133,500	132^6	74,000
GM	64^2	49,900	63^7	42,800	64^4	62,000
WX	22	29,100	22	7,700	22^5	17,800

On Thursday the Dow Industrial volume had increased to 1,929,100 and on Friday 1,938,900. Without any question this told me specialists had begun heavy short selling in Dow stocks. The volume from NYSE stocks was:

Monday	15,100,000	Thursday	25,960,000
Tuesday	16,400,000	Friday	23,760,000
Wednesday	24,570,000		

Ultimately, everything the investor wants to know about the circumstances surrounding a bull raid and the decline that follows it can be learned from the general truths surrounding the five Dow stocks I have selected:

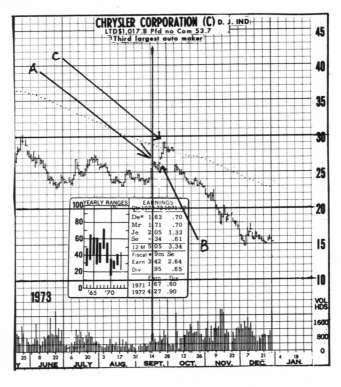

Chrysler rose 1⅜ points to 25½ on September 14, the Friday before the week the rally began. That afternoon the plant was "unexpectedly" hit by a strike. On Monday the 17th, Chrysler rose another point to 26½ (A) on the rumors of a fast settlement. Whereas the stock had traded 25,000 and 31,000 shares at the beginning of the previous week, Monday's volume of 98,500 shares indicated the specialists in this stock had emptied their trading accounts and established short sales.

Because of the existence of this short position, the stock was taken down during the first week of the market rally on progressively lighter volume, trading 54,200 shares on Thursday the 20th. On Friday it went across the ticker tape at 25 and closed at 26¼ (B) on an increase in volume to 88,700 shares. This indicated *several* things to me. Had he wanted to, the specialist in Chrysler could have taken the price down to or just below 20 in order to cover his short position. That he chose to complete his short covering at 25, only 1½ points under the Monday high, and then resume his stock's advance meant time was important.

If he was to profit from the bull raid, he would have to hurry things along or he would miss the chance to distribute at higher prices the inventory he had acquired in the course of the decline from the January high at the 44 level. In a manner of speaking, his attitude toward his short position and his willingness to sacrifice additional profits here in order to participate in the advance then under way, so as to sell out his inventory at higher prices, summed up his attitude toward the duration of the rally. Had he thought it would be longer, the probability is he would have allowed prices to decline over a longer period of time in order to cover the short sales at lower price levels.

Both the numbers theory and my charts suggested 29 as the logical price for selling the stock. On Tuesday the following week (September 25) the stock reached 27⁵ on a volume of 70,000 shares. The following day it advanced to 29 on reversal volume of 114,300 —with big blocks at the high of the day (C). This left no doubt in my mind that this specialist unit, which I cited earlier for its massive short selling on August 17, 1971, had begun to establish major short sales. Any time big blocks appear at the high of the day you can be assured that the specialist is not accumulating for a rally but rather distributing and/or shorting for a further decline. That this short-selling continued through the rest of that week and the *whole* of the following week indicated he was making plans for a *major* decline. Accordingly, when he dropped the price of Chrysler on October 5 on an opening gap of two points, the mechanism for guaranteeing his profits as the stock declined was set in motion. The precipitousness of the drop made it impossible for sellers to get out near the high. Many investors held on, hoping it would recover a point or so before they sold, merely illustrating the danger of this kind of wishful thinking. Ordinarily traders might have considered a purchase of this stock at 21. The extent of his specialist's short sales at 29, however, would have prevented me from making such a purchase, since the possibility existed he would have had a larger than necessary short position in this stock to cover public selling at the 20 to 21 level. Under the circumstances, Chrysler should be examined for possible purchase only in the course of a major reversal of the over-all market's downtrend—and then only in relation to the possibly more profitable investment opportunities provided by other stocks.

There could be no better illustration of the wholly conscious purpose of the specialist system to mislead investors than that provided by Chart 10–3 showing Dupont during the September–October bull raid on the market. Dupont was advanced 41 points from 162 to approximately 203. By itself this stock contributed approximately 26 points to the advance of the Dow index from the 880 to the 990 level.

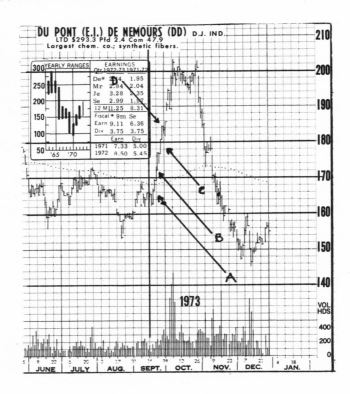

On September 18, the day before the rally began, the stock was dropped from the previous day's close of 165½ on 6,300 shares to 162⁵ on 17,900. On the first day of the rally the stock advanced to 167 (A) on only 11,800 shares, suggesting that it would advance considerably higher before the advent of reversal volume appeared. Automatically, according to the theory of numbers, a minimum target area of 180 became likely. At the end of the week Dupont closed at 172¼ (B) on an increase in volume to 23,900 shares.

On the following Wednesday it reached 180⁷ (C) on 28,000 shares—closing at the day's high, suggesting it would open higher the following day. Thus the Dupont specialist was signaling he intended to take his stock higher than the 180 level. Under these circumstances, and because of its over-all impact on the Dow average itself, the stock had to be examined carefully.

My analysis of General Motors, which was at this time the most strategically important Dow stock, gave me the clue to the probable direction of Dupont. Two factors were relevant: The first was that General Motors had not yet advanced to 69, the level my charting and the numbers theory suggested as the price at which the specialist in GM would halt the advance with short selling. Second, General Motors tended to precede other Dow stocks in establishing short term reversals (whereas at the end of an intermediate or long term movement General Motors tends to be one of the last of the Dow stocks to move into a decline).

My analysis therefore told me that Dupont had at least several additional days of rally ahead of it. On Thursday the 27th it advanced to 184⁶ (D) and closed at 184½ on 37,800 shares. General Motors advanced to 69 on the same day. The next two or three days would tell the story. Prices declined on Friday to 183⁴. GM declined to 67. On the following Monday, while GM continued to decline (to 66⁷) Dupont advanced to 185⁶. On Tuesday it advanced to 190³. According to the numbers theory, the minimum target was now 200. The closing price and volume action for the rest of that week was as follows:

Wednesday, Oct. 3		Thursday, Oct. 4		Friday, Oct. 5	
Price	Volume	Price	Volume	Price	Volume
194½	82,400	189³	100,400	198	117,800

Considering that the price of GM was 66½ after Friday's close, orders should have been entered to sell Dupont at the Monday morning opening "at the market." On the following Monday, October 8, the stock established a high of 203⁴ on 75,400. The big blocks at this price level left no doubt that specialist short-selling had once again been able to deny the authority of demand. As in the case of Chrysler, the conservative trader should have paused to consider the extent of the short sales established at this stock's highs before planning a price target for commitment.

The dramatic advance in this one stock had masked the fact that a number of the Dow's battle wagons had already been torpedoed by their specialists and were sinking fast. The strategy of the Exchange had been to maintain and increase an over-optimistic public's buying by using Dupont as its Judas goat to keep the Dow up. The fact that the Judas goat changes its name for every rally explains the permanence of the Stock Exchange.

Investors can quite justifiably ask why Eastman Kodak (Chart 10–4) proceeded to decline a few days after the rally began and then advanced as the majority of Dow stocks moved down from their highs.

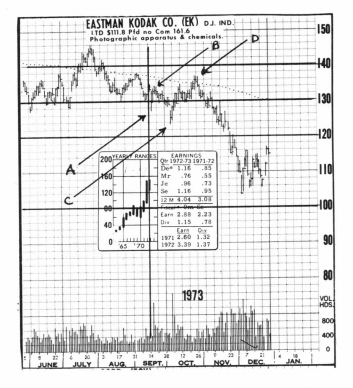

We note that, on the day before the rally began (Tuesday, September 18), EK declined from 133¼ to the 127 level (A) on 133,500 shares—a large increase in volume from the previous day's 43,600 shares. The reason for this increase was that the specialist had cleaned out his book down to the 127 level in order to acquire the stock waiting to be sold if the price dropped under 130. This would provide him with a larger inventory of stock, which he would be able to sell in the course of the rally. It would also help eliminate many of his inventory problems on his next decline through that area.

Having acquired a large inventory under 130, the specialist then advanced the stock's price to the 134 level (B), where he disposed of it. Then, once again he proceeded below 130 to the 124 level (C), thereby cleaning out his book in order to eliminate the inventory problems that would ultimately have to be faced on a decline through this level. Obviously, this specialist was thinking of the hard months ahead, when he would have to struggle to lower stock prices without unleashing an avalanche of public selling at a time when it would be doubly difficult to resell. Although it was already failing, the specialist in EK was still able to employ the euphoria of the rally in order to unload the inventory acquired at the 124 levels by advancing his price to the 137 area (D).

The tape-watcher would have thrown in an order to purchase "at the market" on October 4, when he saw the big blocks going across at the 124 level (total volume 160,200 versus the previous day's 39,400). Employing my charting techniques and the numbers theory, the tape-watcher would have entered his order to sell this stock at the 136 to 137 level, where he would have seen the big blocks crossing the tape.

By moving counter to the majority of other Dow specialists, the specialist in EK, along with the specialist in Dupont and a few others, helped hold the Dow average up. Under the screen provided by this index, the majority of the Exchange's stocks were able to decline without the incidence of heavy selling.

GM Chart 10–5 provides a brilliant statement of the manner in which a highly active stock tends to decline in 5-point stages. Thus, while the major thrust is invariably in terms of 10-point intervals, an immediate accommodation to the specialist's inventory problems is also effected at 5-point intervals.

The way the specialist in General Motors resolved his inventory problems in the course of the rally was basically according to the same formula as that employed by the specialists in the previous examples. The reader should study this chart and apply the foregoing principles to determine his own buying and selling areas. In order to facilitate the application of my charting techniques to this situation I have included the appropriate charts for GM in the book's charting section.

The overwhelming need to unload inventory has the Westinghouse specialist lined up at the starting gate with all the others.

Like a dray horse burdened down with garbage, he too will move up the mountain to dump it somewhere out of sight (Chart 10–6).

During the first week of the rally, note that he pulled the stock's price down to the high-volume selling area just above the 30 level, thereby accumulating enormous quantities of stock into inventory. In order to divest himself of these shares at higher prices, he launched his advance on the second day of the rally by opening his stock on a one-point gap at 32⅞. He closed the day's trading at 34 (B) on 100,500 shares (versus 57,500 for the previous day).

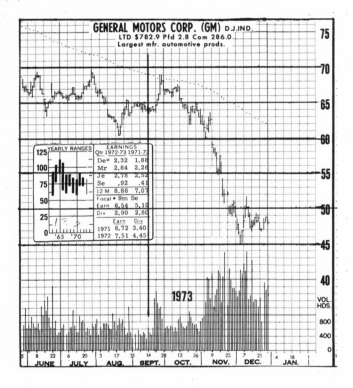

Over the course of the Dow rally, he established his high in this stock quite logically, according to the numbers theory just under 40, at 39⅞ (C) on October 9 on a volume of 67,500 shares. Obviously he had opted to leave unfilled the sell orders he saw on his book at 40 and above. When the tape watcher saw the big blocks crossing at the 39 level, realizing they included specialist short sales, he could have joined him by throwing in his own order to sell short. By employing the charting techniques and the numbers theory, he would be able to see that the specialist's ultimate objective could very well be targeted at the 20 level. The numbers theory would also, however, have indicated to the tape-watcher that the specialist would in all probability be forced to rally his stock from the 30 level. He would therefore anticipate covering his short just above this level.

The following day, October 10, the specialist dropped his price to 36⅝. On the next trading day he allowed expedience to override the requirements of appearances by dropping his stock's price to 33½ (note gap in chart). Apparently, he knew he could not risk the inventory problems that would be created by a routine decline back down from 39⅞ to the low thirties. By dropping his price in this manner, he assumed an inventory that was large (volume for the day was 549,500) but only a fraction of what it would otherwise have been had he not done this. There is no question but that traders leapt in at that price, thereby helping him unload a great part of it that day and on the following day's rally high to 34⅜ (**D**).

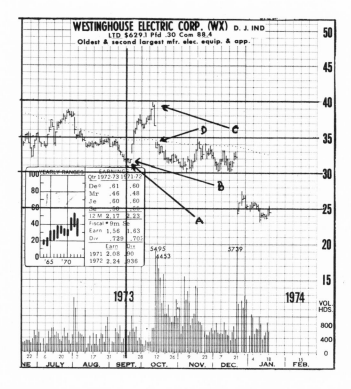

During the ensuing two months it became apparent that, if the Westinghouse specialist was to "catch up" with the time schedule of the other specialists, he would not be able to pursue routine procedures to reach the 20 price level. Employing the tonic myth that a decline in his stock's earnings sanctions catastrophe, he dropped his stock's price 7⅜ points to 24⅞ on an announcement of a decline in earnings. Again it is certain that traders relieved him of a considerable portion of this inventory. Volume for the day was 573,900 shares. On the next two trading days, he rallied the stock and, it would seem, unloaded either all or the great bulk of his inventory (note volume).

These in barest outline are the principles that operated in the bull raid of September–October, 1973, and the market crash that ensued. There was no essential or radical difference in performance between the other Dow stocks and those listed here. Basically each specialist used the occasion to employ the cherished principles of stock merchandising in order to solve the logistical problems that existed in the present because of their inventory accumulations in the past. The same sense of urgency at one time or another always determines the use of the same strategies by all specialists.

To illustrate a further instance of this similarity, I will show how the specialist in GM employed the same merchandising strategies as the specialist in WX to avoid major inventory problems. To this end I am including several excerpts concerning GM from my daily market journal. I would also like to introduce to the reader the concept of maintaining a journal in which he makes daily entries of his market observations. Few things can better serve to clarify the investor's thinking or provide him with a record of his personal progress than to set his thoughts down in writing. Following are a few excerpts from my entries concerning the specialist's strategies in GM:

> *Friday November 2, 1973:* . . . Market closed. GM is set for penetration of the 60 price level having closed at 61½; same is true of GE now at 64 and EK at 130. PG at 102½ is probably destined for penetration of 80 level along with Sears now at 93.

> *Friday, November 9, 1973:* Several things worthy of note: After a delayed opening and having closed yesterday at 62⅝ GM opened at 58½ (down 4⅛ points) on only 46,000 shares. This volume is incredibly small when it is realized that a downside penetration was effected at the critical 60 level. With this shrewd move, the specialist solved his inventory problem by bypassing the limit orders to sell on his book from 62⅝ to 58½. Had the specialist effected transit of 60 in routine fashion he could have accumulated anywhere from 800,000 to 1,000,000 or more shares thereby necessitating a rally. At one time I thought a purchase just under 60 would be a bargain. Now it seems probable he will take it down to at least the 50 level.

Monday, November 26, 1973: The specialist in GM employed the same strategy, opening his stock at 50 on only 68,400 shares having closed it at 52⅛ on Friday. As on November 9th, his decision to *avoid* accumulating an inventory means only one thing. He's going lower.

For further confirmation of the information provided by the theory of numbers and tapewatching, there is the evidence supplied by my charts. I attach immense value to them. In this connection I stated earlier that not only were the approximate price objectives of specialists during the September–October bull raid on the market defined by the theory of numbers when applied to the five stocks selected to illustrate the theory, but these prime objectives were confirmed by my charting techniques. The charts that follow can be seen to do just this.

By studying the charts that have been selected, the reader will learn that it is the consistent alignment of certain angles formed by the specialist's past activity in a stock that enables the Exchange to codify and preserve into the future a stock's angles of advance and decline. In other words, the behavior patterns of a specialist in the past give the chartist an indication of his probable behavior patterns in the future. What is particularly interesting about the following charts is that the predictive value of the angles that have been formed in the past function just as well on a long term (forty-year) chart as they do on a short term chart.

This means that the forces that determine specialist activity in the past are so demanding and definable to him that they are able to exercise a dominating influence over the major direction of his stock's price in the future. Within the limitations imposed by the secrecy in which government has shrouded specialist activity, I can only speculate that these forces are related to such different elements as the trading activity in the stock, its price structure and public supply and demand. Together, these are some of the factors that give each stock its distinctive pattern as the specialist contends with them in solving the inventory problems that lie in the path of his predetermined long term price objectives.

Allowing for the fact that every stock has its own basic personality type in terms of its own angles, which differ in some respects from all other stocks, the ensuing analysis provides a logical demonstration of the fact that the essential rhythmic character of trend does not change with changing economic conditions once it has been established. Unquestionably trend is solely a function of the specialist's long term price objectives and changes only in response to the fact that the specialist has attained these objectives.

The use of these charting techniques by the investor is critically related to the use of the theory of numbers and tapewatching as tools for determining the timing of his investment decisions. The theory of numbers and the charting techniques pinpoint areas of probability regarding the specialist's price objectives. They alert the tapewatcher to critical price levels at which he should watch for confirming price and volume patterns on the ticker tape. Employing the charts as a supplementary tool to the theory of numbers, in conjunction with tapewatching, the investor is able to construct an image of the setting in which the specialist solves his inventory problems.

I would like to point out that I have simplified the charting methodology discussed in *The Wall Street Jungle.* There are basically three angles in operation for both advancing and declining phases in all stocks. In the following sample charts, line AB in Chart 10–7 is the "principal" angle and is formed by drawing a line from a stock's major long term low to its preceding high and measuring the difference between that line and the base of a 90° angle.

CHART 10–7

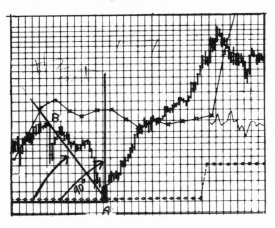

Principal angles can be formed from all major lows in a stock. It should be understood, however, that each principal angle taken from each major low has a function that distinguishes it from the other principal angles of a stock. Angles taken from more recent lows tend to have greater applicability for short term trading purposes. The Chrysler charts are a case in point. Generally speaking, the larger the angle employed, the shorter the term will be over which its trajectory operates. Conversely, the smaller the angle, the more it will tend to be applicable over the longer term.

Chart 10–8 illustrates what I call the "secondary" angle and is formed by drawing a line from a major long term low or to the low preceding the major low and measuring the difference between that and a 90° angle.

CHART 10–8

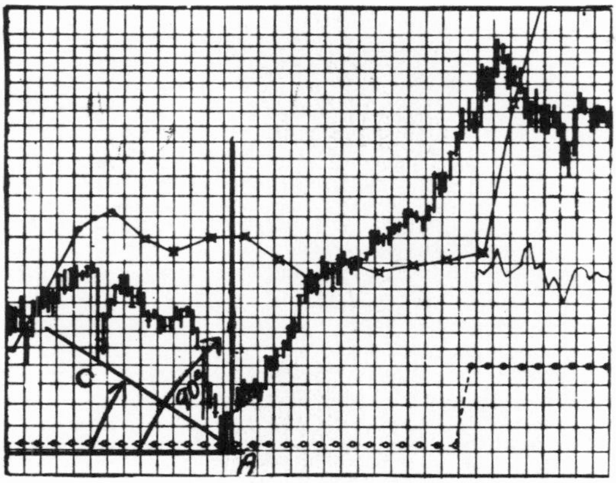

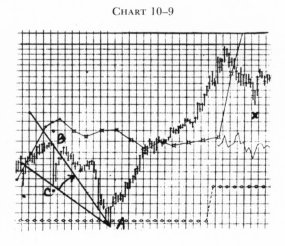

Chart 10–9 shows the "acute" angle, which is the angle between lines AB and AC.

CHART 10–9

For those who are interested, I use a Vemco V-Track Drafting Machine to plot my charts. For a picture of its three major assemblies (the horizontal track, the vertical track and the protractor head), the reader can consult the book's photographic section.

The major point of departure from the technique described in *The Wall Street Jungle* is the use of a concept I refer to as the "complementary" angle of a stock's principal angle. The complementary angle moves at right angles to the principal angle. Thus, if the principal angle from a stock's low is 60, the complement will be 30° (90° − 60° = 30°).

CHART 10–10

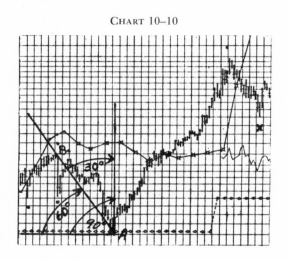

Although the complement of a stock's secondary angle is operative at times (as can be seen from the General Motors example), of the two, the complement of the principal angle will be seen to dominate. As a matter of fact, although all the angles described must be examined for their potential applicability to each individual stock pattern, it is the complement of the principal angle whose functions tend to dominate all others.

It is important to note that, when these angles are employed on the same chart and intersect, the reader will observe that these points of intersection tend to indicate the attainment of a price objective which reflects itself in a change of trend. An example of this can be seen in the chart of United Aircraft.

Our first two examples, (General Motors and Eastman Kodak) will provide illustrations of all the possible angles which might apply toward an insight into the specialist's future trend objectives. The remaining charts provide further illustrations of these angles in operation and also serve to emphasize the dominant nature of the complementary angle of the principal angle.

There is no question but that, in conjunction with tapewatching and the theory of numbers, the investor can go a long way to solving most of his practical investment problems by putting the progressive principles underlying these charting techniques to work.

The best additional advice I can give the reader is that he read the technical chapters over again, study them, the charts, and the further implications that can be drawn from them. If he does this, he can begin to learn and experience the market directly instead of through his newspaper's financial page. The chapters represent a certain freedom and potential fulfillment. They can go far to opening the mind to a broad horizon of facts about the market, the Stock Exchange and the delusions and inner contradictions held for more than a century about both.

For his "when to buy" and "when to sell" signals, the theory clearly marks the "entry" and "exit" signs to the market. By reading the chapters over and applying the principles and techniques to other rallies and declines, the investor can learn not to confuse one for the other as he does now.

Use the chapters as a guide and handbook in order to overcome the inevitable moments when you will be assailed by a sense of weakness and contingency—and remember that you will be subject to the misery of anxiety and failure only insofar as you allow yourself to be dominated by the Exchange's myths and the insurmountable obstacles these myths place in the investor's path.

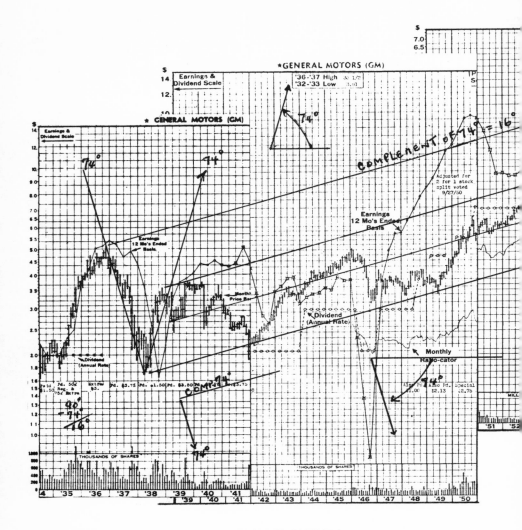

GENERAL MOTORS
SECTION ONE, CHART ONE

Chart One of General Motors shows the dominant influence of the complement (16°) of the main angle (74°—line AB).

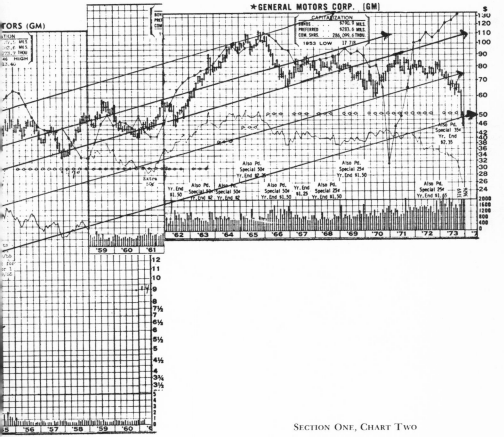

★ GENERAL MOTORS CORP. (GM)

SECTION ONE, CHART TWO

Chart Two of General Motors shows how the complement (16°) of the main angle pinpointed the September–October bull raid high. Note how this angle functions just as well on a monthly chart as it does on a yearly chart.

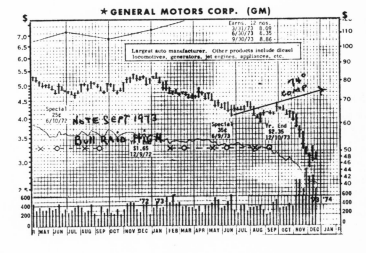

★ GENERAL MOTORS CORP. (GM)

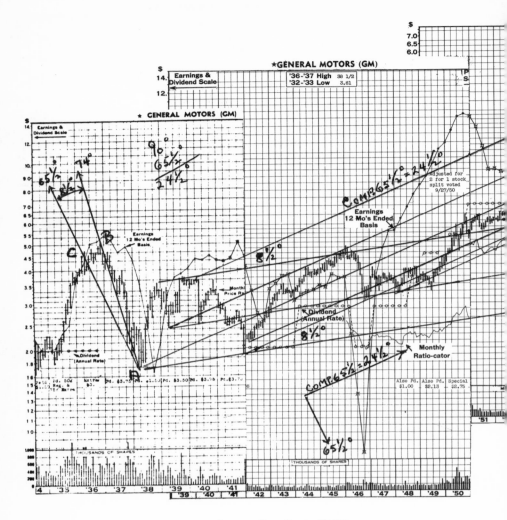

SECTION ONE, CHART THREE

Chart Three of General Motors illustrates the predictive value of both the acute angle ($8\frac{1}{2}°$) and the complement ($24\frac{1}{2}°$) of the secondary angle ($65\frac{1}{2}°$—line AC).

196

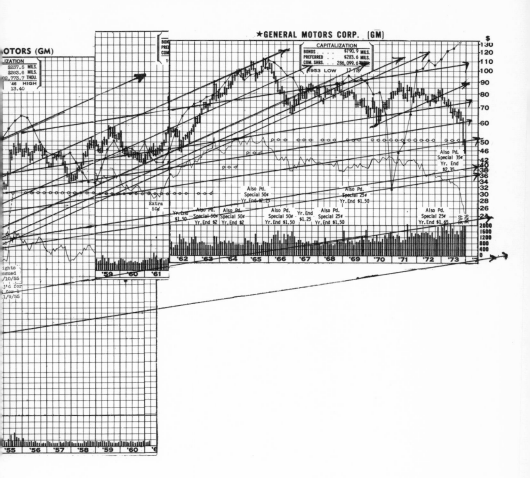

★GENERAL MOTORS CORP. (GM)

CAPITALIZATION
BONDS . . . . $790.9 MILS.
PREFERRED . . $283.6 MILS.
COM. SHRS. . . 286,099.6 THOU.
1953 LOW 17 7/8

MOTORS (GM)
IZATION
$237.5 MILS.
$283.6 MILS.
82,773.7 THOU.
'46 HIGH
13.40

Extra
50¢

Yr. End
$1.50

Also Pd.
Special 50¢
Yr. End $2

Also Pd.
Special 50¢
Yr. End $2

Also Pd.
Special 50¢
Yr. End $1.25

Also Pd.
Special 50¢
Yr. End $1.50

Yr. End
$1.25

Also Pd.
Special 25¢
Yr. End $1.50

Also Pd.
Special 25¢
Yr. End $1.50

Also Pd.
Special 25¢
Yr. End $1.65

Also Pd.
Special 35¢
Yr. End
$2.35

ights
ssued
/10/55
d'd for
for 1
1/9/55

197

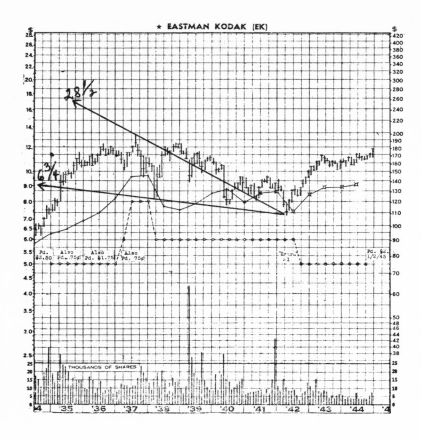

EASTMAN KODAK
SECTION TWO, CHART ONE

The charts of Eastman Kodak illustrate the remaining two angles which are operative in certain cases. Chart One shows the formation of the principal angle (28½°—line AB) and the secondary angle (6¾°—line AC).

SECTION TWO, CHART TWO AND CHART THREE

Charts Two and Three of Eastman Kodak show the principal angle (28½°) and secondary angle (6¾°) in operation during two ten-year time spans. → What is particularly interesting in this example is that instead of the complement of the principal angle being employed we employ the principal angle itself. In the present instance were the complement of this angle employed, the angle of development (at 61½° would obviously be too steep for a development meant to extend over more than a century time span.

198

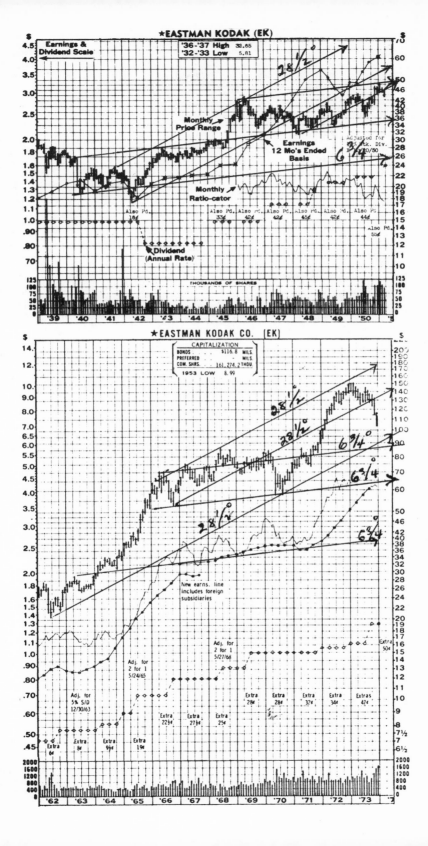

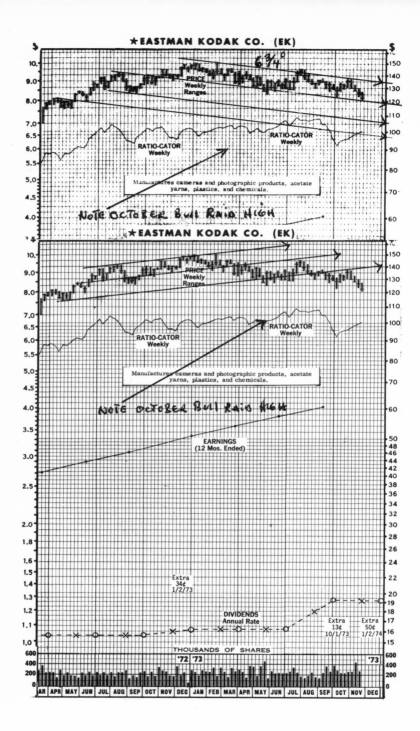

★EASTMAN KODAK CO. (EK)

200

SECTION TWO, CHART FOUR

Chart Four of Eastman Kodak shows the secondary angle (6¾°) pinpointing in both the advancing and declining phases the October bull raid high.

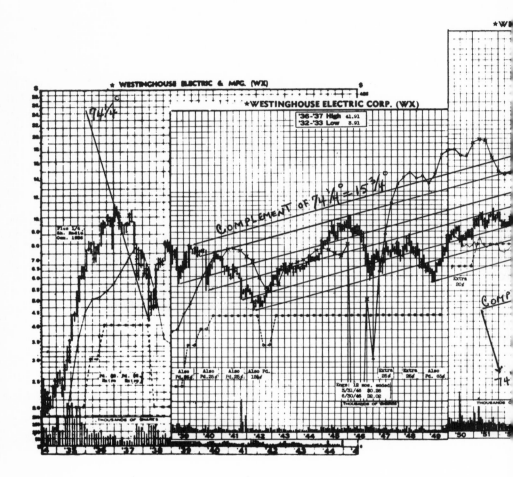

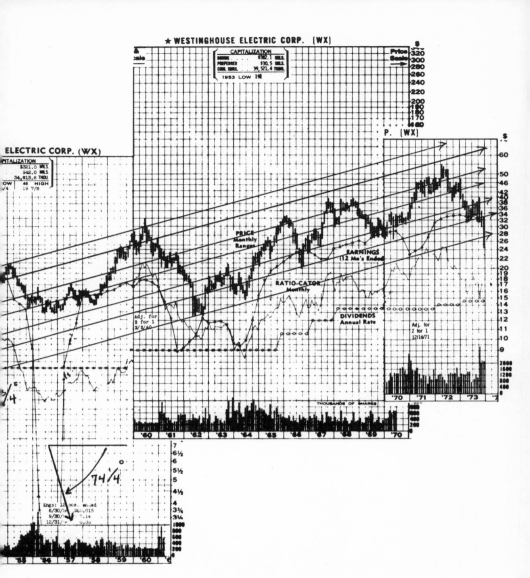

WESTINGHOUSE ELECTRIC
Section Three, Chart One

The charts of Westinghouse provide illustrations of both the acute angle and the complement of the principal angle. In Chart One, note the dominance of the complement (15¾°) of the principal angle (74¼°—line AB) in Westinghouse Electric's advance.

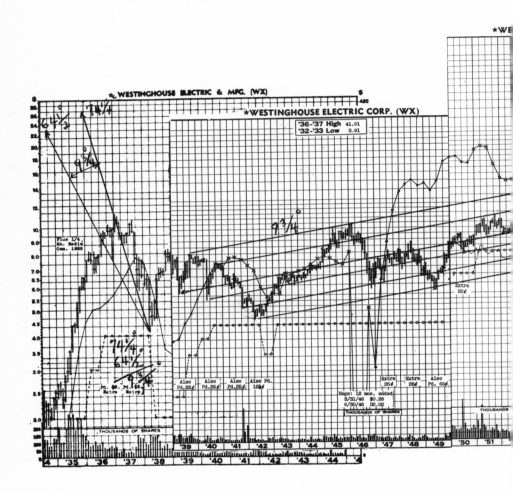

★WE

★WESTINGHOUSE ELECTRIC & MFG. (WX)

★WESTINGHOUSE ELECTRIC CORP. (WX)

'36-'37 High 41.91
'32-'33 Low 3.91

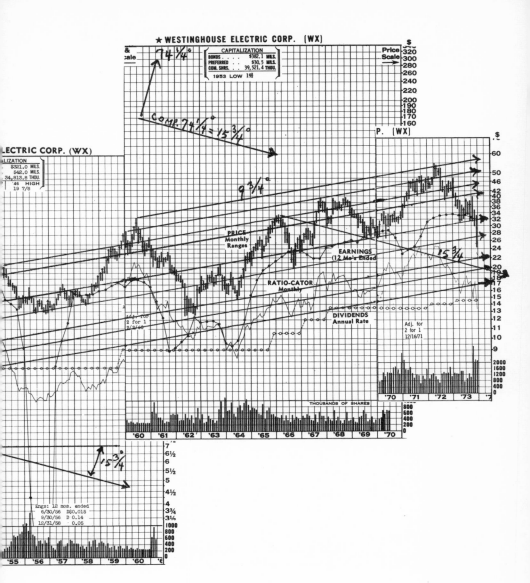

SECTION THREE, CHART TWO

Chart Two of Westinghouse Electric illustrates the operation of the acute angle
(9¾°) in a forty-year time span. The complement (15¾°) of the principal angle
(74¼°) in operation on the downside trend is shown in only one instance in order
not to clutter the chart. The reader should study the chart for other points of
applicability.

205

SECTION THREE, CHART THREE

Chart Three of Westinghouse Electric shows the acute angle operating to pinpoint the October bull raid high in this stock.

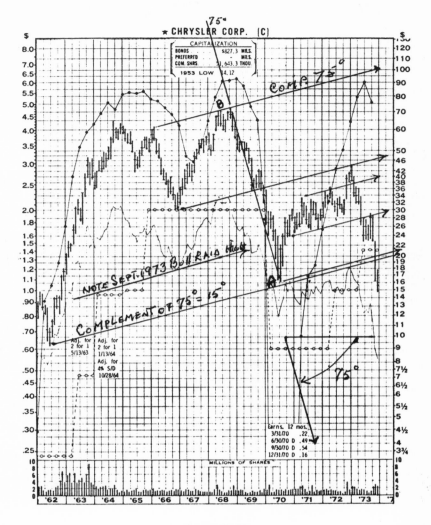

CHRYSLER
Section Four, Chart One

In the Chrysler examples, the 1970 low in the stock has been employed with the 1968 high in order to demonstrate that principal angles may be obtained from the existence of any *major* low. Chart One of Chrysler shows the use of the complement (15°) of the principal angle (75°—line AB) in Chrysler's advancing phase to pinpoint the September–October bull raid high.

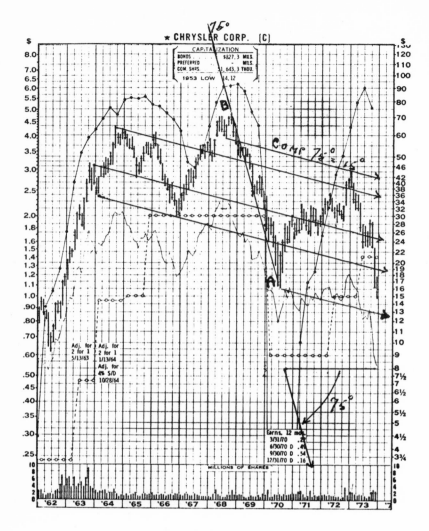

SECTION FOUR, CHART TWO

Chart Two of Chrysler shows how the complementary angle (15°) of the main angle (75°—line AB) indicates probable support and resistance levels in the stock's downtrend.

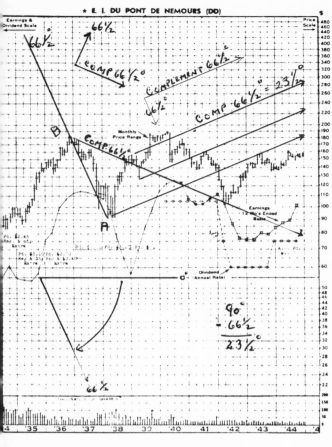

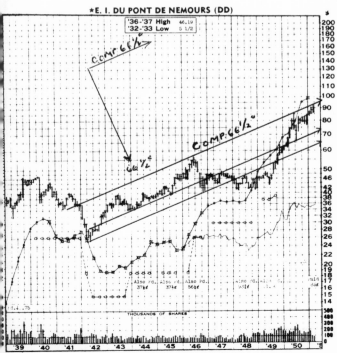

E. I. DU PONT
DE NEMOURS
SECTION FIVE,
CHART ONE AND TWO

Each of the Du Pont
charts illustrates the use
of the complement of
the principal angle.
Charts One and Two
illustrate the use of the
complement $(23\frac{1}{2}°)$ of
the principal angle
$(66\frac{1}{2}°$—line AB) in the
stock's advancing phases
through the 1938 to the
1951 period.

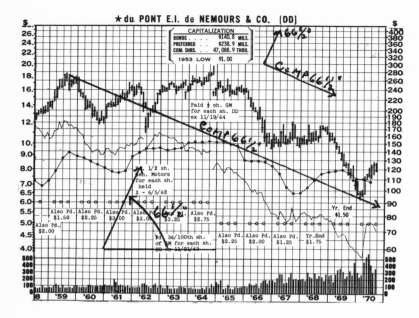

SECTION FIVE,
CHART THREE

Chart Three of Du Pont illustrates the use of the complement (23½°) of the principal angle (66½°) in the stock's long-term decline phase.

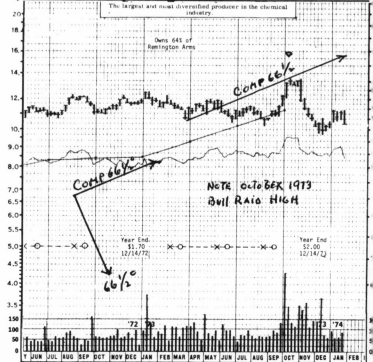

SECTION FIVE,
CHART FOUR

Chart Four of Du Pont shows how the complement (23½°) of the principal angle (66½°) served to pinpoint the October bull raid high in this stock.

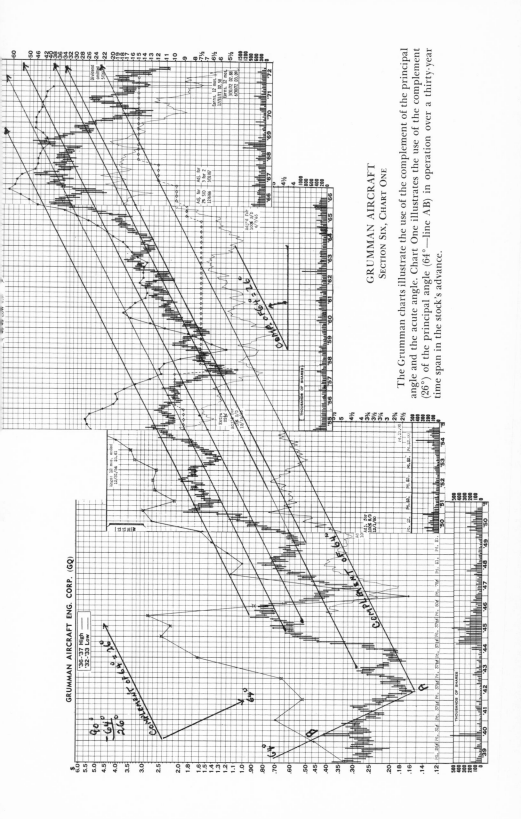

GRUMMAN AIRCRAFT
SECTION SIX, CHART ONE

The Grumman charts illustrate the use of the complement of the principal angle and the acute angle. Chart One illustrates the use of the complement (26°) of the principal angle (64°—line AB) in operation over a thirty-year time span in the stock's advance.

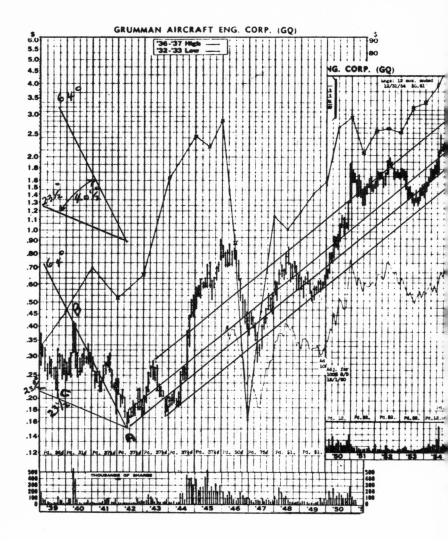

GRUMMAN AIRCRAFT ENG. CORP. (GQ)

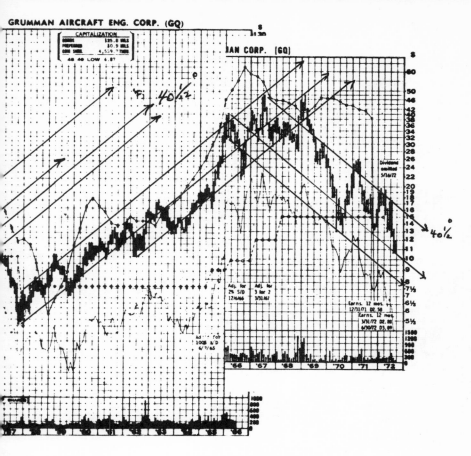

SECTION SIX, CHART TWO

Chart Two of Grumman exhibits the function of the acute angle (40½°) in the stock's long-term advancing phase. Its operation in the declining phase is illustrated only in one area in order to preserve the visual image of the acute angle in the advancing phase. The reader should study the chart for further instances of applicability.

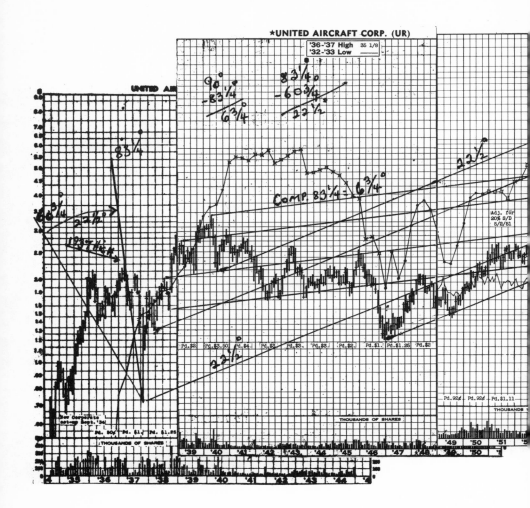

UNITED AIRCRAFT
SECTION SEVEN, CHART ONE

The chart of United Aircraft illustrates the interaction of the complement ($6\frac{3}{4}°$) of the principal angle ($83\frac{1}{4}°$—line AB) and the acute angle ($22\frac{1}{2}°$). To see this interaction in operation, I would suggest the reader observe the way the stock's price structure advanced along the complementary angle from 1959 until it came in contact with the acute angle in 1963. The reader will be able to observe other instances on this chart where these two forces interacted.

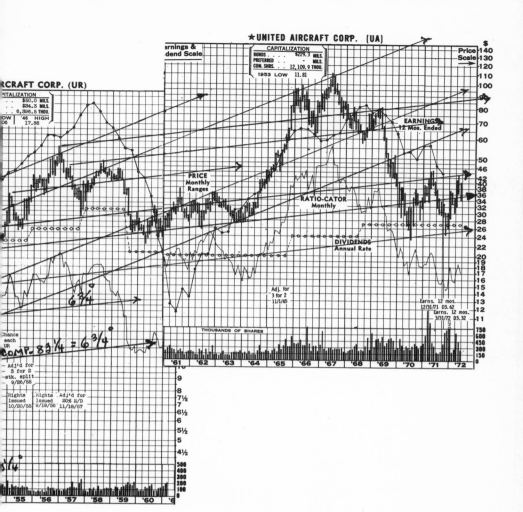

★ UNITED AIRCRAFT CORP. (UA)

CAPITALIZATION
BONDS . . . . $229.3 MILS.
PREFERRED . . . - MILS.
COM. SHRS. . . . 12,109.9 THOU.
1953 LOW 11.81

Price Scale →

Earnings & Dividend Scale

RCRAFT CORP. (UR)
CAPITALIZATION
. . . $50.0 MILS.
. . . $54.3 MILS.
. . . 6,396.5 THOU.
OW '46 HIGH
06   17.88

PRICE
Monthly
Ranges

RATIO-CATOR
Monthly

EARNINGS
12 Mos. Ended

DIVIDENDS
Annual Rate

Adj. for
3 for 2
11/1/65

Earns. 12 mos.
12/31/71 D3.62
Earns. 12 mos.
3/31/72 D3.32

6¾

Chance
each
UR

COMP. 83¼ = 6¾

Adj'd for
3 for 2
stk. split
9/26/55

Rights
Issued
10/20/55

Rights
Issued
9/19/56

Adj'd for
20% S/D
11/18/57

8¼

THOUSANDS OF SHARES

'61 '62 '63 '64 '65 '66 '67 '68 '69 '70 '71 '72

'55 '56 '57 '58 '59 '60

215

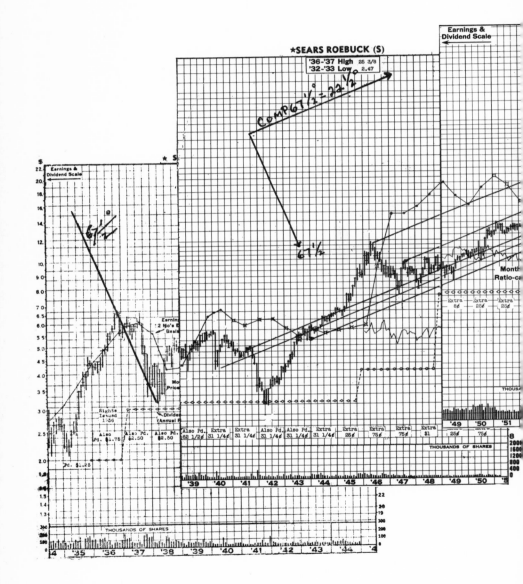

★SEARS ROEBUCK (S)

'36-'37 High 25 3/8
'32-'33 Low 2.47

COMP 6⅛ = 22 ½

216

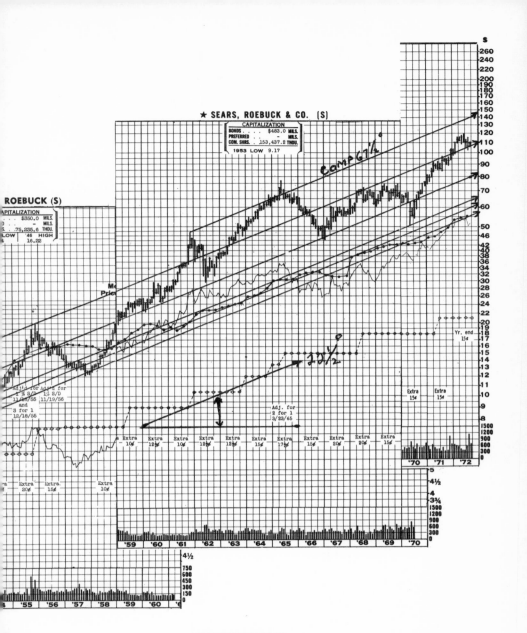

SEARS ROEBUCK
SECTION EIGHT, CHART ONE

Sears serves to further illustrate the operation of the complement (22½°) of the principal angle (67½°—line AB). It should be noted that the reason for the greater precision in the way the price structure follows the blueprint established by the complementary angle can be attributed to the fact that there is much greater trading activity in a stock like Sears than in a stock like Grumman. It is this greater activity that enables a stock's specialists to exercise greater control over that stock's price movements.

11. Litigation: The Ultimate Weapon

*In which the value of litigation is shown to be that
it's the only activity in which the stockbroker must
take reality into account.*

The great achievement of those who exercise control over the
Stock Exchange is not their great power and wealth; it is that they
have adapted their strange caperings to the framework of a society
suffering from prefrontal fraud. We have seen how, in relating
means to ends, they employ a succession of deceptions and schemes
to defraud the vulnerable interests of those to whom they are
legally liable.

In almost every area, the investor's ephemeral well-being has
been destroyed by those in government who, with indecent haste,
seem perversely determined to identify with the boxoffice interests
of the Exchange community. Without the active consensus of government it would be impossible for the Exchange to exercise such
an astonishing succession of controls over investors.

In the beginning, the consensus that now exists within government may have been as uninformed as most investors about the
nature of the Exchange's practices. But there is no question that,
granted the power to choose, during the last forty years the regulatory agencies have persistently and stubbornly chosen to sacrifice
the well-being of the investor for their own self-interest. The fact
is, the levers of financial control have been placed beyond the
grasp of the average investor by the mocking rituals and limiting
potentials of the Exchange and its remote governmental agencies.
The total result is that investors now find themselves faced with a
financial conglomerate that behaves according to certain irresistible
laws, all of which are bent on the investor's destruction.

Regrettably the SEC's deep commitment on behalf of the Exchange has irrevocably interlocked it with the Exchange and the

conditions that surround its routines. Granting priority to the Exchange's objectives, they have translated them into the over-all direction of regulatory policy. So that, thanks to the regulators placed in power to protect the investor, the essential materials and tragic source of all the investor's problems can be largely defined as stemming from regulatory principles that are in plain contradiction to the statutory intent of the securities acts.

This raises the question, Do investors have standing to press claims in court against the Exchange on the basis of existing securities laws? Certainly, it seems to me and to securities lawyers to whom I've addressed the question, Exchange misfeasance fits within the criteria of the antifraud provisions of the 1934 Act. Certainly the sections in this act declaring it "unlawful for *any* person directly or indirectly by the use of *any* means to employ *any* device, scheme or artifice to defraud . . . in connection with the purchase or sale of *any* security" were intended to have the broadest possible application. As I intend to show in the final chapter, due to the special responsibilities the Exchange insider has for the well-being of the invstor, I believe that sections of this act apply to the practices of the Exchange insider and therefore give the investor grounds for suit.

I continue to be astonished, however, that so many millions of investors, untroubled by questions of principle, are reluctant to involve themselves in litigation even when they find themselves brought to the pitch of despair by the frauds of those who pretend to serve them. Perhaps this is attributable to public ignorance of what constitutes an infringment of their rights. Most stockbrokers are familiar with what constitutes fraud; managers and partners of brokerage firms know what should be done to *avoid* fraud. They also know that their customers are largely ignorant of their merchandising techniques, and they exploit this ignorance. For these reasons I have prepared the chapter that follow. While it is hoped they will cause an awakening for many investors by quickening some dark corner of their thinking, nothing could be more in error than to assume that I am attempting to end the book with a magician's flourish that places a rabbit in every investor's hat.

I am not a lawyer. I am, however, aware of the practical problems faced by investors and the general nature of the information they need about the securities laws and the remedies available to them. I have sought, therefore, to open up to public inspection legal principles relating to the conduct of the brokerage business and some of the courses of action that are available to investors when they believe they've been defrauded. I shall also provide examples of the action taken by other investors when they encountered problems in this area. Lastly, I shall provide some of my thoughts on the court system and securities lawyers, and on how I think the investor who needs a lawyer should proceed to select one.

First of all, the investor must have some understanding of what constitutes fraud and of the more commonplace kinds of fraud investors are likely to encounter. For this it is important that he have some acquaintance with the securities acts.

An understanding of Stock Exchange and stockbroker fraud cannot be improvised. It is the product of vigilant insights into the principles of right and wrong, of adaptation to existing law and above all to the clarifications of precedent-establishing litigation. In the absence of these insights and this understanding, hundreds of new laws can be passed and although the financial establishment's lawyers will have learned a great deal in the process, the investing public will not have added one iota to the body of knowledge needed to keep the frauds of the stockbroker community within bounds.

The investor must then learn how to employ the existing criteria of ideas, proposals, and measures that have been successfully put forth by others to counter the consequence of fraud. In many respects the indignation, frustration, and despair of the stockbroker community and the manner in which these cases are being fought by brokerage firms are reminiscent of Napoleon's rearguard action at Waterloo.

More than ever before, the whole apparatus of due process gives the investor access to and utilization of substantive findings, opinions, and precedents that can phrase his sense of outrage far more effectively than useless complaints, grief resumés, or obscenities directed at the heads of his brokerage firm. Insight is wanted, not invective.

The investor, unaware of the body of emerging law that buttresses his authority, invokes nonlegal principles such as custom, fair play, and tradition. He operates on the assumption that self-regulation can keep self-interest within bounds. His naïveté has served to accelerate the breakdown in the relationship between market insiders and the public.

In far too many instances investors don't realize they are being subjected to manipulative practices in which their accounts are being mismanaged primarily for the purpose of increasing commissions. They are also unaware of the common law principle known as "respondent superieur." This rule of law places liability on the brokerage firm itself for the "tortuous" behavior of its stockbrokers when they are "acting within the scope of their employment of apparent authority."[1] One important implication of this principle is that a brokerage firm can be held *financially* liable for the actions of its salesmen. What the 1934 Securities and Exchange Act did was to make general statements about rules of conduct which should exist for the Stock Exchange and the corporate insiders in relation to the public. In recent years these generalizations, because of one lawsuit after another, have begun to acquire definition. For example, Rule 10b-5 of the act now reads:

> It shall be unlawful for any person, directly or indirectly, by the use of any means or instrumentality of interstate commerce, or of the mails, or of any facility of any national securities exchange,
>
> (1) to employ any device, scheme, or artifice to defraud,
> (2) to make any untrue statement of a material fact or to omit to state a material fact necessary in order to make the statements made, in the light of the circumstances under which they were made, not misleading, or
> (3) to engage in any act, practice, or course of business which operates or would operate as a fraud or deceit upon any person,
>
> in connection with the purchase or sale of any security.

In addition, SEC rule 15c1-7(a) prohibits the use of any manipulative devices in connection with the offer, sale, or purchase of securities. It also condemns the use of "any device, scheme, or artifice to defraud," along with "any practice or course of business which operates or would operate as a fraud or deceit." According to the SEC, "the term 'manipulative, deceptive, or other fraudulent device or contrivance' . . . is hereby defined to include any act of any broker or dealer designed to effect with or for any customer's account in respect to which such broker or dealer . . . is vested with *any* discretionary power over *any* transactions . . . which are excessive in *size* or *frequency* in view of the financial resources and character of such account."

In and of themselves the securities acts of 1933 and 1934 did very little, if anything, to eliminate the fraudulent practices of Wall Street's wealthy criminal classes. Obviously, the rules prohibiting fraud are very general and meant to cover all possible exigencies. Often, a suit for fraud is dropped because it is merely a case of the customer's word against the broker's.

Fortunately for investors, guidelines and legal precedent have been established for the most common fraud, churning. In the SEC rule cited above, the Commission stipulated that churning was the favored manipulative device used by brokers to increase

[1] *Mosedrelli* v. *Stamm,* EDNY, 1968.

commissions. In one case, a Court of Appeals stated, "We cannot visualize any circumstance to which the statutory phrase, 'manipulative device, or other fraudulent device or contrivance' applies more aptly than (churning)."[2] Here at last we had a definitive statement regarding an area where a great deal of doubt had existed. The way the securities acts were worded had allowed the industry to weasel its way out of cases in which investors sought to equate churning with a "manipulative" or "fraudulent" device. Gradually the stockbroker was being pitted against the inexorable force of a body of law. The possibilities were improving for a new relationship between investors and the securities industry.

There is not the slightest question that the present system of compensation should be changed. A broker's income should not be tied to the volume of his customers' transactions. It is absurd to have the SEC preaching "investor protection" while it sanctions a form of compensation that causes brokers to be directed toward aggressively increasing their commissions. By the same token, the "incentive commission" paid brokers for the distribution of big blocks is another form of militant treason against investors. Yet, because it helps the Exchange member to unload large blocks, the broker is encouraged to collect an "incentive commission" regardless of the cost to his customer. There is a resounding absurdity to a situation in which the Exchange insists brokers observe their fiduciary obligations and then uses the incentive commission because it "invites special brokerage efforts."[3] It must be apparent to any judge who is willing to see things as they are that under these conditions all standards of value are reversed, that such devices serve only to enable the Exchange to "manipulate" the broker into conflict with the intent of the antifraud provisions of the securities acts. According to another court's findings; "Doubtless, considerable injury to the investing public is not only possible but inevitable when a salesman is compensated in direct proportion to the volume of transactions he handles."[4]

Because brokers work on a commission basis or on a salary plus bonuses based on the amount of their business, the Exchange has created a rat race for the customer's dollar. It is impossible for the broker to observe his fiduciary obligations without upsetting the system. As for the broker who consistently refuses to push big blocks that Merrill Lynch contracts to sell, he would be looked upon as so much useless lumber, as well as something of an embarrassment. It is absurd, for example, to suppose that the general

2 *Norris and Hirshberg* v. *SEC* (D.C. Cir.), Aff'g 21 SEC. 883 (1949).
3 "Investment Manager's Handbook," published by the NYSE.
4 *Lorenz* v. *Watson* (E.D., Pa., 1966).

counsel of a brokerage firm is speaking from the heart when he protests against the calculating self-interest of brokers who churn their customers' accounts when they can see the heads of their firms exhausting their energies in a search for "high-producing salesmen." There are rules that can measure a man's qualifications to function as a "fiduciary." There are also rules that measure a man's qualifications to perform as a top producer. It would be naïve to suppose the former have anything to do with the latter.

On February 14, 1973, the *Wall Street Journal* ran a story on an internal memorandum from the executive vice-president of Bache & Co. According to the *Journal:*

RAIDING ON WALL STREET
REVIVES AS FIRMS SEEK
HIGH-VOLUME SALESMEN

Bache & Co. has revived a policy of offering bounties to certain of its personnel who woo away high producing salesmen from other firms. . . .

The bonus will be paid only after the first year of the new man's employment, and *only if he produces at least $50,000 in gross commission in his first year* while meeting Bache's employment standards. [Emphasis added.]

It is impossible for a brokerage firm to prevent churning when its emphasis is on acquiring what Bache in its advertisements refers to as "super-salesmen."

A memorandum sent on February 22, 1972, by Howard Sprow, general counsel of Merrill Lynch, to its stockbrokers reveals the Stock Exchange member's attitude toward broker production and churning. Having assembled a vast array of facts concerning securities violations, Sprow concentrated them within the confines of four short pages. Aware that there are as many mad customers lurking outside his boardroom's doorways (with their lawyers) as there are misfits in the brokerage end of the securities business, and that many of these have already breached the bare edges of legal solvency, he couches his words in circumspect legalese. He bears on his stockbrokers' difficulties in a way that reveals as much as possible to them and as little as possible to the customers. He is more cautious than candid. Yet the candor is there.

One may observe its extent as he diagnoses the primary ailment of the brokerage industry—*"too many commissions!"* Having pinpointed the cause of the infection, he suggests the remedy by striking straight at the root of Merrill Lynch's problems, that calculating piece of clay, the stockbroker:

GENERAL COUNSEL INFORMATION MEMORANDUM
February 22, 1972

OFFICERS:
OFFICE MANAGERS:
DEPARTMENT MANAGERS:
ACCOUNT EXECUTIVES:
HOLDERS OF OPERATIONS MANUAL:

TOO MANY COMMISSIONS

Churning is easier to define than it is to identify. We can define it as "excessive trading in an account which is induced by a broker for the purpose of generating commissions." As you can see, much of that definition is subject to interpretation. What, for example, is excessive? How do you determine when trading is induced? How do you determine the motivation or intent of the broker? To attempt to measure these matters, the SEC devised certain guidelines which it used in many of the administrative proceedings it brought against brokers on churning charges. Although in the past relatively few cases of churning reached the courts, there have been an interesting number within the past two years, and the court decisions plainly rely heavily upon these unofficial SEC guidelines. The result of this has been to hold brokers to higher standards of accountability than had been the case a few years ago. Let us examine these guidelines and see what they can tell us.

1) Control by account executive--in order to sustain a charge of churning, the customer must be able to demonstrate that the account was "controlled" by his account executive. If the account executive exercises discretion either formally, or with the tacit acquiescence of the customer, he has control over the account. An account executive also can exercise control without exercising discretion. This occurs where the customer relies to such an extent upon the account executive's recommendations that he rubber stamps suggestions which are offered to him. The SEC put it this way: "It has long been established that a broker-dealer or salesman

who uses his relationship of trust and
confidence to a customer to cause an
excessive number of transactions in a
customer's account commits fraud upon the
customer, whether or not the account is a
discretionary one."

2) Relationship between commissions and
profits--the second guideline is the
establishment of a high ratio of commissions
as compared to the customer's profits. In
other words, who benefited from the
activity: the broker or the customer?

3) Turnover Rate--the third guideline is a
mathematical formula called the rate of
turnover. This is calculated by taking a
total of the dollar value of purchases during
the period under review--whether it is three
months or three years--and dividing it by the
average equity in the account for the same
period. The figure carried out to two decimal
places is the "turnover rate." There is no
"acceptable" turnover rate for obvious
reasons, but the courts have considered a
rate of turnover of slightly over twice a
year to be excessive. Naturally, the turnover
rate would be greater for an account with a
small amount of money invested.

It is important to note that in any case brought by
the SEC, all three of these elements were present.
It was not simply a case of establishing any one of
them.

Let us turn now to some of the more common defenses
which brokers have attempted to raise against a
charge of churning. One of these is the fact that a
customer may have made profits during the course of
the activity. Both the SEC and the courts have
dismissed this. In one recent case a U.S. District
Court stated: "The fact that an account may have
showed a net profit is not an absolute defense to a
charge of churning." Several recent suits have been
based upon the theory that if the account had been
left undisturbed instead of trading, the

good-quality securities which the accounts had at the inception of the activity would have increased substantially in price. The courts have not thus far been sympathetic to this hindsight type of reasoning and so they have not required brokers to reimburse their customers on this basis. However, the courts have also taken the position that a customer's inability to recover these alleged damages does not absolve the broker of responsibility for churning an account. The broker may be required to pay damages based upon a different type of yardstick. Often these damages have consisted of a refund of commissions and interest on debit balances charged during the period.

Another possible defense is the sophistication, wealth and desire of the customers to trade. The SEC's notion of what constitutes a sophisticated customer differs markedly from the ideas of some brokers. In some cases, individuals who were considered unsophisticated by the Commission were persons of considerable education and stature within their own professions. These included a trade publication editor, a school teacher, an engineer and a comptroller. The SEC's theory was that knowledge or expertise in their own vocations did not necessarily make them knowledgeable where securities were concerned. The customer's wealth also is irrelevant to whether or not the account has been churned. The SEC has said unequivocally "that the customer may be of substantial means is no defense of a charge of excessive trading." Finally, the customer's own desire to trade must be considered against his knowledge of the risks involved in trading. For an unsophisticated customer--using the SEC's definition of that term--it may be that short-term trading can never be justified.

What can we say then about our own desire to serve our customers' interests and at the same time avoid regulatory fallout? The conscientious use of our monthly activity reviews and the Code 8s is our first line of defense against the mishandling of

an account. Several aspects of that review take a
particular significance in light of the foregoing
discussion.

1) Control over the account, as we have seen, is
   an essential ingredient in the charge of
   churning. We can see then that the question
   on the first page of the Code 8, relating to
   where the customer gets his ideas, is not a
   frivolous one. This question ought to be
   taken seriously and the answers to it must be
   truthful.

2) The background information about a customer
   can give us an indication of his
   sophistication. The information regarding his
   other accounts, his experience, occupation,
   objectives, and worth are all clues, but
   probably the only accurate means of making a
   judgment are through a personal contact by
   the manager with any account which is
   particularly active. Again, we have to keep
   in mind that trading is not for everybody.

3) The turnover rate and profitability of an
   account is an essential clue to any possible
   complaints alleging churning. Although
   profits in themselves, as we have seen, are
   no defense, it is rare that a customer who is
   making money will complain. The time to slow
   down an overactive customer is while he is
   making money and not after his capital has
   been wiped out. An integral part of the
   monthly activity review is a profit and loss
   study and analysis of the turnover rate.
   Another useful guide is a comparison of
   commissions with the amount of capital
   invested. If commissions over a period of
   several months are equal to a significant
   portion of the customer's capital, the
   account ought to be examined carefully. No
   review of an active account is complete
   without an examination of the statement.
   Such signal flags as day trading, frequent
   in-and-out trading, late payments, and

> short-term losses will be obvious from even a glance at a statement.

Churning may not be easy to describe, but it can and should be prevented.

HOWARD T. SPROW

As he sets about his tasks, Merrill Lynch's chief counsel tells his brokers only what is useful to them. He lays down three principles to indicate the general lines along which they must solve their problems. First, if their customers pay them the compliment of asking what stocks to buy and they supply the answer, they have immediately become infected. They have what is called "control." This is one of the most dangerous viruses in the commission business. Second, if the "profitability" of the account is such that the customer makes $1,000 on his investment during a twelve-month period and the brokerage firm makes $1,500 in commissions and interest, the broker can be said to be in need of surgery. Third and last, if the total dollar value of his customer's purchases during this twelve-month period is $30,000 and if the average equity in his account during this period is $10,000, then the turnover rate is 3 times. In that case, since "the courts have considered a rate of turnover of slightly over twice a year to be excessive," it can be said that his ailment is no longer operable. Under the circumstances the best thing he can do for Merrill Lynch and for himself is to seek a change of locale under a different name.

While Sprow discusses the broker's difficulties with his customers and illustrates them admirably, he wisely refrains from trying to explain how the broker is to survive if he builds up the "fiduciary" side of his operations at the expense of his commission business. Nor in his memorandum does he tell his brokers that Merrill Lynch will dismiss them if they are caught churning (since all accounts are supervised it can be assumed Merrill Lynch *knows* which brokers are churning). He leaves the course of action up to them (instead of their supervisors) by telling them, "Although profits in themselves, as we have seen, are no defense, it is rare that a customer who is making money will complain. The time to slow down an *overactive* customer is while he is making money and not after his capital has been wiped out."

In the following examples I will show that, while there may be fundamental differences of character, upbringing, and education among investors, they are all basically highly vulnerable because of their ignorance of the market. Although a "good" broker can get to a man as easily as to a woman, most women exhibit too great a willingness to come under the control of their stockbrokers in the decision-making process. Widows, almost without exception, can be counted upon to be too trusting to begin with and uproariously indignant when they find their trust has been betrayed. It would seem at first glance that the widow's shortcomings as an investor are the inevitable consequence of her inability to cope with the financial problems suddenly thrust on her. The history of widows, however, is symptomatic of the average investor's plight. However overwhelming the evidence pointing to her vulnerability, the explosive truth is that the widow's tragic experience equates with those of doctors and other supposedly more sophisticated individuals. There is only this difference: Once they become widows they become little islands of money surrounded by stockbrokers. With them as his target, the broker need scarcely take aim. They are everywhere.

The average widow's condition in the market can be attributed to the SEC's, the New York Stock Exchange's and the media's desire to inspire confidence in the market. A widow living in Minnesota wrote to me as follows:

> I never had a chance in the market and I lost ten thousand dollars, a tragedy for me because I am a widow well along in years and needed to conserve my capital. Frankly, I never dealt with an ethical stockbroker. They all took advantage of my ignorance of the stock market and didn't care about anything except their commissions.
>
> A year ago I reported to the Securities and Exchange Commission that a stockbroker had made fraudulent statements to me . . . and the only thing the SEC did was to turn over my correspondence to the counsel of the brokerage house, which, of course, accomplished nothing.
>
> Recently I wrote the New York Stock Exchange that unsophisticated, trusting buyers are not protected from unethical, greedy stockbrokers, and that it is a scandal for such a huge and lucrative industry to prey upon the unwary.

The tragedy is that she became involved in an enterprise in which nobody cared whether she survived or died.

All one can do to help in such a situation is recommend that, if she can afford an action at law, she must seek the advice of a competent attorney to determine whether or not she can sue with any chance of recovery. For practical purposes, letter writing is a waste of time unless it's by a lawyer. The brokerage industry has discovered that his letters can't be ignored. Unfortunately, this lady could not afford an attorney. If she could have, however, she would still have had to contend with the fact that all too few attorneys know anything about the securities industry.

A second letter is from another widow in Orange County, California. She and her fellow plaintiffs (also widows) were transported from riches to rags by their stockbroker. This is what she has to say:

> Please find [enclosed] the clippings of a pending case I am involved in with Mrs. —— and Mrs. ——. These two ladies are elderly, and Mrs. —— earned the money she put in the market by nursing and walking the halls of hospitals, making as little as fifty cents an hour, in years gone by.
>
> I myself have cancer and this money was left to me as insurance by my husband, an air force major killed in Vietnam.
>
> While I was in the hospital with my second mastectomy and much other surgery, this person was really ruining me. . . .
>
> I have teenagers and am living on social security and VA compensation. This is hard. . . . I feel these teenagers deserve more than this as it was their father's wish and he provided it.
>
> I did not know or understand what was going on, and I was with [my broker] only 97 days. But he really fixed me. I was very ill, also . . . we do need our money. I am ill and the others are elderly.

The clippings told me that her broker had also been the brokerage house manager and at long last was about to get his comeuppance. He'd been arraigned in Superior Court on charges of grand theft and violation of California securities laws and was being kept under lock and key in the county jug. All three widows had caught him purring over their widow's mite as though it was a saucer of milk. The deputy district attorney commented: "An analysis of the five client accounts . . . showed that the broker 'turned over' one 80-year-old woman's stock portfolio 5.26 times in 21 months without her knowledge, and switched her investment from conservative 'blue chip' stocks into more speculative issues." He added "Other customers' accounts had similar histories." This widow and her co-plaintiffs had been victimized of $180,000. On November 15, 1971, they were awarded $36,000. But they were unable to collect. The brokerage firm went bankrupt, and the broker skipped.

I spoke to the widow's attorney and asked him why the SEC had not stepped into the case in order to protect his clients, why, in fact, they allow such brokerage firms to continue under the principle of self-regulation. His thoughts add to our stock of benign insights into the workings of that institution:

> The SEC is a piece of _ _ _ _. Their effectiveness is getting less and less every day. I have another stock fraud case going now and they're doing the same thing. These people are out and out thieves and they'll never get prosecuted. . . .

That's why these stock frauds consistently occur. Only because of the SEC. Not in spite of, but because of the SEC. These people are smart enough to know that the very worst thing that will happen to them is maybe there will be an injunction against them from selling their rotten stock. . . . And that's the extent of the punishment.

I should perhaps state, parenthetically, that if this highly accomplished lawyer speaks in the vernacular, it is possibly because he ruminates on images of bureaucratic neglect and indifference that he cannot banish, and because fair play toward his clients is the substance of his life. His words are a fresh image of an expert's view on the matter.

Having worked in the capacity of an expert witness with a number of lawyers, I must confess that the brokerage industry's lawyers tend to make Christmas pies out of those retained by the public. But there are exceptions. In the following chapter we describe how one such lawyer's awakened intelligence about securities law turned the tables on the stockbrokers who swindled his client. Indeed, all investors for generations to come should be reminded that

> There once was a widow named Hecht
> who by her stockbroker was wrecked
> she became so overwrought
> she haled him to court
> where the judge said "O Lord this
> sure smells of fraud
> and fraud by gawd is a tort."

12. Bertha Hecht Borrows the Financial Establishment's Pot and Cooks Its Goose in It

In which it is shown that, although the determination of what constitutes damages must all too often be compatible with the self-interest of the judge who has jurisdiction, the unhappy investor's best investment opportunity may still lie in grasping the favorable occasions presented by the courts for exploiting his disappointments.

The Bertha Hecht case is important because it involves the common-run fraud of overtrading or "churning" of the sort encountered by most investors. Since it represents the most ordinary kind of fraud, the case is a mother lode for investors who have been similarly exploited. The unexpectedness with which it was uncovered, its extent and duration, and the infinite variety of techniques employed by the stockbroker should make it of inexhaustible interest to investors.

The Hecht decision was handed down in 1970. It made an enormous contribution to the body of securities law. By raising the hazy, half-assimilated ideas surrounding over-trading to the level of a "deceptive and fraudulent practice," it gave the investor a weapon that would enable him to press future lawsuits based on the secure footing of legal precedent.

In the past the findings of self-regulatory bodies like the National Association of Securities Dealers have tended to favor the interests of the defendant brokers. This was inevitable: Their members are individuals whose backgrounds, indoctrination, and instincts caused them to identify with stockbrokers instead of their customers. Accordingly, their findings, along with the extent and degree of punishment for securities violations, are never as harsh as they can be when justice is handed down by the courts. For this reason if you are an investor, you would have to be pleased with the findings and precedents established by Judge Sweigert, the presiding judge of the United States District Court for the Northern District of California. As a vehicle to the recovery of damages, *Hecht* was ideal. It showed where the case against securities fraud had come from and where it was going.

The words of Thomas Fuller, seventeenth century English clergyman, bring into sharp focus the interior drama of Bertha Hecht and her lawsuit against Harris-Upham: "Take care how thou offendest those raised from low station." The words have a peculiar relevance to the explanation of why a widow in her seventies would be willing to risk what remained of her inheritance to conduct a lawsuit against this totem of the financial establishment.

Bertha Hecht was born and raised in England. In 1914, at the age of twenty-three, she moved to Canada to work as a private tutor. Shortly afterward she came to the United States.

She settled in New York, where she supervised manual training for young children. Years later she moved to San Francisco, where she worked as a saleswoman in a department store. In 1923 she became housekeeper and governess for a San Francisco family. At the end of fourteen years she left to assume the position of tutor in a school for girls.

In 1939, at the age of forty-nine, she was recommended by her school principal for the position of housekeeper and tutor in the home of Herbert Hecht, a resident of San Mateo County. Mr. Hecht's wife had just died, leaving him with a teen-age daughter. He was in the export-import business and, like most businessmen, dabbled in stocks. Although he was of sound mind and body, he also gambled in commodities. His securities and commodities accounts were both maintained at Merrill Lynch. His stockbroker was Asa Wilder.

In 1953 Bertha married Mr. Hecht, and they lived together for two years until he died of a heart attack in 1955. He left a large estate, which was divided equally between his wife and his daughter.

Although her salary during her years as a housekeeper was never more than $125 a month, Bertha allocated a considerable part of that amount to the purchase of stocks. She also maintained a small margin account with a brokerage firm from 1931 to 1936 in which she conducted about four to ten transactions a month. In 1936 she transferred her account to Walston & Company, with whom she remained until 1955.

In a period of sixteen years, from 1939 through 1955, there were thirty-two security sales and forty-one security purchases. In no single year were there more than five sales. More often there were fewer, or none at all. Starting with about $2,000, Mrs. Hecht increased the value of her account from 1931 to 1955 to approximately $65,000. Years later she would come to realize how much better she would have done in the market had she continued to follow the investment patterns of the odd-lot investor; her big-time broker's advice, like alcohol, was no more than an anesthetic against reality. In fact, she would have done much better had she used a ouija board to select five out of the thirty Dow Jones industrial stocks.

Stockbroker Wilder's acquaintance with Mrs. Hecht grew out of his relationship with her husband and developed after his death in both a social and a business sense. In her deposition Mrs. Hecht claimed Wilder had persuaded her to open a commodities account with him; in June, 1956, she wrote to him saying, "Start me on the soy beans when you think it is the right time." Several months later, in August, 1956, her account (maintained at Hooker and Fay at the time) was supplied with the stocks distributed to her from her husband's estate, having a market value of $486,620. This brought her account to a net value of $526,659. Mrs. Hecht dealt with Hooker and Fay for a period of twenty-one months. In May, 1957, Wilder transferred her account to Harris-Upham, where he had been made the brokerage firm's San Francisco manager of commodities. Mrs. Hecht's account by then had a net value of $533,161.

She continued to deal through Wilder with Harris-Upham for six years and ten months, until March, 1964, when she learned from her income tax accountants that the net value of her account had dropped to $251,000. Sounding her trumpet, she went to war. She brought suit against Wilder, Harris-Upham, and others for alleged violations of the Securities Acts of 1933 and 1934, the rules of the National Association of Securities Dealers, and the common law of the State of California. Her case, as the financial establishment was about to learn, had much to recommend it.

Lowenthal and Lowenthal of San Francisco were the attorneys for Mrs. Hecht. Beyond the circumstances of Morris Lowenthal's function as an attorney versed in securities law lay the more general attitudes of a great and liberally oriented gentleman. His briefs have established the syntax and vocabulary for landmark Supreme Court decisions involving the First Amendment. While it was not possible for him to present Mrs. Hecht in the context of stark naïveté, he so conclusively demonstrated not only the absence of integrity and judgment in Asa Wilder but also the mastering design of deception that Judge Sweigert entered a judgment in her favor. Harris-Upham and its representatives then appealed. The Appeals Court held that the brokerage firm and its salesmen were liable for damages caused by churning of the account and by conversion of the customer's securities through fraud and deceit.

It was revealed during the trial that in September, 1959, Wilder procured 102 shares of a savings and loan association stock from Mrs. Hecht (along with twenty shares he failed to deliver) just before a ten-for-one split. Mrs. Hecht had paid him $15,000 ($125 per share) for these shares. After the split, the old shares were worth about $360 per share. With characteristic foresight, just prior to the split Wilder obtained from Mrs. Hecht a transfer to himself of her shares together with the twenty undelivered shares. He contended they were a gift to him; Mrs. Hecht denied this. The court found she was entitled to recovery of $45,920!

Earlier, in November, 1958, Wilder purchased 100 shares of ITEK stock at $94 per share. The purchase was unlawful, since the stock had not been "blue-skied." When this was called to his attention, he called on Mrs. Hecht, told her the stock was speculative, and redeemed it from her, knowing that ITEK had declared a 400 per cent stock dividend, as of January, 1959. As a result the stock appreciated in value from $94 to $300 a share. Wilder gave Mrs. Hecht a check for $9,400, had her endorse the new shares over to himself, and placed the shares in his wife's account. Later he sold the stock for $25,400. The court required Wilder to return the difference between the $9,400 he paid Mrs. Hecht and $30,000, the market value at the date he purchased the stock from her.

As for the over-trading, while Mrs. Hecht was prevented from asserting that Wilder's trading for her was "unsuitable," it is important to understand why the brokerage firm was held liable for losses caused by churning and why, although the imposition of punitive damages is customary in cases of willful or intentional tort, the courts refused to do so on this occasion. There is reason to believe the court erred in this respect and that future decisions in similar cases will award exemplary damages.

According to the trial transcript,

> the account . . . was very actively traded, both in securities and commodities. During the 6 year and 10 month period, over 10,000 transactions occurred, with a gross dollar volume of about $100,000,000. About 1200–1400 of these transactions (with a dollar volume of 9½

million) involved transactions in 200 different corporate stocks. About 9000 transactions (with a gross dollar volume of about 90 million) involved transactions in various commodities.

In the course of these transactions, plaintiff's account showed an overall profit during the period on the securities side of about $164,773. On the commodity side it showed profits of about $515,000, but losses of about $690,000—an overall loss on commodities during the period of about $176,000. Thus, plaintiff's account showed an overall net loss of about $12,000 in the combined securities and commodities accounts.

Although Mrs. Hecht's losses amounted to only $12,000, court testimony brought out the fact that Harris-Upham had received *$295,800* in commissions and interest from her during this period. According to Judge Sweigert, her stockbroker had "grossly and unfairly churned her account for no justifiable reason other than to generate profits for the firm and, indirectly, for himself." The judge also pointed out that, had her portfolio been left intact, it would have had a net value of $1,026,775 by March, 1964.

What makes *Hecht* so interesting is that in so many respects it is a perfectly routine case of the stockbroker exploiting his customer's ignorance. The court record states:

On an account of about $500,000 plaintiff paid commissions and markups of $189,000 in security and commodity transactions and interest of $43,000—a total of $232,000, or about 40% of the size of the account, without considering plaintiff's capital gain taxes, which further affected the possibilities for net gain.

Commission's earned by Harris, Upham Co., on plaintiff's account on security transactions—$76,000—were more than any other of the firm's 8000 to 9000 security accounts in the San Francisco office—except 11–14 other accounts—and amounted to 39% of all security commissions generated by Wilder.

Commissions earned by Harris, Upham from plaintiff's account on commodity transactions—$98,333—were more than any other commodity account at its San Francisco office—31% of all commodity commissions at that office, and 59% of all commodity commissions generated by Wilder.

Although plaintiff's account represented less than 1/10 of 1% of the accounts in the San Francisco office, the commissions ($174,000) and the interest ($43,000) charged plaintiff represented at least 4.7% of the total income of the San Francisco office . . . about 50 times the average charged a customer during the period.

In the course of 1200–1400 security transactions and 4457 closed commodity transactions, Wilder generated 51% of the total commissions earned by him for Harris, Upham.

Regrettably, there is no precise rule or formula for defining churning. Nonetheless, criteria established by the volume and frequency of trades, the nature of the account, and the needs and requirements of the customer can indicate to the court whether the broker's trading was excessive so that he might derive profits for himself, or whether he was more concerned about his customer's interests. Bertha Hecht's case contributed greatly to a definitive understanding of what constitutes churning. According to Judge Sweigert:

> Where a customer so relies upon the recommendations of the broker that the broker is in a position to control the volume and frequency of transactions, and the broker, abusing the confidence reposed in him, recommends and induces an excessive number of transactions, involving multiple trading in the same security, and switches from one security to another, on which commissions and profits are taken without regard to the needs and objectives of the customer, then there is a device, scheme or artifice to defraud within the meaning of Securities Act of 1933 and Securities Exchange Act of 1934.

The SEC and the courts have insisted that individuals highly qualified in their respective professions can be as ignorant in matters pertaining to the stock market as their social, intellectual, or professional inferiors. According to the courts, this can be true of a doctor, lawyer, accountant, teacher, or, in one case, a state official in charge of enforcing the state's securities laws!

Most stockbrokers will fail to understand that, even though their customers do not vest formal discretionary authority with them, they still exercise "control" over that account if the customer is not a sophisticated trader. Judge Sweigert declared:

> Although control by representative of brokerage firm over account is essential to finding of churning, such control need not amount to formal vesting of discretion in representative, and degree of control sufficient to warrant protection may be inferred from evidence that customer invariably relied on dealer's recommendations, especially when customer is relatively naïve and unsophisticated.

It should be possible for most intelligent individuals to acquire enough expertise in the market so that ultimately they might be considered "sophisticated." Under the Exchange's system of censorship of all information coming off the floor of the Exchange, however, such expertise is not possible for any except a few professionals. Even the SEC has been obliged to concede that very few individuals fit this category. Nor has the investor's length of experience in the market anything to do with expertise. The truth of the matter is, the longer the investor is in the market the more false information he tends to accumulate, and the more "inexpert" he becomes. Unfortunately, he is all too often unaware of his lack of expertise. It is to be hoped that the courts will begin to base their conclusions concerning sophistication on the realities of the market. That will occur when it is understood that *any approach to the market is uninformed unless it is based on knowledge of what floor traders, specialists, their bankers, and others are doing on the floor of the Exchange for their own accounts.*

Bertha Hecht was helped in her case by an earlier decision in another case that found the habits of a certain broker fraudulent. The case concerned the revocation of the broker-dealer license of Looper & Co. by the SEC for excessive trading, secret profits, and extension of credit (April 15, 1958). We are indebted for these findings to the Chicago regional office of the SEC, *not* the Washington office.

As it applies to the Hecht case, the Looper case is important because it established the precedent that defined a turnover rate and what was considered "excessive." It is referred to as the "Looper interpretation":

> The turnover rate is computed by dividing the cost of the purchases by the average investment, the latter representing the cumulative total of the net investment in the account at the end of each month, exclusive of loans, divided by the number of months under consideration.

"Excessive" turnover was defined in *Looper* with the simple remark that, "in the period Looper acted for Friedman [another stockbroker], an average investment of $12,373 was turned over *2.4 times from October 1952 to April 1953 when trading ceased."* Thus we find that the SEC looks upon a turnover rate of *slightly more than two times* as excessive. Although Looper churned accounts considerably in excess of 2.4 times, 2.4 times is now the basic figure.

In addition to the turnover rate, Judge Sweigert concluded:

> Another consideration in determining churning is to inquire whether there has been a pattern of in-and-out trading, i.e., a sale of all or part of the customer's portfolio with the proceeds immediately reinvested in other securities followed in a short period by the sale of the newly acquired securities.

According to Judge Sweigert, the final consideration in determining whether an account has been churned or not is *"to compare the dealer's profits with the size of the customer's investment."*
Many brokerage firms maintain that excessive trading is not a

fraud on the customer when the customer's account shows a profit. The implied principle here is that crime in a good cause is honest, or all's well that ends well. Judge Sweigert has a different view:

> The mere fact that in the course of an account profits are made from time to time—or even the fact that an overall net profit is made—does not necessarily justify the churning of the account. Whether churning has occurred must be determined by the handling of the account as a whole.

The stockbroker's duty is to see to it that *all* things tend toward one final end—that end, of course, being the well-being of his customer. Judge Sweigert's decision places the brokerage business on notice that, while churning may make for happiness, it does not make for goodness.

To sum up, we can say that the factors that determine a pattern of churning are:

(1) whether the customer is sufficiently expert to exercise *control* over the account, or whether in fact the broker exercises control
(2) the number of times that money invested in the account is turned over
(3) whether this has been a pattern of in-and-out trading
(4) a comparison of the dealer's profits with the size of the customer's investment and the customer's profits

Harris-Upham sought to assert the defense that Asa Wilder's trading in commodities did not come under the jurisdiction of the acts of 1933 and 1934. Sweigert's decision, upheld by the Appeals Court, was that the true historical role of trading in commodities is to generate commissions for stockbrokers and brokerage firms. It stated:

> Excessive trading . . . in both securities and commodities did constitute a single scheme. . . . Wilder was able to effect an enormous amount of commodity trading by transferring a total of $245,360 from her security account to the commodities account. Thus, the security and commodity transactions were inextricably co-mingled. . . .
>
> Whatever may be the inherent differences between a security transaction on the one hand, and a commodity futures transaction on the other, there is no reason to say that churning, which has to do, not with single transactions, but with the volume and frequency of a series of transactions, can occur in a security account but not in a commodity account. The test in either case is whether under the circumstances the trading in the account [is] "excessive."

> . . . [That] where a registered representative, handling a securities account, induces a customer to open a commodities account to provide an additional opportunity for generating commissions, the commodity account may be regarded as a mere device for churning the securities account. . . .
>
> [That] the only reason for Wilder's encouragement of plaintiff . . . in the commodities market . . . was to . . . generate commissions. Wilder's knowledge of plaintiff's situation, needs and objectives was such that, regardless of plaintiff's acquiescence, any other reason for such trading in highly speculative commodities for a retired widow . . . must be ruled out.

Prior to the *Hecht* decision there had been considerable differences of opinion among existing authorities over the extent to which the different sections of the securities acts and the findings of regulatory bodies could be made applicable to the Hecht case. The primacy of one authority's sections over those of another (for example, of a state's statute of limitations over that of the securities acts) was more a matter of expediency than of law. The investment industry naturally wanted (and generally got) application of the shortest possible statute of limitations for suits on securities violations. *Hecht* contributed enormously to settling this and other questions to the investor's advantage.

While it is true that the legitimacy of the opinions in *Hecht* were based on the lawmaking authority of the acts of 1933 and 1934, the findings of the SEC (the "Looper interpretation"), and the findings of the NASD, such matters as suitability, due diligence, churning, the waiver of rights, statutes of limitations, and liability of brokerage houses were only some of the issues never before conjoined in a case brought by an individual investor under such unique circumstances.

The findings of the Appeals Court pointed out that Stock Exchange Rule 405 requires general partners or other persons designated by the firm, such as managers, to "use due diligence to learn the essential facts relative to every customer, every order, every cash or margin account carried by such organization [and to] supervise diligently all accounts handled by registered representatives."

Yet when a conscientious stockbroker (and there are some) attempts to observe "due diligence" and refuses to sell his customers highly questionable new issues or to purchase stock for them in a down market, more often he brings down upon himself the branch manager's wrath.

Many brokers allow their branch office managers to push them to increase the volume of transactions. Nor are most branch man-

agers the least bit hesitant about the kind of stocks they are willing to push or the suitability of those stocks for their firm's
customers. Because he wants to keep his job, the broker generally
does what he is told. He should, however, realize that the failure
to exercise "due diligence" will sooner or later lead to fraud, even
if it is unintentional. That being so he should cock his eye at the
Appeals Court's findings:

> The gist of an allegation of churning of securities account is fraud
> in law and is different from common law fraud in that a specific
> intent to defraud is unnecessary . . . where a single fraudulent
> scheme based on excessive churning of customer's account involved
> both securities and commodities, court was entitled to award cus-
> tomer damages for entire loss.

Stockbrokers should remember this. Despite the fact that it was
the manager or the partner who placed you in an uncompromising
position, he won't help you when the worst comes. At that time,
he will execute a remarkable *volte face* and suggest you betray the
trust he placed in you—and you will be fired.

But what about Harris-Upham in all this? It appears it felt put
upon. It protested it could not be held liable for the willful acts of
its agent. The court held otherwise. It decided that the primitive
compulsions of employer and employee were linked together at
the expense of a third person, Bertha Hecht:

> Although Wilder testified in his deposition that he was on a *straight
> salary* and that he had received *no bonuses* or *salary increases* during
> the period of the account, it was established during the trial that
> Harris Upham gave him two bonuses—one of $5,000 in June, 1961,
> and another of $5,000 in January, 1962, and further, that he did in
> fact receive an increase of salary in March, 1961, from $1,250 to
> $1,500 a month which remained his salary until March, 1963, when
> it was restored to $1,250 a month and, further, that in June, 1964,
> three months after the loss of the Hecht account, *his salary was
> sharply reduced to $850 a month*. It thus appears that to this extent
> Wilder was being indirectly compensated by Harris Upham in pro-
> portion to the volume of transactions and the amount of commis-
> sions generated by him for the firm.

Harris-Upham and Wilder also tried to evade responsibility for
Mrs. Hecht's losses by maintaining she

> had acquired a familiarity with security trading . . . as early as 1928.
> [They said she was] *"a veteran gambler,"* well aware of the risks
> involved in trading, not only in securities but also in commodity
> futures. [They said she knew that you can] "lose your shirt" in the

commodities market . . . that all the extensive trading and speculation in her account was upon her insistence and with her . . .
approval.

On the other hand, Mrs. Hecht's lawyers suggested that none of
this meant anything. To paraphrase their statement, they suggested that, if their client had a head of her own, so did a pin.
Thus the battle raged. Judge Sweigert listened to the lyric out-
pourings of counsel for the plaintiff and counsel for the defendant
and expressed himself accordingly:

> This case is a classic example of the trial process wherein able
> counsel for the respective parties have polarized the issues by their
> extreme and undiscriminating contentions concerning plaintiff's
> alleged competence or her alleged ignorance. . . .
>
> Actually, plaintiff was neither as "dumb". . . as plaintiff's counsel
> contends . . . nor was she as . . . informed as defendant's counsel
> would make her out to be.
>
> The truth concerning this issue lies in between and . . . we hold
> that her knowledge and experience, together with the information
> at hand, were *at least sufficient to . . . put her on . . . notice . . . her
> account was being handled in a manner contrary to her claimed
> understanding.* . . .
>
> Having . . . permitted Wilder and his firm to continue handling
> the account on this basis . . . for nearly seven years, *the Court finds
> that plaintiff's conduct is such that she is barred . . . from suddenly
> taking the position that such trading of the account in securities
> and commodities was unsuitable for her needs and objectives,* con-
> trary to her instructions and should never have occurred. . . .
>
> For this reason the Court considers her contentions (that Wilder
> purchased speculative and low grade securities in place of dividend-
> paying securities, effected the purchase and sale of commodities
> without her knowledge or comprehension as to their significance
> or suitability, and sold securities short for tax maneuvering pur-
> poses) to be unfounded *except insofar as such transactions were a
> part of "excessive" trading of her account by Wilder—a subject to
> be presently discussed.* . . .
>
> This court is satisfied that, although her experience and com-
> petence were such that she knew her account was being actively
> traded . . . her comprehension of market operations and business
> affairs beyond that was so meager that she still had to rely upon
> Wilder concerning whether trading in any particular volume or
> with any particular frequency was reasonably suitable or, on the
> contrary, whether it was excessive under the circumstances. . . .
>
> Whatever market knowledge she had was mainly jargon picked
> up from those who handled her account . . . her husband, Wilder—
> and from financial columnists. . . . This Court finds that . . .
> although plaintiff had enough experience to tell from the confirma-

tion slips and monthly statements that she was paying commissions and interest on transactions in her account, *she just did not have the sufficient competence to understand whether the frequency and volume of the transactions might be "excessive."* [Emphasis added.]

The Appeals Court concluded that the damages of $439,520 awarded by Judge Sweigert should be reduced by $143,000. It stated that it was limiting *damages to the amount of the commissions involved "because this is the only element of damage which was proximately caused by defendants."* The court merely insisted that what was stolen be returned, and all would be forgiven. Such findings provide a conspicuous example that our court system conforms to the abiding interests of the financial class. It accounts in large measure for the rise of securities violations, frauds, and thefts by Stock Exchange members.

Judge Powell of the Appeals Court took exception to the view of the majority. He stated in his dissent:

In narrowing recovery for churning solely to commissions earned (plus interest on the margin account) the Majority overlooks the fact that the dealer in his zeal to earn commissions may have caused damage unrelated in amount to what he earned in commissions . . .

The Majority has decided that Mrs. Hecht's commodity account was in fact churned but that any loss beyond that of cost of commissions was due to the risks of commodity trading of which she had knowledge. . . .

The trial Judge . . . found that there was an excessive transferring of money from the securities account into the commodities account, and that the action was pursuant to Wilder's fraudulent scheme to generate commissions. Mrs. Hecht was therefore more deeply involved in commodity trading than she knew. As a consequence her losses were just that much greater. For that she was entitled to redress. The trial court awarded her $78,000—the net commodity losses.

The loss of $78,000 could very well have been a substantial profit considering the size of the account and assuming it was properly traded. The evidence in this case discloses churning of a grand magnitude. In the eight years the commodity account was with Harris Upham & Co., total sales and purposes exceeded $89,000,000; commissions charged to Mrs. Hecht were $98,338; and the account profited in only two of the eight years. . . .

To the degree that she was in commodities beyond her knowledge and as a result of Wilder's scheme to generate commissions by the excessive transfer of money from the securities account to the commodities account she was entitled to recover damages. The award of $65,000 was not clearly erroneous and in my opinion should be affirmed. . . .

In my judgment the award of $78,000 for commodity account losses is sustained by the evidence. While the damages may have been difficult to compute ". . . the risk of the uncertainty should be thrown upon the wrong-doer instead of upon the injured party."

Judge Powell's dissent is further proof that new patterns of power are emerging.

The Appeals Court nonetheless stated in this case that "one of the principal congressional purposes of the Securities and Exchange Act is to protect the investor in this highly sophisticated field and . . . it is the duty of the courts to be alert and to provide such remedies as are necessary to make effective congressional purpose." It would have demonstrated a greater desire to "protect the investor" had it properly penalized the brokerage firm for its malfeasance.

More than any other recent decision, however, the court's findings in this case had an ominous reverberating authority, if only because it alerted investors to their rights at law—and because it pointed the finger at a way of life in which respectability is oftentimes the essence of imposture.

When the decision was rendered in September, 1970, the financial press soft-pedaled its comments about the case. The Stock Exchange refused to comment about it. Despite Judge Sweigert's statement that Harris-Upham had "grossly and unfairly churned" the Hecht account, having conducted "more than 10,000 transactions" in a period of six years and ten months, Mr. Harris contended there was "no evidence of churning" by his firm. It must have been impressed on Mr. Harris that silence is the safest lie. He gave no further interviews.

The need to protect the naïve gambler in stocks from the unscrupulous stockbroker has long been understood. But to this present all too few expedients have been devised to neutralize his influence. The orderly and wide ranging rules that exist, in theory, make these general points:

(1) The stockbroker has a responsibility to check the *source of his customer's funds.* In other words, it must be determined that the money the investor is about to lose in the market was not embezzled or stolen and that it comes to the brokerage firm properly intact from the customer's savings.
(2) The stocks the broker trades for his customer must be "suitable" for him.
(3) The customer's stocks must not be churned by the broker.
(4) The stockbroker's activities will be carefully supervised by the branch manager.

But threats of fines, censure, or temporary suspension for infringement of any of these rules have proved inadequate to check the dire effects of what amounts to a spoils system. The reasons are not difficult to understand. There is nothing to fear when it is understood that the courts will censure but not punish. Cervantes said, "He who has the judge for a father goes into the court with an easy mind." Why forgo the opportunities to acquire the wealth, power, and authority sanctioned by, and so easily obtained under, such a court system?

Judge Sweigert, however, is representative of a small band of jurists who have begun to renovate the judicial system by moving it into a healthy period of transition. They are providing a treasure trove of precedent-establishing decisions that have begun to pound relentlessly away at Wall Street's wealthy criminals and their "use of manipulative devices in connection with the offer, sale, or purchase of securities."

It is important for the investor to understand, however, that judges like Sweigert and Powell (and Sirica!) are still the exception. Most judges are information systems whose image of reality is predetermined by their interaction with the financial institutions in their community and the "happenings" and feedback from these institutions. Thus, while we must hope for the Sweigerts to provide practical remedies for the stockbrokers who seek to exploit the market's Bertha Hechts, and to establish the legal criteria and prohibitions that make it more difficult for stockbrokers to justify or rationalize their trading practices in terms of the old arguments, the investor must be prepared not for the Sweigert, but for his opposite, for the judge who is wheeling and dealing his way toward a higher court.

13. Judge Kaufman and the Wall Street Connection

In which it is shown that the habits of most judges are arranged on the same principles as most financial editors.

It is no use lamenting the conflict that exists in our court system between human nature and due process. We must learn to live with it. But, unless the investor is able to trace the condition of the court system to its hidden origins and purposes he will not be prepared to cope with the irritating and often abrasive manner of most judges and with the problems their natures present. The investor must reorient his conception of justice to accommodate the perplexing insight that it is not the law he must fear, but the judge. The law can be on his side, whereas the judge often won't be. In such cases he will be confronted with an establishment puppet whose duty is to render justice but whose aim is to delay it.

The events and emotions in the lives of most judges are those of businessmen. They are lawyers with a different label. Despite the symbolic representations and noble metaphors implicit in the word "judge" it must be recognized that most judges obtain their appointments because they understand their functions in the syntax and grammar of the financial establishment; and that their advancement depends on their willingness to conform to the traditional demands of its hierarchy and their mini-minded, money-mad plots. As such they represent a fairly commonplace variant on the ethic of the businessman. Accordingly they tend to be as reactionary as, and in total sympathy with, the precepts and principles of institutions like the Stock Exchange and its brokerage firms. In a context in which their behavior is perfectly acceptable, and indeed demanded of them, by the financial establishment, like the stockbrokers they serve, they soon come to want justice far less than they want money. Nor are they necessarily any better or more advanced ethically than the stockbrokers, dope pushers, and embezzlers who bribe them to get off.

Viewed in this context we can begin to understand the schizoid behavior of the court system: why, as in the Hecht case, it allows the district court to give something with one hand, while the appellate court then takes something back with the other hand.

Because the public lacks knowledge of the courts and the financial system underlying it, it is unaware of the demands made on the court system by the financial system, or the manner in which these demands then merge into and transmit information to the surrounding culture.

Because judges identify with the mental processes and practices of the financial system, court cases involving stockbroker fraud can be a nightmare for the investor who is unprepared to accommodate himself to the alien values and hangups of such judges. A brief account of my own encounter with such a jurist may be useful.

The particular judge to whom I refer is the quintessential specimen of the humorless tyrant, totally unaware of any personal limitations. I was to serve as an expert witness in a case involving the churning of a widow's account. It became apparent before I took the stand that he meant to fix in my mind the danger of any enterprise that opposed the interests of those in the financial establishment who had placed him in power. First, he sought to disqualify me by stating that since I did not spend most of my day in a brokerage house boardroom I could not qualify as an expert. The plaintiff's attorney asked him if he had read my book *The Wall Street Jungle,* and he replied, "I don't have to. I can tell from the title it is biased."

His own qualifications as a market analyst rested solely on his reading of the financial page. The courtroom, in consequence, was subjected to an assault course in financial clichés. Under any other circumstance his arrogant ignorance might have been a source of laughter.

He placed the plaintiff on the stand and sought to show that her expertise was as great as his own, thereby establishing her "sophistication." Only after she had lost all hope and crumpled before him did he move on to the next course. At that point he "persuaded" her to accept a small settlement. Like a handyman in the Stock Exchange household he pointed to the high costs of further litigation and the advantages of accepting the brokerage firm's "generous" offer of a settlement. He finished with the threat that, if she didn't accept the settlement, she stood a good chance of ultimately losing the case.

The pathetically small settlement having been accepted, he then issued an order binding everyone present to keep secret his name, the name of the defendant brokerage firm, the circumstances surrounding the trial, and the findings of the court. This, I later learned, is not unusual in such court cases, which is one of the principal reasons so little is known of the major frauds of member firms. I should also point out that, despite requests for press coverage from local newspapers, the media made themselves conspicuous by their absence. This is also not unusual, since they are reluctant to embarrass their sources in the brokerage business.

As an investor, you must recognize that years of immunity from regulation have fostered an enviable contempt for the law by the financial system. Therefore, when you establish your right to fair play by taking your case to court, unless you play your cards carefully you will almost inevitably prove fair game for the hard-core judge and his friend the Wall Street lawyer.

But before the lawyer is brought in, the manager of the brokerage firm, recognizing the threat of imminent litigation, will almost surely suggest that a deal can be made, or that "I'll make it up to you on the next hot issue." If that doesn't work, he will shrug his shoulders and say, "Okay, let's take it to arbitration." For you to accept this offer would be to fulfill his most pernicious dream.

Whenever the manager does turn the investor's thoughts to arbitration as a vehicle to recover, the investor will almost surely learn that for all its pretensions of public service, of existing to place at the investor's disposal, and at the lowest possible cost to him, the services of a nonpartisan panel of fair-minded administrators, arbitration proceedings are rarely, if ever, a way of obtaining even-handed justice. On the contrary, it is the best possible vehicle for serving the interests of stockbrokers who don't dare risk having their frauds brought to court.

Regrettably, most investors sign margin agreements with their brokerage firms stipulating they will submit all disputes between them to arbitration. This, of course, is a form of evasion (and fraud) perpetrated on investors. In 1970, on a visit to Washington, D.C., I brought to the attention of the SEC that in 1953, in *Wilko* v. *Swan,* the Supreme Court ruled that investors have the option of deciding to litigate or to arbitrate, and a customer's agreement to arbitrate future disputes with his stockbroker is an impermissible waiver of that customer's rights to seek recovery for damages in court. Further, the existence of a prior agreement to arbitrate which causes the customer to assume he is under obligation to arbitrate and has no alternative but to arbitrate is a further fraud on investors. The Supreme Court had, in fact, declared such arbitration agreements not only invalid but illegal.

The SEC advised me it was aware of the Supreme Court decision and was "studying the matter." In contrast to its frank and frontal perception of fraud when it occurs among the small fry of the securities industry, there is nothing like the way the explosive disclosures of Stock Exchange guilt are subtly defused by the Commission.

More than twenty-one years after the Supreme Court's decision and forty years after the passage of the first securities act, the brokerage community continues to deceive investors into thinking they must accept arbitration. Nor do investors recognize that the balance of power in such arbitration proceedings is weighted heavily on the side of the broker since the arbitrating panel is composed mostly of stockbrokers selected by the New York Stock Exchange.

The SEC acknowledges the Supreme Court's decision but fails to implement it despite the fact that a reading of all brokers' margin agreements shows the brokerage firms to be currently in violation of the Supreme Court's ruling. The Dean Witter agreement, for instance, states:

> Any controversy between you and the undersigned arising out of or relating to this contract or the breach thereof, shall be settled by arbitration, in accordance with the rules then obtaining, of either the Arbitration Committee of the Chamber of Commerce of the State of New York, or the American Arbitration Association, or the Board of Arbitration of the New York Stock Exchange, as the undersigned may elect.

The bones of many an investor are oft interred in these words. The history of arbitration proceedings is one long lament. Investors employ them in the belief they are just as good as a court trial in the presence of a jury, and a great deal less expensive. The fact is they are great in what they promise, absurd in what they provide.

When the investor takes Broker A to arbitration, Broker B, presiding as judge, will inevitably see to it that Broker A gets no more than a slap on the wrist since he (Broker B) may well be up for arbitration before Broker A, presiding as judge, the following week. The mild and fragile processes of broker back-scratching places the conscious self-interest of the brokerage community at the center of all such proceedings. Obviously, this is not the way to carefully and honestly subordinate the clear and unprejudiced view of an impartial tribunal.

A typical instance of how the Stock Exchange conducts its arbitration proceedings is laid out for autopsy in the case of *Sobel* v. *Hertz-Warner & Co.*, Second Circuit, November 28, 1972. The customer agreed with his broker's request to take his complaint to arbitration. He charged his broker with market manipulation and the creation of false market activity. The customer's broker was ultimately indicted for this. But it was only *after* the arbitration proceedings were terminated that he pleaded guilty to the charges. In its hearings with the customer however, the arbitration panel summarily defined its intent with these words: "Having heard and considered the proofs of the parties [we] have decided and determined that the claim of the claimant be and hereby is in all respects dismissed."

Sobel asked the arbitration panel to tell him the basis for their dismissal of his complaint. He was advised the board's decision was final and that no reasons would be given. Not surprisingly, Sobel assumed the decision of the arbitrators would not hold up in court, where he proceeded to seek clarification. The district court demanded that the Exchange's arbitrators provide an explanation for their decision. It noted there was insufficient evidence available to decide whether or not their decision was legal. The district court judge stated that he could not tell if there had been "manifest disregard" of the law by the arbitrators. If there had been, this would require a reversal of the arbitration panel's findings. He then remanded the case to the arbitrators and asked for "an indication, now wholly lacking from the record, of the basis on which the petitioner's claim was dismissed." Sobel assumed he had won his case.

The findings of arbitrators may be dismissed under the United States Arbitration Act when they have been arrived at by what are considered "undue means" or when they have "exceeded their powers." In the event such proceedings have exhibited "manifest disregard" for the law, according to the Supreme Court, their findings may be subjected to judicial review. The judge had also stipulated that his findings involved

> a controlling question of law as to which there is substantial ground for difference of opinion, namely whether an arbitration award in a case involving federal securities law standards which fails to provide some indication of the basis of the arbitration panel's decision may be set aside and resubmitted to the arbitration panel . . . and that an immediate appeal from the decision may materially advance the ultimate termination of this litigation.

He then stated, "The court's ruling possibly may have widespread ramifications for the conduct of arbitration generally, and hence it may be in the interest of justice to present the Court of Appeals with an opportunity to consider and answer the questions raised at the moment in the litigation when they may be most clearly framed." In other words, he passed the buck to the Appeals Court. This was just what the Exchange wanted.

Now, with the help of the judges who preside over the Second U.S. Circuit Court of Appeals, the Exchange turned the proceedings into something worthy of a lab slide. It began by filing what is called an *amicus curiae* brief. This is done by someone who is not a party to the litigation but who volunteers or is invited by the court to give its opinions on the matters pending before the court. In the present instance the Latin translation of the phrase, "friend of the court," is highly appropriate.

The Exchange exhibited its attitude toward arbitration in its brief with the following: "The active trader or large scale speculator with ample fiscal means *requires little protection*. He is both free and, as a practical matter, able to assert his claim in the courts in the first instance." [Emphasis added.]

Sobel must have asked himself what it all meant. "They forced me to go to arbitration. How can they now cop a plea by saying that I should have gone to court if I wanted 'protection'?" Properly understood, the implied principle in the Exchange's statement that the investor "requires little protection" should enlighten those concerned with the principles of self-regulation.

The Exchange also made it apparent that its arbitration procedures are secret proceedings whose findings are never disclosed. It maintained that because of the costs of litigation the "smaller investor" is not in a position to go to court and it is "in order to keep costs down" that boards of arbitration should not be required to give customers the reasons for their decisions!

The appeals court behaved as though it had been infiltrated by stockbrokers. It stated that "the first issue before us is what is the issue before us?" It then went on to state: "the issue before us is whether the arbitrators here are required to disclose the reasoning underlying their award." Although the lower court had maintained that, if "manifest disregard" of the law was to have any meaning, the Exchange was under an obligation to state the reasons for its findings. The Appeals Court was disposed to think otherwise. It reversed the decision of the lower court stating that "in the circumstances of this case the arbitrators have no . . . obligation to explain their award." The case was then sent back to the lower court. The admission of guilt by Sobel's stockbroker was ignored by the court as having no intrinsic merit. That must have bewildered Sobel.

The court's decision has tremendous implications for the future of all arbitration proceedings. Writing about this case in the *New York Law Journal* of February 2, 1973, a highly qualified expert in the field of corporate and securities litigation, Edward Brodsky, stated, "If ever a naked decision of arbitrators *screamed* for explanation, it was under the facts in Sobel v. Hertz-Warner & Co., a recent decision of the Court of Appeals for the Second Circuit."

The court, however, adhered to the Stock Exchange view that arbitrators need not explain their decisions, even at the sacrifice of "legal precision."

The true objectives of the judiciary, particularly in New York, can be seen in its bias on behalf of the stockbroker and the different degrees of zeal with which it pursues justice when the defendants are not stockbrokers. The problem of judges who sympathize with criminals is a subject for pathologists. As for arbitration proceedings, thousands of investors are still unaware that Stock Exchange insiders look upon them as the extension of a machine that allows them to turn the market's little pigs into sausages.

Buttressed and armed against arbitration, the investor must prepare himself for the next hurdle, the court system that exists in the United States and the manner in which its judges envelope themselves in legal sophistries to justify themselves, the Stock Exchange, and its members' practices.

In his book, *Lawyers' Ethics,* sociologist Jerome Carlin quotes a lawyer talking about the Wall Street law firms: "I've been shocked by members of the large firms who bring clients here and suggest that we go in and try to put in the fix."

Paul Hoffman, in *Lions in the Street,* quotes Carlin and comments on the questionable methods of trial judges and their discriminatory practices:

> The belief that there is a double standard of discipline in the bar is widespread—and with good reason. Consider these two statements:
>
> 1. "There are so few trial judges who just judge . . . who rule on questions of law and leave guilt or innocence to the jury. And Appellate Division judges aren't any better. They're the whores who become madams. . . .
>   "I would like to [become a judge]—just to see if I could be the kind of judge I think a judge should be. But the only way you can get it is to be in politics or buy it—and I don't even know the going price."

2. "I shudder to think what a Martian astronaut . . . would think of our courts and what goes on, or does not go on, in them. As to the judges, what would he think of certain of them, in theory elected by the public but in fact hand-picked by political leaders for purely political purposes irrelevant to merit?"

The language of the first may be more vivid, but their import is the same. The first was made by Martin Erdman, a Legal Aid Society lawyer who works in Manhattan's Criminal Courts Building. As a consequence, he was censured by the Appellate Division. The second was made by Francis T. P. Plimpton, then president of the Bar Association, at the association's Centennial Convocation. Naturally, no action was taken against him.

It is just the double standard. As Joseph Borkin defined it in *The Corrupt Judge*: ". . . The selective application of the Canons, with one code for the Brahmins of the law and another for its lesser servants, with a soft impeachment for knavery on the grand scale and a swift, harsh discipline for the fumblings of the petty shyster."

I should perhaps point out that, although our court system is shatteringly corrupt all over the country, especially where it concerns securities law, it is a sinking ship in New York. This, of course, is due to its proximity to and domination by the Wall Street crowd. The *New York Times* stated in an October 2, 1973, editorial: "The court system in this city and state is a disgrace." According to Paul Hoffman in *Lions in the Street,* the prestigious law firm of Arnold and Porter filed motions to have a case shifted from Washington to New York where *"both lawyers and judges are more familiar with the complexities of securities law and more sympathetic to its practitioners."* (Emphasis added.)

On October 15, 1973, a news story in the *New York Times* quoted Maurice Nadjari, the special state prosecutor appointed by Governor Rockefeller in 1972 to investigate corruption in the criminal justice system Mr. Nadjari states that "graft and payoffs to judges were involved in some of the over 200 investigations that may mature into indictments. The entire criminal justice system is tainted and perhaps it's by reason of the way it is created [largely through] the powers of the prevailing political party."

Nadjari chose the right institution to pick on. We should perhaps add that, when he speaks of judges and the court system in general, he is speaking about judges who also handle securities cases. When you meet one of them socially he will probably behave like Santa Claus. But meet him in court on a securities case and he may affect you quite violently. All of which brings us to Judge Kaufman.

Because of his all-important appointment as top man on New York's Second Circuit Court of Appeals, Judge Irving Kaufman has written practically singlehanded the manual that sanctifies the merchandising practices of those who worship in the main temple. It is a good bet that a member of Wall Street's wealthy criminal class can have a lower court's verdict reversed on appeal to Judge Kaufman's court—or, at worst, escape with a slap on the wrist.

Thus, in a case involving the financial penalties devolving on those guilty of transmitting inside information (*Schein* v. *Chasen,* May 10, 1972), we have the curious spectacle of Judge Kaufman, in.an astonishing dissent from the majority opinion, seeking to exempt the one individual who is most likely to be culpable— the stockbroker.

According to the *New York Law Journal* of Monday, June 25, 1973, the majority opinion of the court held that "a 'mesne' tippee [i.e., a broker who obtained the inside information and passed it on to a client] would be equally liable to the corporation for its tippee's profits." What delighted Wall Street and astonished the bar was Judge Kaufman's incomprehensible dissent. In the words of the *New York Law Journal:* "Judge Kaufman, in a vigorous and almost incredulous dissent, characterized the majority (Waterman, Smith, JJ.) view as a *'totally new concept'* which is *'extraordinary, expansive and incorrect.'* " (Emphasis added.)

One could only wonder at Judge Kaufman's astonishing obeisance to the tellers of the Great Counting House. On what basis is the majority's opinion "extraordinary, expansive, or incorrect"? Given the practical need, which was acute, the courts had long ago held brokers liable in such cases.

The case was sent back to District Court Judge Harold R. Tyler, who in 1971 had dismissed it. Judge Tyler, like Judge Kaufman, urged the same ultimate conclusion. The case involved Lum's; its chief executive officer, Melvin Chasen; and Lehman Brothers (September, 1973). Chasen, the president of Lum's, a Florida-based corporation engaged primarily in restaurant franchising, addressed a securities industry seminar and gave them an estimate of company earnings. About six weeks later he called a Lehman Brothers broker named Simon and told him he expected lower earnings. The broker telephoned a friend at the IDS mutual fund complex, who then sold out its holdings (86,000 shares) in Lum's.

Judge Tyler affirmed Judge Kaufman's curious principle that, while the cause of justice must be served by imposing liability on IDS for using the inside information provided by Lehman Brothers, there is nothing in the way of evidence suggesting that

Lehman Brothers should be held liable for supplying the inside information. According to the *New York Law Journal* of September 18, 1973:

> The decision last week by Judge Harold R. Tyler, Jr., of the U.S. District Court for the Southern District of New York finding violations of Exchange Act Section 10 (b) and Rule 10b-5 thereunder by Lum's Inc. and its Chief Executive Officer, Melvin Chasen, should not come as a surprise to securities industry personnel or their counsel. The same cannot be said with reference to the court's conclusions concerning Lehman Brothers, one of whose salesmen transmitted material information concerning Lum's to IDS, a large institutional holder of the Lum's stock.

It seems the court's opinion dealt only with Lum's, Chasen, and Lehman Brothers, as all others had settled charges against them out of court. Chasen and Lum's were found guilty. As for Lehman Brothers, the court found that the complaint was "barren of any reference of Lehman's participation in or knowledge of the acts constituting the offense other than the bare allegation that it was Simon's employer." The court added that, while Simon's position was admittedly fraught with conflicts of interest, "it is difficult to determine what other supervisory procedures could have been implemented to prevent the isolated, ambiguous leak which did occur—short of imposing a rule that salesmen are not to contact the management of companies whose stocks are held by clients."

It has been well established, however, that persons engaged in a joint enterprise to commit a wrong are both individually and jointly liable for damages and can be held to account for the profits of the other participants in the wrongful act.

Sound research, common sense, and equal justice before the law were more forcibly illustrated in *Hecht* v. *Harris-Upham,* when Judge Sweigert stated: "A stock brokerage firm can act only through its various partners, employees and agents, and the acts of its employees and agents, in the course of their employment, are the acts of the firm."

Judge Tyler had talked from both sides of his mouth and played both ends in order to turn his court into a comfort station for Wall Street's illuminati. Everyone in the Lum's case who had sought to evade reality was cast out of Eden for tasting of the forbidden fruit—everyone, that is, except Lehman Brothers.

Lehman was represented in court by the giant (144 lawyers) Wall Street law firm of Simpson, Thacher, and Bartlett. Its senior partner is Whitney North Seymour, Sr., a close friend and supporter of Richard Nixon. Whitney North Seymour, Jr., also a member of the firm, who recently resigned as U.S. Attorney for the Southern District of New York, is also a close friend of Richard Nixon. Under the circumstances, if you were an ambitious judge and involved in this high-stakes game, would you have played your ace and cited Lehman or, in a mood of carefully adjusted benevolence, given an imbecile twist to what should have happened by holding back your trump card and playing the two of clubs, thereby agreeing with Judge Kaufman in allowing Lehman Brothers to walk off with the pot? With this kind of mental agility one could in time acquire enough momentum to land in the Supreme Court.

In his book, *The Finest Judges Money Can Buy,* Charles Ashman provides seventy examples of what he refers to as "judicial pollution." Where it concerns securities violations, it would seem that judges function, as do stockbrokers, through instincts contagiously set in motion by Wall Street financial interests. Thus we find questionable behavior not only by judges on the New York Supreme Court (one of whom stated, when it was found he had violated antifraud provisions of the Securities Acts, "I have no excuse. I was just greedy"), but all the way up to the U.S. Supreme Court, to Justice Abe Fortas, who resigned under fire for taking what his critics referred to as a $20,000 payoff[1] and who now lobbies for the stockbrokerage firm of Loeb, Rhoades.[2]

On June 1, 1972, after wealthy stockbroker John Loeb pleaded no contest to three of eight counts charging him with failure to disclose campaign contributions, Judge John Cannella of the U.S. District Court for the Southern District of New York denied the government's request that Loeb be photographed and fingerprinted. "For the life of me, I don't see why it should be done," Judge Cannella said. When it came to sentencing on June 8, Judge Cannella fined Loeb $3,000. Loeb could have been sentenced to three years. He was represented in court by former Attorney General Herbert Brownell, senior partner of the Wall Street law firm of Lord, Day, and Lord—and Abe Fortas.

Judges understand power; they know where it resides and who exercises it. Their anonymity and the anonymity of those they serve, coupled with the public's ignorance of the law and the power they wield within their jurisdiction, is what makes each of them the ideal financial weapon. They have a vested interest in their connections with Wall Street. Hence, they look upon its institutions, its policy-makers, and their legal counsel as the ultimate reality. They are the power brokers of the financial establishment. Their politics is Wall Street.

[1] Charles Ashman, *The Finest Judges Money Can Buy,* p. 219.
[2] Paul Hoffman, *Lions in the Street,* p. 216.

Reproduced by permission of Paul Conrad and the *Los Angeles Times*.

Perhaps most significant about the Lum's case is not the way our courts mocked those who believed in their myths, nor even the failure of a judge like Kaufman to muffle the aches of injustice. It is the failure of an idea that matters most—the idea that our courts are willing to distinguish between what is right and what is wrong.

The failure of such ideas is caused by man's inability to suppress the subtle tyranny of the nature locked in the dark recesses of his psyche, and the connection it forces him to make with others to serve its demands. Perhaps, among other reasons, the failure of the idea in the Lum's case was due to the Wall Street connection in Judge Kaufman's psyche that could be traced to a father's pride in a son who is a successful stockbroker with the New York Stock Exchange firm of Loeb, Rhoades.

14. So You're Going to Sue Your Broker

In which it is shown that, since the nation's best law schools have become assembly lines for Wall Street law firms, it may well be that the best lawyer available to the investor is the one he looks for and can't find.

The lesson that emerges from the conventional plot movement cases like *Sobel* v. *Hertz Warner* and Lum's is clear. A crisis of values is discernible. The public is faced not only with rigged stock prices and rigged arbitration proceedings, but with a rigged court system as well. The fact is, the more insight the public is able to gain into the practices that melt into each other on the floor of the Exchange and the more access it gains to sources of information that until now only insiders have possessed, the closer the Exchange and its court system come to a day of reckoning.

It seems strange that so little attention has been paid to the fact that what the Exchange preaches has nothing to do with what it practices, or that when this establishment—including the media—indulges in arbitrary deception, it is violating the antifraud provisions of the securities acts. If deception is the mainspring of the Exchange's alien environment, then investors must look to litigation as their ultimate weapon. Litigation is the only rejoinder to the Exchange's carefully staged purse-snatchings.

Thus far, a court system functioning in blind homage to the Exchange has served to domesticate public passions by resolving almost all of the problems presented by litigation. But newly appointed state prosecutors and highly accomplished authors have begun to focus a bright light on the inward drift of these courts and on their judges' expectations. Can investors' understanding of these matters then lag far behind? Will they not observe and take issue with a condition in which deception functions at one end of the financial establishment only because of a corrupt court system at the other end?

For the present, and although the stockbroker bias of most judges cannot be pinpointed, the investor would do well to spare himself, as much as possible, the mastery that the Exchange is able to exercise over the New York and adjacent court systems. With that in mind:

(1) The investor must try to effect a change of venue when his case is assigned to a court of Stock Exchange jurisdiction.

(2) Because there *are* honest judges, an attempt should be made to have the case held in one of their courts. A review of cases involving securities litigation will yield the names and jurisdictions of these judges. The information can be found in the nearest university law library.

(3) Investors have at their disposal the best means of effective competition with the Exchange—trial by jury. Juries are composed, for the most part, of individuals dedicated to the cause of justice.

(4) Most important of all, the investor must engage counsel who understands the practical difficulties that must be surmounted if the truth is to override the special claims and subterfuges employed by the Wall Street lawyer on behalf of the defendant stockbroker. He must be highly articulate, a man who has enough chutzpah and class to capture a jury's will to believe, who so forcefully employs the criteria and rules of reason for establishing the truth that only the most willfully subversive member of a jury can reject them. He must be able to anticipate and counter the stratagems of the Wall Street lawyer. He must also be a lawyer who has demonstrated, in similar cases in the past, an ability to obtain a simple utilitarian verdict of "guilty as charged."

In the remainder of this chapter, I would like to discuss first the manner in which I believe the investor should go about finding his lawyer, and what he and his lawyer should expect of each other and from opposing counsel. Second, there is a great deal the investor can do to prepare himself better for trial by jury. Inadvertently, he can hamper a jury's thinking and bring discredit on himself and his case. By working to help the jury to a better understanding of the issues involved and by putting it in touch with the realities of the securities laws, the investor can involve the jury in a quest for enlightenment that will make a just verdict almost inevitable. I would have liked to be able to recommend class action suits as vehicles to recovery, but they have become entangled with so many restrictions that they may no longer be the best alternative for investor actions.

The number of investors who believe their lawyers sold them out is legion. More often than not they are wrong. They think as they do because, on the basis of the facts, they filed a suit in which the obviousness of the fraud made a favorable verdict seem inevitable. With this conclusion as their starting point, when they lost their case they could only conclude it was because of malfeasance.

Granted, Wall Street lawyers have from time to time bribed or in other ways seduced their opposition, such instances have to be rare. That it may *seem* to the investor who loses what he thought was an open and shut case as though his lawyer has made a private deal with the stockbroker's lawyer is more directly related to the competitive skills of the opposing attorney. The truth is that certain inevitable, highly predictable conclusions were probably apparent before the case began. Invariably, the investor retained counsel whose inexperience in the field of securities litigation made it impossible for him to distinguish between questions that established his client's allegation of fraud and questions that failed to cast sufficient light on the dispute.

One major difference between the investor's attorney and the Wall Street lawyer is that the former is too often concerned with the bread-and-butter problems relating to his fee. On the other hand, lawyers from a firm like Milbank, Tweed, Hadley, and McCloy, representing the Stock Exchange, or from Gibson, Dunn, and Crutcher, representing outfits like E. F. Hutton, have a longer reach. They are attached to their cases on a retainer basis and are in court as much to prevent social change as to represent their clients. They are as concerned about the long-term implications of their cases as they are with serving their clients. When they go into court to defend a violation of the securities acts, the investment community is also on trial. Therefore, they will enlist the aid of their entire firms to jealously protect their case.

The fact is, their grip on the language and syntax of the market is decked out to a disturbing degree with every trick of the legal trade. Coming up against this dominant fact, the investor is tempted to back down. The soft menace of their tone, a compound of fabrication, force of suggestion, and the master strokes that come of a chapter-and-verse understanding of securities law, causes most investors to believe they are beaten before they start. For this reason, and because the investor is imprisoned in fear, he will often agree after one or two days of trial to settle his case for nothing or next to nothing.

The more important the stockbroker defendant, the more formidable his legal counsel. No matter that the client's guilt has been clearly established, he will bend every effort and use every legal device to persuade the jury and the judge that his client is an extraordinarily open and generous individual, so driven by his swollen integrity as to be incapable of deception. The brutality counsel demonstrates in the course of taking depositions and his deceiving gentleness before the jury are the final proof that he brings to his task the ideological approach and cash value of a dedicated SOB. This is also reflected in the fact that most financial establishment lawyers consider themselves members of an elite for whom the rules of law and order do not apply to them as they do to the common man. As it happens, this is not so much the characteristic of an elite as the garden variety organization mentality that has submitted to the bulldozing dominion of power and money. Accordingly, they are bent on preserving the cosmetic appearance of Wall Street. If their standards do not fit the needs of society, the concrete reality of their situation is that truth and fair play are irrelevant to the underlying assumptions of the investment industry.

This mentality has its genesis in the most unsuspected and ivory tower-like areas of social behavior, i.e. the nation's foremost educational institutions. To insure survival, the law firms that represent the financial establishment have snapped up each year's harvest of the best brains graduating from the country's best law schools. The legal and social conditioning of these graduates is the key to continuing social control. Since they maintain their personal contacts principally with other members of the financial establishment, these young lawyers soon are morally sideswiped into becoming the financial establishment's best weapons. From the moment they go to work on securities cases, they are kept busy marshaling precedents and half-truths to mask the hocus-pocus of their clients. In time they adopt the average stockbroker's point of view: To be successful in business one must have a body of law that is respected by the community—but one you can get around.

It is against this mentality the investor pits himself as he goes to court. The investor and his lawyer face the communal character of a corrupt establishment. The courts have been turned into the legal instrument of a demolishing culture. Their function is to perpetuate that culture. It is very difficult for an opposing attorney to make the jury see that truth and half-truth are being mingled with omissions and misstatements of material fact. Unlike the Wall Street lawyer, the lawyer who is inexperienced in securities matters is unable to pinpoint the subtle differences that exist in the rituals of the stockbroker and that distinguish aggressive business practice from fraud.

So the investor requires the services of an attorney whose success as a securities trial lawyer is already recognized by his contemporaries. He must also be the kind of lawyer who knows how to handle a dirty fighter. Interestingly enough, I know of several such emancipated individuals, men who in their arguments have persuaded juries to resolutely reject the defenses raised for fraud.

You might seek help from your local county or state bar association in finding such a lawyer. It's my opinion that the best place to look is in a university law library. With the help of the reference librarian, it should be a simple matter to track down the important cases successfully pleaded against Stock Exchange members or their brokerage firms. An important source of information is the Securities Report Service published by Commerce Clearing House. Information on such cases can also be found in the files of the regional offices of the SEC. It has been my experience that, unlike those who move into and out of the SEC via executive appointment, those who staff the regional offices are eager to help the investor.

The general expectation among investors is that, once they've been defrauded by their stockbroker or the Stock Exchange, the best lawyers should be willing to work for them for nothing, next to nothing, or on a contingency basis. The best lawyers are not likely to do this. Under extraordinary circumstances, they *may* accept the case on a contingency basis.

When you meet your lawyer for the first time, therefore, you should understand at the outset that he has a family to support and an office to maintain, and the more successful he is, the higher his fees must be to maintain what, in all probability, is a high standard of living. Be sure of one thing. If he's the best, whatever he charges he is worth it. For one thing, this kind of lawyer won't take your case unless he believes he can win it.

After talking to him, if you feel you would like to move forward but lack sufficient funds, there are ways to obtain the money needed for legal fees. If you have standing in the community, good credit, and, in the lawyer's opinion, a *great* case, you might consider going to your bank for a loan. It might, perhaps, also help if you brought your case to the attention of other investors who are using the same brokerage firm. This can, of course, be done through advertising, in interviews with the press, or by having your attorney obtain a list of the stockbroker's clients and contacting them. If you give tremendous exposure to your case, chances are you will find others ready to join you. Four or five investors sharing the cost of legal fees can lessen the burden of litigation considerably.

The first thing your attorney will want to know when you have presented your evidence to him will be the attitude of the brokerage firm when you confronted it with your complaint. If you are like most investors, you will have discovered that, although you made every necessary effort to acquaint the brokerage firm with your difficulties, all you received in return was an effort to delay any action on your part. You will have received a form letter indicating your complaint is being examined. When, after a period of weeks or months, nothing was done and you wrote the main office, chances are you received a letter from the firm's attorney denying any and all wrongdoing. Your prospective attorney will want to know these details. Don't try to keep any relevant facts from him. Be absolutely truthful about everything. Bring everything out into the open, realizing if you don't, opposing counsel will.

Listen carefully to his advice. Follow it, but don't try to give him complete control of the case. He probably won't want it. There are decisions he will want you to make and that you should make. They can be easy decisions, such as when a brokerage firm makes an absurd offer of settlement. This is what happened in the Bertha Hecht case. Harris-Upham made Mrs. Hecht an inadequate offer. Her attorneys advised her to turn it down, and she did. Had Harris-Upham offered her a sizable settlement, she would have had a difficult decision to make—and only *she* could have made it. As it happened, Harris-Upham's lawyers seemed to have forgotten that the Wall Street lawyer's safest course of action is to keep his client out of court. We can only be thankful that they failed to observe this caveat. Generally, if counsel is a successful securities lawyer, he knows that it can be a dangerous course of action for him to let his client risk going to court, particularly when the case involved has enormous implications for the entire investment industry.

These are thoughts to fly by as you go to meet your lawyer. If he has a reputation as a successful securities lawyer, you must realize he is your ace card. Therefore, even if you are in Mississippi and he is in San Francisco, don't let his location deter you from retaining him.

According to the best authorities on the subject of securities law, the complaint for a successful lawsuit for securities violations should be drafted to include common law and state securities acts. Concerning punitive or exemplary damages, Stuart C. Goldberg, in the *New York Law Journal* of November 10, 1972, stated that they are generally awarded in cases involving intentional tort. He points out that, since churning has been cited as being "one of the most injurious types of fraud possible" and "deserving of the severest condemnation," punitive damages serve as an ideal means of indemnification and as a deterrent to future actions of a similar nature.

Goldberg is concerned that punitive damages have not been awarded in churning cases. He suggests that the reason may lie in the attorney's complaint, which cites only violations of the anti-fraud provisions of the Exchange Act. The argument for punitive damages becomes much stronger when the antifraud provisions of the Securities Acts are included in the complaint along with the common law and state statutory provisions that grant punitive damage for intentional tort.

The findings of appropriate court actions and SEC opinions are also important, as is the requirement that such actions be filed within the statute of limitations of the sections, rules, or provisions of the acts, or (and this is important) the state in which the action is filed. For example, the rule in the Exchange Act that specifically cites churning as a manipulative device insists that the suit must be filed within one year of discovery of, and under no circumstances more than three years after, the event. (Securities Exchange Act of 1934, Section 29b). Another point: a suit filed under this statute *would involve only churning in the over-the-counter market.* For this reason, the lawyer expert in this field will file his actions for churning under the sections of the Federal Securities Acts that form the hard core antifraud provisions of these acts, i.e., the Securities Act, Section 17(a) and the Exchange Act, Section 10b and rule 10b-5.

The investor must realize that the legal privileges surrounding fraud are not self-executing; the crock of gold at the rainbow's end goes to the plaintiff who not only is great on direct examination but who also stands up as straightforward and honest under cross-examination. For the rest, all the investor can do is conduct himself in court in such a way as to stimulate the jury's interest in him and his case, and avoid making the egregious bloopers I have witnessed that totally estrange a jury. In this connection, I would earnestly suggest that investors obtain a copy of *How to Win Lawsuits Before Juries* by Lewis Lake (Englewood Cliffs, N.J.: Prentice-Hall, 1954). While it is written principally for attorneys, it is an indispensable guide to the layman on how to conduct himself properly before the judge, what his demeanor should be toward opposing counsel, actions that disturb jurors, and how to prepare himself for trial.

For my part, I have sought to show that the investor's place in the securities market hinges on his demand for decent and fair treatment and on his awareness of his evident and concrete rights. It has been my purpose to suggest the re-creative potentials of litigation, which, because of his ignorance of the law, the investor has allowed to remain idle. The more he has neglected his rights, the more they have, like an unused muscle, diminished in the eyes of the stockbroker community. In seeking to distinguish between Wall Street lawyers and the lawyers available to investors, I have endeavored to point out that, however noble sounding, the stockbroker's lawyers are committed to the service of clients who require their most ruthless and merciless efforts.

Though I could only touch on the matter briefly, I have tried to show why the investor going to litigation requires the experience and perceptions of the most highly skilled securities lawyers. Only an attorney versed in the subtleties of prosecuting a securities case can strike successfully at the fixed customs of most courts. The brief references made here to the way the complaint should be filed are elementary and are included merely to give the investor an idea of the directing dynamism of the antifraud provisions of the securities laws. In any case, the skilled securities lawyer will exercise an autonomy that is all his own.

There is one additional thought of tremendous implication, which I believe can have the most profound repercussions not only on the well-being of investors but also on the character of the stock market. We have seen that the fear of financial loss caused by litigation is the only viable deterrent to stockbroker fraud. I shall explore in the next chapter the potentials of litigation as they address themselves to the practices of Exchange insiders.

15. How to Sue the Stock Exchange

In which it is shown that as long as there is a New York Stock Exchange no great lawyer need ever complain of a want of opportunity.

From its beginnings Western civilization has been locked in the bear hugs of naked power. Man the optimist, plagued by an uneasy feeling he will die clinging to the cliff's edge, has nonetheless tried to fashion a life that allows him to assert some control over his wants. Uneasily conscious that he is free only in his imagination, he submits to the myths of power that mask the money manager's authority.

Nor is there anything else he can do. His energies are, of necessity, devoted wholly to the problems of survival. He must balance himself as best he can on his precarious perch or land in the dust heap. Except for a slap here and a tickle there, he has neither the time nor the inclination for anything else. At the bottom of the pyramid of power and in the light of existing experience, he begins to wonder why he bothers at all. Riding the upthrusts and convulsions of one economic breakdown after another, he mistakenly thinks that the structuring of his misery has its origins solely in the blunders and follies of government's brute power.

He is unaware that the pattern and order of services that surround the scheming and deceptive rituals of the businessmen and money managers who run government have set determinate limits to his hopes. Rarely does it occur to him to think of the trumpet blasts of his bureaucrats and demagogues as the pragmatic response to the fiats of big money's authority. His innocence surprisingly undiminished, he submits to the spoils system of the greedy gangs whose economic controls become more far reaching and more malign with the passing of time. The favoring condition of a corruptible bureaucracy always being present, new arrangements of power differ from the old only in that they are, of necessity, more covert and more devious.

What is more natural than that our insights into the way of today's world should reveal that, if it is man's good that is wanted, something is missing; that the privation and hardship that exist at one end of the scale can be attributed to the same age-old source of menace at the other end. As always, the thwarting potentials, common characteristics, and hidden impact of the businessman's economic-political mechanism are still asserting themselves at the expense of the powerless. His propaganda machine, credit organizations, financial institutions, and impersonal monetary controls are still tragically transforming the character of government, whose irreversible processes, we are told, are the end product of power by consensus. But behind the democratic fable the dominant contours of the Great Adding Machine are still determining the means and ends of mass man's material world. The ultimate traps and tragic consequences of uncontrolled financial power can be seen working themselves out on the New York Stock Exchange, the twentieth century's refined model of the robber baron prototype. To the accompaniment of the ever recurring phenomenon of a slapstick bureaucracy, enlisting the gestures and sound effects of American free enterprise, the power strategies of the money man's conspiratorial gatherings have bounced into the present like hard rubber; and once again, apprehensive about reality; fragmented by taxes, inflation, and unemployment; helpless in what he is told is the heartland of freedom, man is doomed to the radical insecurities and desperate contingencies of a crisis situation.

The folk spirit incarnate in those who hold the reins of power within the Exchange establishment (and I am here referring to the heads of the Eastern banking establishment as well as the heads of the Stock Exchange) represents a phenomenon of profound significance to investors. Their strategies have established them as the financial establishment's—and the government's—ultimate policymakers. By their covert use of power they have added new dimensions to the old assaults of the dictator.

Their power can be neutralized only by the force of a greater power. This fact is obvious and leads us to wonder if there is another power within the established order of things that can prevail over them. If we think along these lines, we must inevitably come to the conclusion that there is, just possibly, one such force, that is, the gospel of law already in existence, from which Exchange insiders *derive* their power. It is a compensatory gospel and contains, to begin with, a fact of law to which few insiders will wholly accommodate themselves and from which, in fact, most will shrink. It is a law that is a necessity in the nature of things, where billions of other people's dollars are concerned. I am referring to the body of law governing the conduct and liabilities of the *fiduciary*—a person to whom property and/or power *is entrusted for the benefit of others.*

Stock Exchange insiders have, of their own volition, assumed a trust. At the very least they have a statutory obligation to "maintain a *fair* and orderly market." Thus, the relationship between Stock Exchange insiders operating on the floor of the Exchange (or in an administrative or executive capacity) and the investing public is fiduciary in nature and imposes on these brokers and those who govern them the duty of acting in the highest good faith and integrity toward their investor customers. In fact, their obligation of diligent and faithful service is no different from that imposed upon trustees.

Although, judging from his behavior, he would appear to be free of any responsibility, the Stock Exchange insider has the same fiduciary responsibilities as the corporate insider. This is important since the SEC has seen fit to regulate the activities of corporate insiders in a manner not yet extended to Stock Exchange insiders. Legal precedent, therefore, has been established in connection with corporate insiders, which, I believe, can be stretched to fit Exchange insiders.

In the past, nonstatutory responsibility rules engendered by Section 10(b) and rule 10b-5 of the 1934 act treated the question of insider disclosure ambiguously. In fact, a careful investigation of rule 10b-5 fails to turn up any use of the term "insider." However, as it involves the obligations and responsibilities of those who ought to be considered insiders, they are now dealt with authoritatively by the SEC and the courts. *An important expansion of insider rules is the imposition of a positive obligation on all insiders to disclose their inside information before engaging in any securities transactions in which that information has a material bearing.* Failure to disclose such information from whatever source, i.e., governmental, corporate, or economic, is itself a violation of the insider's obligations to the investing public. Regrettably, neither the SEC nor the courts have seen fit to expand the insider concept to include members of the Stock Exchange corporation. It nonetheless seems clear that, since they have expanded the potential classes of persons to whom duties and liabilities under 10b-5 run, it should be only a small step to include Stock Exchange insiders under this rule as well.

Using the logic employed by the SEC in 1961 in the Cady, Roberts and Company case, a brief can be made for the view that Stock Exchange insiders have a fiduciary responsibility to their customers, the public. In Cady, Roberts a stockbroker used information supplied him by a director of the Curtiss-Wright Corporation concerning a reduction in dividend as the basis to sell the shares of this stock in accounts held by him on a discretionary basis. The broker argued he did not violate rule 10-5b since he had acted only in the best interests of his own customers, to whom, he said, he owed a fiduciary duty. While conceding that he "undoubtedly occupied a fiduciary relationship to his customers," the SEC maintained that "this relationship could not justify any actions by him contrary to law." According to the SEC the duty he owed to the public as a whole was "primary" and greater than his duty to his immediate customers. The SEC further stipulated that "clients may not expect of a broker the benefits of his inside information at the expense of the public generally." With this statement the SEC opened wide the doors of the mind, allowing thought to rush in. Had the information from the director of Curtiss-Wright caused the broker to sell his own shares of Curtiss-Wright, would that not have compounded his misfeasance in the eyes of the SEC? He would most assuredly have been acting in a totally self-serving manner to benefit himself from the use of inside information "at the expense of the public generally."

Having made this exploratory thrust, is it not now quite logical to substitute for the stockbroker in Cady, Roberts the Stock Exchange specialists and other insiders on the floor of the Exchange? Do they not have a fiduciary obligation to place themselves in a position of trust with respect to the public, whose benefit they and the Stock Exchange are in business to serve, and to whom as their principals they should be required to account for any profits personally derived from the use of information not first applied for the benefit of their principals?

In the Cady, Roberts case, the SEC maintained that "the obligation" of the insider "rests on two principal elements: first the existence of a relationship giving access, directly or indirectly, to information intended to be available only for a corporate purpose *and not for the personal benefit of anyone;* and, second, the inherent unfairness involved where a party takes advantage of such information, *knowing it is unavailable to those with whom he is dealing.*"

Thus we find that the legal obligation of the corporate insider as a fiduciary is one of good faith and fair dealing to his shareholders. To effect this there can be

1. *No conflicts of interest*
2. No competition with those for whom he is acting as a fiduciary
3. No exploitation of his insider position for his own financial advantage
4. Full disclosure of all material information

The analysis is provocative, for the importance of what the SEC has just laid down as law is not what it says about stockbrokerage firms like Cady, Roberts and Company but in what it said—and continues to say between the lines—about Stock Exchange specialists who trade on the basis of inside information provided them by the heads of the corporations in whose stocks they trade (and by other specialists who have acquired inside information in their stocks) or who acquire inside information from government sources about forthcoming economic announcements. The SEC could hardly be more precise in describing the violations of 10b-5 by those insiders on the floor of the Exchange and by the executives of corporations like GM, Alcoa, U.S. Steel, and Standard Oil who were advised by the White House of President Nixon's plan to announce his New Economic Policy on August 15, 1972. In his rough, unlettered way the President can always be found laboring to make the world safe for Wall Street by freeing its members from the restraints of ignorance about his plans. Or consider the way, without disclaimer by the SEC, the pattern for assuring the continued affluence of Exchange and corporate insiders is laid down by their transactions in stocks like Occidental Petroleum in July, 1972, and Gulf Oil in December, 1972. Obviously, if Exchange insiders were obligated to observe the rules laid down by the SEC in Texas Gulf Sulphur and other cases, the fundamental problem, which is to find a way of regulating the securities industry wisely, would be solved.

Actually, however, we are past the point where the present system can be effectively regulated. I am not, therefore, suggesting that all the problems presented by the Exchange can be solved by 10b-5. Excessive commissions are still being swallowed without an anesthetic, and self-regulation is responsible for evils that have spread like a glandular growth. We do not as yet have an effective alternate system in operation that could replace the corruptions of the Stock Exchange's specialist system. Proposals have been put forth, however, for such an Exchange, one by myself, that would fit the needs and realities of American industry on the one hand and investors on the other. In fact the only viable solution will be to develop an alternate Exchange system, strictly regulated, with

specialists, floor traders, and all others replaced by clerks and carefully and publicly programed computers. The machinery of information must no longer be reserved to serve the ignoble and
expensive sentiments of the Exchange establishment's private
club. Everything to do with the public's financial institutions must
be accessible to public inspection. Confidential negotiations between Wall Street and Washington must be replaced with open
agreements openly arrived at.

We know already, however, that this type of reform will not be
brought about by the SEC. When a broker-dealer firm serves
itself too well as principal in competition with its customers by
taking too much of a "spread" or too high a "markup," it is asked
to hold out its wrists to be slapped. But we have seen that the SEC
chooses to act differently where Stock Exchange insiders are concerned.

By now we are also aware that this form of nonregulation is not
due to a lack of ample evidence of Exchange insider fraud. According to the Special Study Report of 1962,

> specialists are at the heart of the problem of organization, manage-
> ment and disciplinary procedures of the exchange. They are domi-
> nant in the administration of the exchange . . . the misuse of their
> fundamental role in the operation of a fair, orderly auction market,
> and the breakdown of regulatory and disciplinary controls over
> them—all are part of a complex pattern of interlocking causes and
> effects. It is for this reason that any program of reform must con-
> centrate heavily on the dominant role of the specialist.

Nor can we resist the last steps in the argument posed by the SEC
as a captive agency. For the long implicit and sometimes revealed
fact is that the Exchange's ultimatums determine the Commission's conclusions.

Senator Harrison Williams (D.-N.J.), in many ways the SEC's
sharpest critic, contemplated this problem and then on January
9, 1973, let loose a barrage at the Commission. He pointed out that
in two critical studies on the stock market's operations the SEC
had significantly neglected to enforce disciplinary procedures
against the Stock Exchange when it discovered substantive infrac-
tions of the rules (i.e., *fraud*). A rundown of the Commission's
derelictions revealed that, in the course of a four-month study in
1970 of specialist performance in handling stock trades, the Commission had singled out eighty-eight large price swings in various
stock issues on different days and had come to the conclusion that
the Exchange should have disciplined fourteen specialists for mal-

feasance. The SEC then proceeded to report to the Exchange suggesting the Exchange take action against the specialists. In response, the Exchange pointedly advised the agency that disciplinary action was *not* warranted. The SEC again asked the Exchange to penalize the specialists. The Exchange again declined. Then, in July, 1971, the SEC sent a final letter asking the Exchange to write standards for specialists "as soon as possible." There the SEC allowed the matter to rest. In the conclusion of its report the SEC stated, "The NYSE has not promulgated such standards and the SEC has not pursued the matter further." Had it done so, James Needham would probably not have been appointed chairman of the NYSE.

In my opinion, nothing better illustrates the fact that the specialist is the end product of a system for rigging and manipulating stock prices than the protean resourcefulness of the rationale he employs as he drops stocks a full point on only 100 shares, only then to revise this rationale so that another stock can be pegged at a fixed price of 26 for six days while insiders sell more than 9 million shares of it.

Add to this the insider's great financial achievements when, in one of his most egregious breaches of manners, he drops prices and cleans out his books prior to a bull raid on the market; or, having committed himself to a prearranged plan, he *raises* prices, scares out the shorts, empties his trading and investment accounts, and then sells short prior to dropping prices so that he can once again felicitously accumulate stock for his investment accounts.

Sufficient examples have been provided in earlier chapters to show that the SEC has allowed Exchange insiders to violate the rules governing their activities. In effect, what we now have on the floor of the Exchange is a state of affairs in which specialists and those associated with them are left perfectly free to follow their own interests in their own way. In view of the large amounts of money involved this is not only contrary to the rules for fiduciaries, it is contrary to common sense. As things now stand, the Exchange's all-powerful specialists are accountable to no higher authority than themselves. Certainly the dress extras who occupy seats on the Exchange's Board of Governors as representatives of the public employ an investment approach that is workable in practice only if they are able to operate in close harmony with specialists. Nor is the SEC totally unaware of the fiduciary nature of the relationship between the Exchange insider and the investor. I wrote the Commission on March 5, 1973, to point out that the market would be far more secure for investors if the customs of its insiders did not clash with their responsibilities as fiduciaries. I quote one paragraph:

> Since specialists serve as fiduciaries—much, in fact, like the heads of corporations, figures should .be provided for transactions in which they are directly or indirectly interested. This, of course, would also include their off-the-floor transactions.

Since the Commission's obligations to the Exchange appear always to override its regulatory obligations, my letter went unanswered.

I imagine, however, that if the SEC were confronted with imminent legislation on this subject it might raise as its main defense the notion that the broker-dealer's credentials and privileged freedoms allow him to act as an agent for the public on some occasions and as a dealer for himself on others; and that, while he is acting as a dealer for his own account, he is exempt from fiduciary responsibilities. This line of reasoning can only lead to the conclusion that the specialist is a creature who is able to so stubbornly restrict himself and the forces of human nature that he can wear both hats at once and in such fashion that the interests that pertain to the agent are blind to the wishes of the dealer, and vice-versa.

Presuming, however, that specialists are able to block the electrical impulses conditioned to flow to the brain on behalf of their public customers so that they do not interfere with the qualitatively different self-serving electrical impulses that, so to speak, seek to dig the investor's grave and bury him in it, it doesn't matter. We must acknowledge the simple fact that once the specialist acts on his own behalf he has set in motion a chain of events that are dramatically in conflict with his role as agent. Certainly it must be obvious that it is impossible to destroy a customer one moment and then, ignoring statistical probabilities, seek to serve him the next. If the specialist has used his book "as a dealer for his own account" by dropping prices in order to acquire the stock of public customers before launching a bull raid on the market, how can he then serve them as an agent when he *"wiped them out"* of his book before advancing prices? Not even the electronic pseudo-brain of a computer could resolve this problem.

The enormous grant of ungoverned power, the ability this power gives Exchange insiders to implement their exorbitant financial aspirations, and a regulatory program of know-nothing and do-nothing have been established as public policy whereas it is an infringement of public trust. Investors are therefore faced with the brutal fact that, while laws exist on the books for their protection, no one has yet bothered to implement them.

Since the Commission operates on the naïve assumption that investors will continue to accept a self-regulatory scheme that is deeply at variance with the real character of their needs, since, indeed, the premises upon which self-regulation rests have been tragically contradicted by the experience of millions of investors and exposed as unworkable, the irreducible fact to which investors must adapt is that they must protect themselves.

There is no resistance to the Exchange's practices from the SEC, nor is there likely to be. That being the case, investors can proceed on the infantile assumption that they are compelled to accept the Stock Exchange's arrogant demonstrations of naked and unlawful power, or they can combine together as a consumer group to force the financial establishment to obey laws instead of their intuitions.

Since the only discipline now observed by the Exchange is custom, it would be absurd for investors not to seek to impose the rule of law, since it already exists. Its utility has been demonstrated in a long series of court cases. What other way has not been tried? Time has run out for the solutions provided by legislative hearings, study groups, compromises with what is right and necessary in order to appease powerful opposing interests. The problem has been laid at the feet of the politicians. They've chosen to step over it or ignore it. Most of them fear the power of Wall Street.

Nothing comes easy. For whatever is wanted a price must be paid. Life, history, even love—all are finally determined by economic arrangements. Thus, if you want to protect your rights, you're going to have to *fight* for them in court. Only the courts can provide the punitive sanctions that can make an unregenerate power structure willing to change in order to become bearable.

Only when the courts have been induced to recognize the importance of the issues placed before them—that the financial impulses of Exchange insiders are at the center of the investor's problems—will high standards of conduct be imposed on that institution. In a business enterprise so totally affecting the public interest that it is, in effect, a public utility, a group of vested interests must be made to justify its practices in a court of law.

It is possible and logically necessary for lawyers dedicated to corporate responsibility to prod the courts into formulating rules of conduct that will make the practices and income of these insiders more visible. While it is possible for persons like myself to profit by exploiting their strategies, the quality of life, the social unrest, the human costs that must inevitably be paid by society as a whole are too great. Only if one attempts to show that one is eating well because one knows how to exploit those who are perpetrating an enormous fraud on others, can one live with the bitter aftertaste.

Nothing changes. Our political standards are still those of the Stone Age. The passions of self-interest that determine the philosophy of government and the calculated cruelty and deception a country's leaders will sanction at the promptings of private financial interests are no different now than they were in the Middle Ages.

It is no exaggeration to say that Americans are moving into a period of the most acute economic crisis, not only because of the absence of creative political leadership but because what limited wisdom our politicians can boast has been placed at the service of the financial and business establishment's privileges and private monopolies. I will not press the point further except to say that the source of this condition can be located in a philosophy of unlimited private profit for businessmen and politicians. Obviously, such a situation flies in the face of reason, since the kind of leadership needed now cannot be found among those whose dismal interests are dedicated to the building of private fortunes for themselves and who, to this end, have so conspicuously suborned themselves and their office to serving the business and financial establishment at public expense.

In the final analysis, the basic difficulty is that everyone wants something but no one wants to pay for it. Most investors would rather not admit this. Or, if they do, it is with an indifferent shrug or a sigh. They want utopia, but they want someone else to build it and pay for it. It is this lapse of reason that has allowed a well-heeled financial establishment to move into Washington in order to organize the politician's passions into serving its ends.

A new outlook is needed. The approach to the issues that now face investors are there, waiting to have life breathed into them. I have sought to show that rule 10b-5 seems capable of being logically expanded to include breaches of fiduciary responsibilities by Stock Exchange insiders and the Exchange corporation. Certainly American investors will have renounced their rights and most vital interests if they do not now attempt to assert control over this institution's arrogant controls and its arbitrary use of the power vested in it as a trustee of the rights of its shareholder customers. Its whole dynamic is in the wrong direction. In a constitutional democracy there is no place for an institution that in ever increasing logarithmic spirals manipulates stock prices up and down in order to buy cheap and sell dear. We are in desperate

How to Sue the Stock Exchange

277

need of change. The right of safe investment in American business, economic equilibrium, control over inflation, secure employment, and a consumer-controlled credit mechanism are all too important under present circumstances for the trial-and-error adaptations that must accompany a rigged stock market.

Index